Knowledge and Mind

Joseph Branse

Portland, Maine

April Fool's Day
2004

Knowledge and Mind
A Philosophical Introduction

Andrew Brook and
Robert J. Stainton

A Bradford Book
The MIT Press
Cambridge, Massachusetts
London, England

First MIT Press paperback edition, 2001
© 2000 Massachusetts Institute of Technology

This book was set in Times New Roman by Asco Typesetters, Hong Kong, and was printed and bound in the United States of America.

Third printing, 2002

Library of Congress Cataloging-in-Publication Data
Brook, Andrew.
 Knowledge and mind : a philosophical introduction / Andrew Brook and Robert J. Stainton.
     p.   cm.
 "A Bradford book."
 Includes bibliographical references and index.
 ISBN 0-262-02475-6 (hc : alk. paper), 0-262-52317-5 (pb)
 1. Knowledge, Theory of. 2. Philosophy of mind. I. Brook, Andrew. II. Stainton, Robert. III. Title.
BD161.B459   2000
121—dc21
                                                            99-38797
                                                               CIP

Contents

Chapter 8

**A New Approach to Knowledge and
Mind**   189

Preface for Instructors

Whenever you read a good book, it's like the author is right there, in the room, talking to you, which is why I don't like to read good books.
Jack Handey

This text covers, at an introductory level, issues in epistemology and philosophy of mind. It is, so far as we're aware, the only contemporary text to do so. It also serves as an introduction to philosophy per se, raising issues about the nature and methods of philosophy and presenting some of the very basic logical tools of the philosophical trade (e.g., modus ponens, reductio ad absurdum, etc.)

In claiming that this text is distinctive, we don't mean to deny that there are a number of textbooks in philosophy of mind available. On the contrary, several have been published in the last few years. But the majority of these are better suited to a more advanced, more specialized, course. Most important, the recent crop of philosophy-of-mind books do not deal with epistemology.

Similarly, what epistemology texts there are also tend to be too advanced for a first-year course. And the epistemology texts do not treat of philosophy of mind.

So far as we're aware, then, despite the numerous texts on philosophy of mind available, there isn't one that adequately discusses knowledge. Still less is there a truly *introductory* text that covers both knowledge and mind. Yet in the present philosophical climate, such a book is required. We want to target the many introductory—i.e., first year, single semester—philosophy courses that focus precisely on these two areas. Moreover, in the age of cognitive science, ever more such courses will surely appear, because epistemology and philosophy of mind are, together with logic and philosophy of language, the philosophical cornerstones of cognitive science. Hence a text that introduces both is called for.

The text has three parts: one devoted to *knowledge*, another to *mind*, a third relating the two. Knowledge and mind are not, of course, unrelated: whereas epistemology addresses the nature of knowledge and what can be known, philosophy of mind deals with the nature of what does the knowing, namely, the mind. (Also, anyone wanting to *know* the nature of mind needs some idea of what knowledge is and how it's attained.) In addition, several of the issues we address clearly overlap the two areas: e.g., knowledge of language (including language acquisition and the relationship between thought and talk) and knowledge of other minds. The book ends with a discussion in the second half of part III of how work on epistemology and philosophy of mind meld together within present-day theorizing in cognitive science.

Other topics could have been chosen, but these strike us as interesting and accessible enough for beginners, while also being of singular importance for those intending to pursue further study in philosophy of mind, epistemology, and cognitive science. Still, some of these choices are non-obvious. Let us therefore explain them, albeit briefly. Discussing the metaphysics of mind and skepticism (both about the external world and about other minds) is standard in philosophical introductions to mind and epistemology, respectively. Choosing these topics needs no defense. Some might wonder, however, at our inclusion of knowledge of language and of free will.

Part of our motivation is to make this textbook connect with the antecedent concerns of readers: both students who are not otherwise philosophically disposed and those who are but have no formal training. Whereas skeptical worries about the physical world or about other people's mental states and events may strike beginners as impractical and pointless, issues like the relationship between thought and language and debates about language learning can, in our experience, capture the imagination and attention of nearly anyone. In a similar vein, whereas mind-body relations might not occur to just anyone, free will and the responsibility that comes with it are issues we all must deal with. (The same can be said, of course, of life after death, another topic we introduce.) Another advantage of including these topics is that students notice the connections between knowledge and mind on the one hand and social/moral philosophy on the other. And just as important, they come to see the relevance of empirical work to philosophy.

The book also contains a section on the nature and methods of philosophy. But, following the advice of nearly every reviewer, we have placed the discussion in the middle of the text, so that students will have done some philosophy before they are asked to reflect upon what philosophy is. This section on metaphilosophy falls at the end of chapter 3. We chose that location because by that point, students have been exposed both to a quite traditional debate about knowing the external world and to a more empirically informed discussion of knowledge, thought, and language. Thus their own experience should accord with our conclusion in that section: namely, that philosophy is a very heterogeneous activity. We take up the same set of issues once more, albeit briefly, right at the end of the book.

Acknowledgments

Our first thanks go to those who read earlier drafts of the book, and provided valuable advice and suggestions. They are Andrew Botterell, Jay Drydyk, Maite Ezcurdia, Tim Kenyon, David Matheson, Jillian McIntosh, Robert Martin, Christopher Olsen and his research group at the University of Toronto, Don Ross, Ian Slater, Daniel Stoljar, Julian Wolfe, and an anonymous reviewer for the MIT Press. Prof. McIntosh deserves special thanks for her particularly thorough and searching comments and suggestions. As a result the book is better in more ways than we can say.

We also owe special thanks to the students and teaching assistants in our introductory courses on epistemology and philosophy of mind at Carleton University (where we both teach) and Bryn Mawr College (where Andrew Brook was Wexler Visiting Professor). In particular, we would like to thank Ian Slater, who kindly provided his detailed class notes. We would also like to explicitly acknowledge our debt to three books that one or the other of us has used in teaching this material: Paul Churchland's *Matter and Consciousness*, Thomas Nagel's *What Does It All Mean?* and Jay Rosenberg's *The Practice of Philosophy*. Our students' reactions to these books, both positive and negative, greatly shaped this text.

In addition, we are grateful to Marie Green for converting Stainton's hand-written lecture notes into electronic form, to Jennifer Schellinck for preparing the index, and to the excellent editorial people at MIT Press. Most of all, thanks to Richard Dickson (who proposed that we write such a text) and to our respective wives, Christine Koggel and Anita Kothari. The book is gratefully dedicated to the three of them.

Work on this project was financially supported by the Social Sciences and Humanities Research Council of Canada. We are thankful for their continuing aid.

All epigraphs but one are taken from the Saturday Night Live skit "Deep Thoughts by Jack Handey," published as *Deep Thoughts: Inspiration for the Uninspired*, by Jack Handey (copyright 1992 by Jack Handey; published by Berkley Books); *Deeper Thoughts: All New, All Crispy*, by Jack Handey (copyright 1993 by Jack Handey; published by Hyperion); *Deepest Thoughts: So Deep They Squeak*, by Jack Handey (copyright 1994 by Jack Handey; published by Hyperion).

Knowledge and Mind

Chapter 1

Introduction to Philosophy, Knowledge, and Mind

If you hit a man over the head with a fish, he'll have a headache for a day. If you teach a man to hit himself over the head with a fish, he'll have a headache for the rest of his life.

This book treats of two subject areas within philosophy. They are EPISTEMOLOGY and PHILOSOPHY OF MIND.[1] Within these two areas this book will discuss specific issues like knowledge of the external world, knowledge of language, the relation between mind and body, free will, etc. Before turning to these, however, we should say something about the two areas.

1 Epistemology

Epistemology is the philosophical subarea that focuses on the nature, extent, and origin of human knowledge. The name is a mouthful, but it's a reasonable label nonetheless: 'episteme' is the Greek word for knowledge, and '-logy' essentially means 'study of'. Hence 'epistem-ology' is the study of knowledge. Traditionally, epistemologists address three central questions:

(1) What is knowledge?

(2) What can we know?

(3) How is knowledge acquired?

At this point we don't want to try to answer these questions: even *introducing* them thoroughly will take the whole of part I of the book. But by way of illustration, allow us to introduce a sample answer for each.

A long-standard response to the first question is that a statement is known by an agent only if she believes the statement, the statement is true, and she is justified in her belief. Thus, on this account, which dates back at least to Plato (b. ca. 428 B.C.[2]), no one can *know* a falsehood: for example, no one can know that two is an odd number. Nor can anyone know something that they do not believe: if someone, say Zoltan, does not *believe* that Hungary is in Europe, then he cannot *know* that Hungary is in Europe. Finally, if Zoltan believes that Hungary is in Europe, but he has no good reason for believing this, then his belief is unjustified, and he therefore does not know it.

This "justified true belief" theory of knowledge may seem odd at first glance, and some philosophers reject it. Other views include the following. Some hold that knowledge is derived from recognized authority—which seems to suggest that a person could "know" something which isn't actually true. (Many philosophers find this result astonishing.) Others insist that knowledge without justification, i.e., knowledge by faith, is possible. And so on. In this introduction, we needn't settle on the right answer to (1). The aim, to repeat, is simply to introduce and explain the question 'What is knowledge?' by considering a classical sample answer.

One radical answer to (2) is that human beings cannot know anything. This kind of extreme SKEPTICISM is rare. A more common skeptical view, one which will occupy us at length in part I of this book, is that, *in certain areas of inquiry*, nothing can be known. For example, one might maintain that nothing can be known about the *external world* or that nothing can be known about *other people's mental states*—their feelings, desires, etc.

Skeptics about a given domain often argue as follows: They assume that (something like) the justified true belief account of what knowledge is, is correct. They then contend that statements of the kind in question (e.g., statements about the external world or about other people's minds) fail to meet one or more of these conditions. For instance, they might argue that statements about other people's minds cannot adequately be justified. Hence, given the definition of knowledge as *justified* true belief, such statements are not known. Or again, skeptics about morality might argue that there are no moral *truths*. Hence, once more, the justified true belief account of knowledge rules out moral knowledge. However plausible or implausible they may seem, these sample answers should help to clarify question (2): what can we know?

The third traditional epistemological question is 'How is knowledge acquired?' There is a classic gradient here: at one extreme are those who think that true knowledge is derived from sensory experience; at the other, those who think, to the contrary, that real knowledge is not sense-based at all. Those who lean towards the former are called EMPIRICISTS, while those who lean more towards the latter are called RATIONALISTS. Extreme empiricists think that there can be no nonsensory knowledge because, to use one famous slogan, the mind is a "blank slate" (i.e., *tabula rasa*) at birth. So, whatever ideas end up in the mind must have been put there by experience. The rationalists, on the other hand, deny that the mind is vacant at birth: they are happy to allow that human minds contain "ideas" (i.e., beliefs, concepts, etc.) at birth. (In fact, rationalists typically downplay the importance of sense-based knowledge, stressing instead knowledge arrived at by "pure thought." Only the latter is, for them, genuine knowledge. The rest is mere "opinion".)

Empiricists and rationalists, in addition to disputing what *contents* the mind has at birth, also typically disagree about the power of our innate cognitive *capacities*. A rough comparison: a factory has both machines, and materials that the machines work on. "Cognitive capacities" are the machines of the mind; while "ideas" are its materials. Empiricists are willing to admit that *some* capacities are there from the start, since without some innate capabilities, no learning would be possible. The ability to remember, for instance, or to associate one sensation with another, are innate mechanisms that even empiricists embrace. But they generally allow *only* these very minimal mechanisms. Rationalists, in contrast, believe that the human mind has very powerful and creative cognitive faculties at birth. It is innate ideas together with these dynamic reasoning abilities that, according to the rationalists, give human beings the kind of knowledge that cannot be obtained via sensation. (Such knowledge purportedly includes mathematical knowledge, moral knowledge, knowledge of God, and knowledge of language—none of which, say the rationalists, is adequately accounted for by empiricist theories of knowledge acquisition by sensation.)

The debate between rationalists and empiricists, notice, is not about what we know. Instead, the issue is *how* we know what we do, as well as what the ultimate foundation of "real" knowledge is: experience or reason. In part I will consider at length some epistemological questions. For the moment, we hope that we have given you some idea of what epistemology is all about.

2   Philosophy of Mind

Philosophy of mind is the other subject area within philosophy that we will discuss in this book. Its focus, as the name suggests, is the mind. Its questions include these:

(4) What is a mind?

(5) How are minds related to bodies?

These are emphatically *not* the only questions in philosophy of mind. (For example, another key one is this: Are minds subject to scientific laws, and scientific study? And, if so, is our reasoning and acting truly free?) But these two give you the general idea. They and the question about free choice will be dealt with in part II. For now, again just to suggest what philosophy of mind is, let us sketch some answers to (4) and (5).

Here's a first pass at an answer to (4): a mind is a thing that *thinks*. It is, to revert to a classical Greek view, the *rational part of the soul*. Of course, if this definition is to capture every kind of mentality, 'thinking' must include a lot of things, e.g., perceiving, believing, reasoning, having sensations, and being conscious. All of these are *mental states and events*.

One problem that immediately arises is, What is the relationship between such mental states and events and *bodies*? This, of course, is question (5). There's clearly some sort of relationship between mind and body: when you drink a lot of alcohol (a physical event), you become confused (a mental state), and when, being completely drunk, you eventually fall down (a physical event), it can hurt (a mental state). *Precisely* what the mind is and how mind and body relate will occupy much of chapters 5 and 6. For the moment, it may be enough to note two radically different answers.

René Descartes (b. 1596), who might reasonably be called the founder of modern philosophy of mind, maintained that mind and body were two wholly different kinds of things. Two radically distinct realms, if you will, about as different from each other as numbers and rocks. (How different are rocks and numbers? Well, have you ever tried throwing a *number* through a window? Or again, how would you go about taking the square root of a *rock*?) This is DUALISM about the mind. Thomas Hobbes (b. 1588), in stark contrast to Descartes, believed that mind and body were essentially the same. Hobbes was a MATERIALIST who maintained that all there really is, is matter in motion. Hence "mind" can be nothing more than this. Descartes had his work cut out in explaining how mind and body can be related. After all, according to him they are *radically* different. Hobbes, on the other hand, had no great problem here. But he was stuck with another concern: mind *seems* so different from body. Our minds think, feel pain, dream, get confused, and so on, but planets and snowflakes do none of these things. So how can our minds be nothing more than matter in motion? The burden of materialism is to give a satisfactory answer to this question. (There is also a third broad position: IDEALISM. This is the view that everything in existence is mindlike. We will consider it along with the other two when we discuss the mind/body problem as a whole in chapter 4.)

Another question that will occupy us is (6):

(6) Can a person ever really know the mind of another?

This question is interesting in part because it involves both philosophy of mind and epistemology and thus highlights the overlap between the two. It is epistemological because it's about knowledge, but it's also about the mind. And how one answers (6) will depend quite a lot on what one takes a mind to be like.

Time to sum up. We began by noting six traditional questions about knowledge and mind. These were the following:

Epistemology
1. What is knowledge?
2. What can we know?
3. How is knowledge acquired?

Philosophy of Mind
4. What is a mind?
5. How are minds related to bodies?
6. Can a person ever really know the mind of another?

These are not, we want to stress, the only questions in these subfields of philosophy. Indeed, you will encounter others as the book progresses. But keep these questions in mind as you read. They will help you keep the big picture in front of you as you work through more specific issues in the chapters to come.

3   Epilogue: Arguments, Philosophical and Otherwise

To me, truth is not some vague, foggy notion. Truth is real. And, at the same time, unreal. Fiction and fact and everything in between, plus some things I can't remember, all rolled into one big "thing." This is truth, to me.
Jack Handey

As the "deep thought" just quoted demonstrates, there is a lot of confusion about truth! Happily, there is a basic technique for getting at the truth: argument. In this section we want to ask: what is an argument? At bottom, it is a *series of statements*, but with a special characteristic: the various statements are intended to stand in supporting relationships, so that, if the earlier statements in the argument are true, the final statements are true, or are more likely to be true. What is supported is called the *conclusion* (or conclusions); what does the supporting is one or more *premises* and some *reasoning* that demonstrates that the premise(s) support the conclusion.

Given this, suppose that someone gives an argument whose conclusion you dislike. What do you do? In legal debates, politics, science, and everyday disputes, it's not enough simply to disagree: you have to *argue* against the conclusion. The same holds true in philosophy. But how does one argue, in philosophy and elsewhere? Well, given that conclusions are supported by two things, premises and reasoning, what you have to do is to criticize your opponent's premises or criticize her reasoning or both. These are your only options for showing that the argument is wrong.

Let's take these in turn, beginning with challenging premises. One way to refute someone's premises is just to gather facts about the sensible world: do experiments, calculations, literature searches, and so on, and show that the opponent's "information" is just wrong. But philosophers don't typically do this, or at least this isn't the only thing they do. Philosophers most often offer *internal* criticism, which means showing that the premise they want to deny conflicts with other presuppositions of the person they are arguing with. If the philosopher can show this effectively, then the person she is arguing against (sometimes called her interlocutor) must give up something, and the philosopher can suggest that her interlocutor reject the premise in question.

An example may help to clarify this question-the-premise strategy. Suppose Chris wants to establish that capital punishment is wrong. He argues like this:

Premise 1 All killing is wrong.
Premise 2 Capital punishment is killing.
Conclusion 1 Therefore, capital punishment is wrong.

A philosopher, we said, can reply to an argument (i.e., a series of statements in a "supporting" relationship) by showing that one of its premises is inconsistent with something that the argument's proponent believes. Here's a case in point. Agnes might say to Chris, "Look here Chris, your premise 1 is inconsistent with something else you believe, namely, that killing in self-defense is okay." If Chris does truly believe that killing in self-defense is acceptable, then there is a conflict between one of his background beliefs and the premise, P1, that he is putting forward. (Throughout the text, 'P' will be used for premises, and 'C' for conclusions.) He must somehow overcome the conflict: believing obvious inconsistencies is not a viable option. Agnes, kind soul that she is, makes a suggestion: what Chris ought to do is to give up P1. Of course, if he does give up P1, he now needs another argument for his conclusion.

But suppose Chris rejects Agnes's suggestion and says instead that to remedy the inconsistency in his purported beliefs, he is going to give up the idea that killing in self-defense is okay. Indeed, whatever case Agnes puts forward—killing in war, killing to save others, mercy killing—Chris sticks by P1: *all* killing is wrong. Then what happens? Here, unfortunately, debate ends. But of course Chris cannot claim *victory*, for he is now relying on a premise that his interlocutor surely rejects. After all, Agnes doesn't believe that killing in self-defense is wrong, so she doesn't accept P1. And Chris can't *convincingly* argue from premises that aren't agreed upon by both sides: his and his interlocutor's. What Chris needs to do if he is to establish his conclusion in the mind of his opponent is to find premises that are accepted by her and then show that *if these premises are true, then the conclusion must be true.* Once the premises are accepted and it's accepted that they lead directly to the conclusion, the opponent can't help but accept the conclusion, on the assumption that she's rational and consistent. (There's no point arguing with someone who's really and truly irrational.)

Let's sum up. There are at least two ways of responding to a philosophical argument: you can question some or all of its supporting *premises*, or you can question the *reasoning* from the premises to the conclusion. Until now, we have been discussing how to go about criticizing premises. Specifically, we said that philosophers often do this by highlighting tensions between the arguer's background beliefs and the premise in question.

We now turn to the other means of response: challenging the reasoning. Jay Rosenberg puts the general point nicely: "Whereas a criticism of content addresses one or some of the premises individually with the challenge 'That isn't true,' this criticism focuses on the *relation* between the conclusion and all the premisses, and its challenge is 'That doesn't follow'" (1984, 14).

Let us start with a definition. An argument—which, remember, is a series of statements—is VALID whenever the following holds: *if* the premises of the argument are true, *then* its conclusion must be true.

Here we need say a word about terminology. (Terminological issues will arise in a number of places in this book because what philosophers mean by a term is sometimes quite different from what the term means in everyday life. Beware!) We are using the word 'valid' in a special, technical sense. You mustn't suppose that 'valid', as used in philosophy, neatly matches its use in everyday talk. In everyday talk, the word 'valid' often means 'fair' or 'justified' or even 'true'. In philosophy, it simply means than an argument is alright *internally*. In particular, as *philosophers* use the term 'valid', someone's point of view isn't "valid" or "invalid": only arguments are valid or invalid. In this sense, an argument can be 'no good' even if it is valid. For valid arguments, in this technical sense, are allowed to have false premises as long as the premises, *were they true*, would guarantee the truth of the conclusion.

Here is a valid argument with a false premise:

Premise 1 Whales are fish.
Premise 2 If whales are fish, then there are building-size fish.
Conclusion 1 Therefore, there are building-size fish.

Clearly the conclusion would have to be true if the premises were true. So the argument is valid, according to the definition. And yet the conclusion is false. How can this be? Because the first premise is false: whales *aren't* fish. They're mammals.

Another bit of philosophical jargon, which will come up again later. A valid argument *that also has true premises* is SOUND. Notice a consequence of this definition: every sound argument must, by definition, have a true conclusion. It's clear why: given what 'sound' means, in this technical usage, every sound argument has true premises, and every sound argument is also, by definition, valid, and given the meaning of 'valid', a valid argument with true premises must also have a true conclusion. (Every valid argument deserves a star. But *sound* arguments are even better than valid ones. They are very hard to come by and deserve at least three stars.)

To simplify for the sake of exposition, you might think about it this way: when challenging someone's reasoning, you are essentially questioning the *validity* of her argument, rather than the truth of her premises. (In fact, the logic of arguments, philosophical or otherwise, is more complex than the valid-invalid dichotomy suggests, but for present purposes, think of attacks on reasoning as questioning validity. We will introduce one of the complexities shortly.) Typically, one questions validity by showing that the *argument pattern* the opponent is using is faulty. Here's how:

• Find a parallel argument, with the same pattern.
• Show that this parallel argument has true premises (or anyway, premises accepted by all sides), but a false conclusion (or anyway, one denied by all sides).

That is, you *model* the reasoning pattern and thereby establish that this sort of argument doesn't guarantee the truth of the conclusion, despite the truth of the premises.

Here's an example. Suppose you want to know whether the skeptical argument in (7) is valid:

(7) *The target argument*
    Premise 1 I am *sometimes* mistaken.
    Conclusion It is possible that I am *always* mistaken.

One way of showing that the target argument is *not* valid is to find a closely parallel argument—an analogy, if you will—whose premise is true and yet whose conclusion is false. And there is such an argument:

(8) *The analogous "modeling argument"*
    Premise 1 Dollar bills are *sometimes* counterfeit.
    Conclusion It is possible that dollar bills are *always* counterfeit.

The conclusion of the modeling argument is false: there wouldn't be such a thing as a *counterfeit* dollar bill if there weren't also *genuine* dollar bills, so it's not possible that all dollar bills are counterfeit. The lesson of the modeling argument is this: you cannot always infer from '*x*s are sometimes *y*' to '*It is possible that x*s are always *y*'. That is to say, this ARGUMENT FORM is not valid. But the target argument in (7) shares this form. So it's not valid either.

Some valid argument forms are highly familiar. So much so that they have special names. For instance, there is MODUS PONENS:

(9) *Modus ponens*
    If *p*, then *q*
    p
    Therefore, *q*

Every instance of the *modus ponens* argument form is a valid argument. For instance, the arguments below both have this "shape," and the truth of their premises guarantees the truth of their respective conclusions.

(10) *Premise 1* If [Stuart's parents smoke] then [Stuart will die a horrible death].
     Premise 2 Stuart's parents smoke.
     Conclusion Therefore, Stuart will die a horrible death.
     p = Stuart's parents smoke; *q* = Stuart will die a horrible death

(11) *Premise 1* If [it's raining or it's snowing] then [Pat and Jeff will stay inside].

Premise 2 It's raining or it's snowing.
Conclusion Therefore, Pat and Jeff will stay inside.
p = It's raining or it's snowing; q = Pat and Jeff will stay inside

Other such familiar valid forms include *modus tollens*, and *hypothetical syllogism*, which have the following shapes:

(12) *Modus tollens*
    If p, then q
    It's not the case that q
    Therefore, it's not the case that p

(13) *Hypothetical syllogism*
    If p, then q
    If q, then r
    Therefore, if p then r

Now we need to introduce the complexity we mentioned above. We defined validity this way: if the premises are true, the conclusion must be true. In fact, that holds, strictly speaking, of only one kind of important argument, DEDUCTIVE ARGUMENTS. In another important kind of argument, the relationship between premises and conclusion is less binding: the premises are *evidence* for the conclusion. What 'evidence' means here is this: if the premises are true, the conclusion is *more likely* to be true but is not guaranteed to be true. Arguments of this type are called INDUCTIVE ARGUMENTS. Here is an example:

Premise 1 There are heavy black clouds in the sky.
Premise 2 The humidity is very high.
Conclusion It will soon rain.

Note that the conclusion does not *follow from* the premises, in the sense that if the premises are true, the conclusion *must be* true. Nevertheless, if the premises are true, *it is more likely* that the conclusion is true than if the premises are false. (If it is really bright and sunny out, it is less likely that it will soon rain than if it is humid and there are heavy black clouds in the sky.)

In a deductively valid argument, the relationship between premises and conclusion is called ENTAILMENT: the premises *entail* the conclusion, which just means that if the premises are true, the conclusion *must* be true. In an inductively valid argument, the relationship between premises and conclusion is called EVIDENTIAL SUPPORT: the premises are *evidence* for the conclusion, which just means that if the premises are true, the conclusion is *more likely* to be true. Philosophers use deductive arguments more than inductive ones, but we will both use and discuss inductive arguments from time to time, too (see chapter 3, section 2, for one example).

In sum, philosophers generally criticize arguments in two ways: first, by showing that some premise is in tension with the facts or with what interlocutors are prepared to grant (attacking the premises); second, by showing that the argument pattern used is not generally reliable (attacking the reasoning). The latter is often done by modeling the argument, and thereby showing that the form of the argument is questionable.[3]

Study Questions

Note: Many of the questions in the study-question sections do not admit of simple answers. They are, rather, designed to provoke reflection and/or discussion. So if you don't "know the answer," this does not necessarily mean that you "haven't understood the text." On the other hand, if you can think of absolutely nothing to say about a question, then you should reread the appropriate sections.

1. What are rationalism and empiricism? Is it possible to mix a little of each? How?

2. Can questions (2) and (3)—about what we can know and about how knowledge is acquired—be answered independently of one another? Can either of them be answered independently of (1): what is knowledge?

3. For an agent to know that *p* is said to require at least three things: *p* must be true, the agent must believe that *p*, and she must be justified in her belief. To illustrate the necessity of each of these, give three examples of not knowing.

4. What are materialism and dualism? In what sense is it impossible to mix them?

5. Define each of the following: 'argument', 'valid argument', 'sound argument'. Give an example of a valid argument that is not sound. What in particular makes it unsound? Can there be good arguments that aren't valid? Specifically, can there be arguments that support a conclusion even though it's not the case that the truth of the premises guarantees the truth of the conclusion?

6. Define 'premise', 'statement', and 'conclusion'. How are they related? Can a statement be a conclusion in one context and a premise in another? Give an example. How might one challenge a premise? A conclusion?

Suggested Further Readings

There are many textbooks that discuss the three key questions of epistemology: What is knowledge? What can we know? How is knowledge acquired? A good starting place is Chisholm's (1989) classic introduction or Bertrand Russell's very readable *Problems of Philosophy* (1912). The readings in the collection by Nagel and Brandt (1965) cover many topics in epistemology—e.g., nonempirical knowledge, skepticism, knowledge of the material world, knowing other minds—and it includes both traditional and contemporary sources. For more advanced and more contemporary readings, see Bonjour 1985, Dancy 1985, Dancy and

Sosa 1992, Goodman and Snyder 1993, Lehrer 1990, or Lucey 1996. A nice general introduction to philosophy can be found in Solomon 1998: it discusses the nature of philosophy, philosophical arguments, rationalism and empiricism, argument forms, and other relevant topics.

Solomon 1998 also contains a guide to writing philosophy papers. Other books on this important topic include Rosenberg 1984, 1996, and Graybosch, Scott, and Garrison 1998. See also Weston 1987.

The roots of rationalism lie in Plato and Descartes, while John Locke and John Stuart Mill are key historical sources on empiricism. See especially Plato's *Theaetetus* (1973 [ca. 399 B.C.]) for a very early statement of rationalism, and John Locke 1965 [1685], for an influential Empiricist critique. As for secondary sources, on the rationalists we recommend Copleston 1946, part 3, and 1960 as an overview, and Kenny 1968 on Descartes in particular. Jonathan Bennett 1971 is a useful, though sometimes controversial, commentary on empiricism.

Our discussion of the nature of argument follows Rosenberg 1984, especially the chapters "The Form of an Argument" and "The Content of an Argument." As for dualism and materialism, they will be discussed at length in chapters 4 and 5, so specific source material may be found at the end of those chapters. For general overviews, see Churchland 1984, Jacquette 1994 and Kim 1996.

Also, for just about any topic in this book, a good starting place is one of the encyclopedias of philosophy. Examples include Edwards 1967 and Craig 1998; the former was the first, the latter is the newest and most comprehensive.

PART I

Knowledge

Chapter 2

Knowing the External World

Instead of having "answers" on a math test, they should just call them "impressions," and if you got a different "impression," so what, can't we all be brothers?
Jack Handey

1 A Skeptical Argument

The first specific issue that we'll look at, within epistemology, is whether, assuming you know your own mind well enough, you can be sure of anything beyond the inside of your mind. We will present an argument whose general conclusion is that you cannot: the only thing you *really know*, if this argument works, is how things *appear* within your mind. Specifically, it will be argued that you do not know anything about the external world.

The argument for this rather extraordinary skeptical thesis is actually quite simple. It requires only two premises:

(1) *The argument for external world skepticism*
Premise 1 All you *directly* know is how things seem to you.
Premise 2 If all you directly know is how things seem to you, then you can't know how things really are outside of you.
Conclusion Therefore, you can't know how things really are outside you.

There can be no question about the *validity* of the argument. In fact, the argument has one of the simplest forms of valid argument, *modus ponens*: if *p*, then *q*; *p*; therefore, *q*. Since (1) has this form as well, it too is valid: *if* its premises are true, then its conclusion must be true. Hence, the only way to avoid the conclusion of the argument in (1) is to go after its premises. So let's start with this: what supports the premises?

Support for P1 of (1) comes from empiricism, a doctrine we've encountered before. According to empiricists, everything you know ultimately derives from your experiences and sense impressions. Notice what *isn't* being claimed here: that everything you know *is* sense experience. That claim is quite implausible, at least at first glance. More initially plausible is the idea that there is *direct* and *indirect* knowledge: very roughly, things you perceive and things you infer on the basis of those perceptions. What the Empiricists say is that the former, the direct knowledge, just *is* sense experience, and all "indirect" knowledge derives from, i.e., is based on, this direct knowledge. Hence all you know *directly* is how things seem.

Why believe this? Because, according to empiricism, there is essentially *nothing* in your mind at birth. Hence whatever ends up there either *is* experience or is produced from experience—specifically, sense experience.[1]

P2 arises from the (reasonable) question of whether it is always (or even ever) justified to infer *how things are* from *how things seem.* What lies behind this question are two worries. On the one hand, there are certain cases in which the way things seem doesn't correspond to the way things are: just think about how things seem while you're dreaming. The whole point about dreams is that from the inside the dream can *seem* so real without what you (appear to) experience actually *being* real: e.g., it can seem that you're on a beach, savoring a cocktail, listening to the soothing sounds of waves crashing on the shore when in fact you're at home in bed. So one can't *always* safely draw the conclusion (infer) 'It's really true that such and such' from 'It seems that such and such'. Or, to take a different sort of case, when you look at a drinking straw in a glass of water, it may look crooked, but despite its seeming bent, it's actually straight. Such cases lead the skeptic to wonder whether the inference is *ever* justified: i.e., it makes her suspect that P2 may be correct.

Error cases are one source of worry. Here's another more generalized concern: how things are and how things seem could simply be altogether distinct realms. Suppose they are. Well, then, to take an example, since you can't safely infer what cows are like by looking exclusively at skateboards (two distinct kinds of *physical* things), you surely can't safely infer facts about how things are from looking exclusively at (the wholly different domain of) how things seem.[2] But P1 says that ultimately all one *can* "look at" are seemings. So there is no way to draw safe conclusions about how things really are.

Fair enough. But, you might wonder, why suppose that seeming and being *are* disconnected in this way? How does the skeptic know that the inference from seemings to how things are is illicit? The answer is, she doesn't know this. But the skeptic doesn't have to know that the inference form in (2) is unreliable.

(2) The way things seem → the way things are

(The arrow '→' means something like 'implies'; i.e., if what is to the left of the arrow is true, then what is to the right will also be true.) She just has to say that *we can't be sure* that it's reliable. Indeed, it's not just that we can't be *certain* about (2). Rather, there seems no good reason to treat the inference as reliable. And now comes the challenge from the skeptic: "Show me that seemings are reliable indicators of how things are. And do this making use only of how things seem, because, as P1 says, that's all one ultimately has available."

Reflecting upon how one might go about this, it becomes clear that meeting this challenge, i.e., justifying (2) on the basis of impressions alone, just isn't possible. For, any such justification would surely *presuppose* (something like) this very inference form. Here's the worry. Form (2) is a claim about the way things are. Basically, it says that seemings provide insight into how thing are. Now the only evidence the skeptic allows us in arguing for (2) is seemings. But to support (2)—a claim about how things *are*—using only seemings, you must already be sure that seemings reflect the world as it really is. So you can't justify (2) on the basis of seemings. But since seemings are all you've got, (2) is wholly unjustified.

The overall lesson: since we're not independently sure that (2) is true, we're not sure about any results achieved from its use, but results *not* achieved by its use are results about seemings, i.e., experiences. Or so P1 says. Hence, seemings are all we can really know.

Consider a parallel argument about knowing the future. The inference form here is this:

(3) The way things have been in the past → the way things will be in the future

Whenever one makes predictions about the future, something like (3) is presupposed. Consider the following case: Juan always buys pizza from Tina's pizzeria. Why? Because every pizza Tina's restaurant has ever made for Juan has been absolutely delicious. So, wanting continued excellence, Juan orders today's pizza from Tina's. Question: why does Juan think that, just because Tina's *past* pizzas were delectable, this one too will be? Because he expects the future to be like the past. That is, he assumes (3).

But what justifies him in thinking this? Here's a bad answer: "Well, in Juan's previous experience, the future was like the past. So he can now expect the future to *continue* being like the past." The obvious problem with this answer is that it *presupposes* (3), and hence cannot justify it: to expect that, as before, predictions based on past experience will come true is to *assume* that past experience gives insight into future events. Hence, it is to assume the very thing that requires justification.

Recall the overall flow of the argument. Empiricism, the idea that all knowledge comes from experience, yields premise 1:

Premise 1 All you know directly is how things seem to you.

Next up, two things support premise 2:

Premise 2 If all you know directly is how things seem to you, then you can't know how things really are outside of you.

First and most obvious, the occasional unreliability of sensations (e.g., in dreams and optical illusions) supports P2. But more fundamental support for P2 also comes from the idea that knowledge of the external world, if it's to be grounded in sensations alone, requires something not achievable, i.e., that (2) be justified only with sense experiences. Putting P1 and P2 together, we get skepticism about the external world: that you cannot *know* how things are "outside you."

It may help to clarify the skeptic's position if we recall the justified-true-belief account of knowledge. On this view, which we'll assume for the sake of argument, you know something only when it's true, you believe it, and you're justified in your belief. What's being questioned by the skeptic is whether those beliefs that are not about experiences are *justified*. The skeptic is not saying that our beliefs about nonseemings are *false*. She's saying that they are unjustified, because they all assume something, namely (2), that is itself unjustified.

Put otherwise, the skeptic about the external world is not claiming that there *isn't* anything outside her own mind. (That would be SOLIPSISM, not skepticism.) Here's why. Unless (2) is a safe kind of inference, you can't know *anything* about the external world from seemings alone. This means, among other things, that you can't know that there *isn't* such a world. If the inference form in (2) isn't reliable—and the skeptic challenges us to show that it *is* reliable—then we can't safely infer anything about what is. We can infer neither that there is "stuff out there" with such and such characteristics nor again that there isn't anything there at all (i.e., solipsism). In brief, the skeptic thinks that a negative claim, to the effect that there is no world outside, would be as unjustified as the positive claim that there is.

Compare the case of knowing about the future: the skeptic who asks for a justification of (3) is *not* saying that there's no such thing as being right about the future. What she says is that *if* no justification of (3) is forth-coming, *then* given the justified-true-belief account of knowledge, human beings cannot know anything about the future, because none of their beliefs about the future is justified. She then challenges the nonskeptic to justify (3) without assuming the very thing in need of justification. And it looks like this challenge must go unmet. In the same way, in asking for a justification of (2), the inference form that yields knowledge of the external world, one needn't claim that there is no external world, but, barring a justification of (2), *knowledge* of how things are "outside one" is not possible. And, says the skeptic, there's no way to justify (2), since any attempted justification will assume (2) itself.

The upshot of all this: while there may be an external world such that human beings *in fact* have correct beliefs about it, we can never *know* anything about it. For, because (2) cannot be justified using the senses alone and (says P1) the senses are all we have, it seems that all claims about the external world rest on an unjustified *assumption*. But knowledge requires justification: you cannot know things that you merely assume, nor can you know things that are simply consequences of things you merely assume. Hence the only thing you really know is how things seem to you, i.e., the contents of your own mind. This is skepticism about the external world.

Before turning to responses to this skeptical line of thought, it's worth pausing to consider the extent of the skepticism. An argument like the one just presented, if it works at all, also establishes that you cannot know any-thing about yourself, in the sense of knowing *your body*. It's not just external objects, understood as physical things at a distance from you, that you cannot know. P1 also entails that you have no direct knowledge of your arms, toes, hair, etc. According to P1, remember, you have direct knowl-edge only of your sensations. Hence, no part of your body is *directly* known.

But now, *indirect* knowledge of your body seems to require an inference form like this:

(4) The way my body seems → the way my body really is

And now the very same problem arises: there is no way to justify (4) on the basis of how your body seems. But unless (4) can be justified, every belief you have about your body rests on an unjustified assumption. This means that none of those beliefs count as knowledge. Moreover, (4) is not so obviously reliable that it needs no defense: to give just one example, sometimes (e.g., in dreams and hallucinations) it can seem that one's body is running or standing up, when in fact it's not.

One final point. Strictly speaking, P1 ought to read, "All you know directly is how things seem to you *right now*." Every other kind of knowledge would seem to be equally based on inferences from how things seem at the present moment. But how can those inferences be justified with the only evidence being beliefs about *present* seemings? They cannot, says the skeptic. Hence, no belief *about your past self*, even in the sense of your past *mental states and events*, truly counts as knowledge. At best all you know is your own mind, right now—if the skeptic is right.

2   Objections to External-World Skepticism and Replies

As the light changed from red to green to yellow and back to red again, I sat there thinking about life. Was it nothing more than a bunch of honking and yelling? Sometimes it seemed that way.

Jack Handey

We now present five replies to the above skeptical argument. Sadly, none of them works.

Objection 1:   Causes

You might be tempted by the following sort of reply to the skeptic: "There must be an external world, or you wouldn't have the experiences you do. For something surely causes your experiences. And the best candidate cause is an external world."

Now, the first worry about this kind of antiskeptical maneuver is this: How do you know that you couldn't have the experiences you do, *without* some cause? What *experience* justifies the claim that everything has to have a cause? Maybe there just is no cause of your experiences.

Moreover, even if there must be *some* cause, how do you know that the cause is the external world? According to P1, the only thing to which you can appeal to justify these claims are, you guessed it, more seemings.

Finally, suppose the skeptic granted that there must be some cause of your experiences, and that this cause must be external to you. This would be cold comfort. For how can you tell, from the contents of your experiences, what the causes are really like? It's not enough to know that there's *something* external that causes, for example, your tree sensations: what you really want to know is that *trees* do this. That is, what you really want to know is not only that there is an external world but also what it's like: that it contains trees, and other people, and so on. And the mere fact—if it is a fact—that your sensations have some external causes will not get you this. For you must admit that seemings sometimes exist without their apparent external causes (e.g., in dreams and hallucinations). So you need an argument whose premises can all be justified by direct experience to rule out the possibility that all experiences are like dreams in not having the external causes that they seem to.

Objection 2:   Science

Doesn't science refute the skeptic? In particular, scientists regularly use general principles of explanation to go from seemings to how things really are. Specifically, scientists draw inferences about the external world on the basis of the explanatory power of their theories: the most explanatory theory is the correct one. Thus, to take an example, scientists believe that there are enormous continental plates deep below the surface of the earth, because the theory of plate tectonics, which postulates such plates, best explains things like the observable shape of the continents, the existence of mountain ranges, the location of earthquakes, etc. One can't directly observe continental plates. But it's reasonable to believe in them because otherwise certain observable phenomenon would be inexplicable.

Notice the general principle here:

(5) Theory T best explains appearances $\rightarrow$ things really are as described in theory T

Notice too the parallel with skepticism: given the truth of (5), this response to the skeptic goes, one can know about the external world from seemings alone because, though we can't directly observe the external world, it's still reasonable to believe in it, for otherwise certain observable phenomenon would be inexplicable. Hence, to repeat, P2 must be false, and the skeptical argument fails.

This move is called INFERENCE TO THE BEST EXPLANATION. The skeptic has a reply to it: (5) itself needs support. But what justifies (5) in a way that respects P1 (i.e., that relies on nothing but sense experiences)? Only this: that, in our experience, the connection suggested in (5) *seems* to hold. It seems to be the case that the theory that best explains appearances is actually true of the world outside. But without (2), the very thing at issue, we can't move from this case of seeming to being. So, to establish (5), and hence refute P2, the objection from science needs to *assume* that seemings correspond to the way things are. And this is to assume that P2 is false.

In brief, this reply to the skeptic BEGS THE QUESTION.

(6) *Begging the question* Assuming as a *premise* what one seeks to establish as a *conclusion*.

To illustrate the problem of begging the question, consider a different sort of example. An atheist asks his religious pal how she knows that God exists. She replies, "I know that God exists because it says so in the Bible." This responses *begs the question* being asked because, unfortunately, what the Bible says has no weight *unless God exists.* So, as philosophers say, "The argument assumes what it is trying to prove," i.e., it begs the question.

Or perhaps the antiskeptic will try to argue this way. We ask her how she knows that P2 is false. She replies, "I know P2 is false because of (5)." And now we ask, "How can you be so sure of (5)?" To which she says, "Well, given the falsity of P2, I can infer (5) from how things seem." To spell this out, the conclusion the antiskeptic wants to establish is that P2 is false:

Premise 2 If all you directly know is how things seem to you, then you can't know how things really are outside of you.

And she uses (5) to argue against it. But for (5) to be true, P2 must already be false. So she is reasoning in a circle—a mistake called CIRCULAR REASONING.

(7) *Circular reasoning* A form of reasoning in which one uses *A* to support *B* and then turns around and uses *B* to support *A*.

So far the antiskeptic is not making much progress.

Objection 3: Ordinary Living

Consider the daffodil. And while you're doing that, I'll be over here, looking through your stuff.
Jack Handey

One might say to the skeptic, "Your talking to me only makes sense if I exist. So you must agree that I do exist. In which case, your own action, e.g., speaking to me, contradicts your skeptical position." To this she may rightly reply either that her behavior might simply not "make sense" or that what she may be doing, for all she *knows*, is having an *imaginary* debate, in order to make her inner life more rich.

This antiskeptical objection does, however, suggest a more general line of attack. The skeptic's ordinary everyday lifestyle seems to be in direct conflict with her philosophical position: she *says* that she knows nothing about the external world, and yet she *acts* exactly like the nonskeptic. One wants to ask, If the skeptic really doesn't think she knows anything about the external world, what keeps her from happily jumping out of the window? Or again, to return to the Tina's Pizzeria example, if the skeptic really doubts that she can know anything about the future on the basis of her experience of the past, why does she, like Juan, keep going back to Tina's?

There are at least two ways to answer this kind of objection. On the one hand, the skeptic might say, "Of course we, myself included, *do* believe things about the external world, about our bodies, and about the future, but that doesn't show that we're *justified* in believing them. And without justification, we don't *know*."

On the other hand one might say, "Nobody really believes skepticism, it's too strange; but—and this is the crux—the arguments for it seem irrefutable." That is, one way of understanding philosophical quandaries is this: one comes to a weird conclusion (e.g., that nothing is known about the external world) from seemingly harmless premises (e.g., P1 and P2), via an apparently faultless argument. This is a paradox, in need of resolution. And, of course, it's no response to point out that the conclusion *is* weird. That's precisely what makes the resulting conclusion paradoxical. What's really wanted is a way to "wiggle out of" the skeptic's conclusion. Either way, the skeptic's argument is not *overcome* by pointing out that it's in tension with the way she actually lives.

Another variant on the "ordinary living" argument goes like this. As G. E. Moore (b. 1873) pointed out, when you find yourself believing two mutually inconsistent things, you must give up (at least) one of them. (For instance, recall Chris from the last chapter: he wasn't able simultaneously to hold both that all killing is wrong and that killing in self-defense is not wrong. One of these had to go.) But, given that one cannot hold two incompatible views, how ought one to go about choosing *which* of the two conflicting beliefs ought to be rejected? Here's a seemingly reasonable strategy: hold on to the more obvious of the two. Let's capture this idea in a principle that we will call MOORE'S PRINCIPLE:

(8) *Moore's principle* If you find yourself believing two incompatible things, reject as false the less obvious of the two.

So far so good.

Now consider: we saw that P1 and P2 together entail that you can't know *anything* about the external world. So, for instance, P1 plus P2 (repeated as (9)) is incompatible with (10):

(9) All you know directly is how things seem to you, and if all you know directly is how things seem to you, then you can't know how things really are outside of you.

(10) You know that there is a coffee cup on your desk.

Because (9) is incompatible with (10), you cannot believe both. You must choose one or the other. Moore's principle says that you must reject whichever of (9) and (10) is less obvious. And now ask yourself: which of these *is* less obvious? Surely, one might say, (9), being a complex philosophical claim, supported only by reflection upon the source and nature of knowledge, is less obvious than (10). To take just one point: P1 presupposes complicated doctrines like empiricism. But which is less obvious, empiricism or (10)? Surely empiricism. Hence what empiricism supports, namely P1, cannot be maintained in the face of an incompatibility between it and (10).

The problem with this line of argument is the one just encountered above: even if it shows that external-world skepticism is incorrect, it does not provide a diagnosis of where exactly it goes wrong. *Of course* the skeptic's conclusion is bizarre and conflicts with our ordinary beliefs—this isn't news. What one wants to know is, How can it be that the skeptic's seemingly flawless argument yields the absurd conclusion that we cannot have justified beliefs? Besides, sometimes things that are "obvious" turn out to be *false*: in dreams and hallucinations, it can be "obvious" that you're on the beach, even when you are in fact at home in bed. Or again, it once struck people as obvious that the seas were full of gods and monsters, that anyone who sails too far on them will fall off the earth, etc. So maybe Moore's "principle" isn't so reasonable after all.

Objection 4:   Direct Perceptual Realism

To me, clowns aren't funny. In fact, they are kind of scary. I've wondered where this started, and I think it goes back to the time I went to the circus and a clown killed my dad.

Jack Handey

A more direct attack on the argument is to reject P1 outright. Until now we have been supposing that P1 is supported by the empiricist claim that there are no innate contents. Hence, we said, everything in the mind arrived there by experience. We took this to imply that the only things that directly enter the mind are "seemings." This is just another way of stating P1. But does P1 really follow from empiricism? Suppose that what one experiences aren't (just) sensations and the like but also external objects like desks and boats. Then even if all genuine knowledge comes from experience, it still isn't true that all we know directly are seemings. To the contrary, we directly know desks, boats, and so on.

Many contemporary philosophers favor this sort of view, called "direct perceptual realism." For them, we do not perceive desks and the like *by* having seemings; rather, we directly perceive them, unmediated. Here is a way of thinking about this direct/indirect talk. It's natural to say that Tiejun has never directly perceived Bill Clinton: he has never met the man, never seen him in person. Still, in some sense Tiejun has perceived Clinton, by seeing representations of him in newspapers, on TV screens, and so on. Hence, Tiejun has *in*directly perceived Clinton: he perceived Clinton *by* perceiving representations of him. Now, some classical philosophers supposed that no one ever directly perceives anyone or anything else. Even Clinton's family, on this view, never really directly perceived him. What they directly perceived were their internal "seemings." Nor has Clinton ever directly perceived Clinton's body. This classical approach yields P1.

Thus, it appears that one way to overcome the argument in (1) is to reject the classical line: contrary to what P1 says, one directly perceives external objects, not just seemings. And yet there are two reasons why the classical approach is hard to resist. First off, consider illusions and hallucinations. When someone hallucinates an apple, their experience is exactly the same as in accurate perception, i.e., perception of a real apple. This suggests that the thing directly known, in both the normal and hallucinating cases, is the same. Yet what is perceived in a hallucination of an apple clearly is not some external apple. Rather, it is something internal: maybe an apple image. Hence, since what is directly perceived in the case of accurate perception is the same as what is perceived in hallucination, in both cases it must be some internal thing that is actually perceived.[3] What internal thing, you may ask? Seemings, of course. Besides, how can the direct perceptual realist convince the skeptic that we do directly perceive boats, trees, desks, and so on? It would seem that any such attempt would beg the question by appealing to human relations to external things.

In sum, direct perceptual realism may have a lot going for it. (Indeed, a great deal more could be said about it.) Nevertheless, P1 isn't entirely easy to resist.

Objection 5:   Meaninglessness
Instead of a trap door, what about a trap window? The guy looks out it, and if he leans too far, he falls out. Wait. I guess that's like a regular window.
Jack Handey

Let's sum up, before continuing on. We presented a two-premise argument to the effect that you cannot know anything about the "external world." The first premise was supported by (one version of) empiricism.

P2, in turn, was bolstered by reflection upon two things: first, that the inference from how things seem to how things are is not *always* reliable (the "error worry"), and second, that this inference form is not *itself* justified by anything. Nor does it appear to be independently *justifiable*. Therefore, every belief whose support requires the use of (2) on page 17, and that's *every* belief about nonseemings, is ultimately unjustified: every such belief rests on an unjustifiable assumption. Hence, no belief about nonseemings is known to be true. Having explained the argument for external-world skepticism, we considered three antiskeptical replies: first, that human experiences must be caused somehow; second, that a scientific inference to the best explanation would show that the likely cause was the external world; and third, that "ordinary living" shows that skepticism isn't a serious option. We then launched a direct attack on P1, in the guise of direct perceptual realism.

Truth be told, all of these replies have been around for quite a while, and none of them has greatly swayed true skeptics. Luckily, there's another tool in the antiskeptic's chest. Maybe skepticism, instead of being *false*, is actually *nonsense*: maybe skepticism can be shown to be meaningless. There are at least two distinct routes to this conclusion. Let's call them the "contrast" maneuver and the "semantic" maneuver.

The former goes like this: the comparison between seeming and being requires that there is some "being" to contrast with the mere "seemings." Without this, there is no distinction between illusion and reality. And, of course, the skeptic, in asserting things like P1 and P2, presupposes just this distinction. Therefore, goes the objection, even the skeptic must take for granted that there's such a thing as the external world, with its unperceived features.

The answers to this objection should be obvious. First up, what the skeptic wants to say is that she doesn't *know* whether there is an external world, or whether it has such and such features. At best, this "contrast" argument shows that she presupposes, in giving her arguments, that there *is* an external world: not that she presupposes that she *knows* that there is. Nor is it obvious that whenever someone presupposes something, they also presuppose that they know it: it surely makes sense to say, "I take for granted that it will be sunny this weekend, but I am not absolutely positive of this." And this is precisely a case of presupposing something (that it will be sunny) without claiming to know it. Second point: sometimes one presupposes something false, in order to argue against an opponent. One way of doing this is the argument form called REDUCTIO AD ABSURDUM:

(11) *Reductio ad absurdum* Accepting a hypothesis for the sake of
argument and then showing that it has absurd consequences, and
hence should be rejected.

Such an argument would, of course, be strong grounds for holding that
the originally assumed hypothesis is false. Hence, the skeptic may be
taken to be arguing as follows: "Suppose, for the sake of argument, that
there is an external world; then there is a distinction between seeming and
being; but, given P1 and P2, we can only know seemings; so we cannot
know the supposed external world." Nothing incoherent here. And also,
it's surely open to the skeptic to concede that there is a distinction between
seeming and being while saying, "On any given occasion, we cannot be
certain that *this* seeming accurately represents the way things are." This
would be cold comfort to the antiskeptic. So, even granting that the
seeming/being distinction is presupposed by the skeptic, antiskepticism
doesn't follow.

On the other hand, it's not clear why the skeptic has to admit that there
really *is* a distinction between how things seem and how things are. All
she needs is this: that people *understand* the idea of the external world and
the contrasting idea of the "realm of seemings." The skeptic does not
further need to admit that people manage to have this understanding by
encountering the real world. (Compare: children understand the *idea* of
Santa Claus and the Easter Bunny. And they are able to contrast these
ideas with other, less friendly, ones like the Bogey Man. Nevertheless,
Santa and the Easter Bunny do not exist.)

This brings us to the second argument for the meaninglessness of skepticism, the one that we've dubbed the "semantic maneuver." It goes like
this. Take the conclusion of the skeptical argument, repeated below:

Conclusion 1 You can't know how things really are outside of you.

It might be argued that this assumption is either meaningless or self-
refuting. Either way, it should be rejected.

The argument starts with VERIFICATIONISM, a philosophical doctrine
held (during some of his working life) by Rudolf Carnap (b. 1891) and by
the LOGICAL POSITIVISTS associated with him. The basic idea of verificationism is that the meaning of a statement is *the observations by which
the sentence may be verified*. This doctrine gains its plausibility from the
following thought: that sentences gain their meaning by being connected
with experience, i.e., with some (possible) observation. So any statement
that is utterly disconnected from experience, and hence has no "means of

verification," lacks meaning. (That is, such statements look vaguely grammatical but actually have no real meaning: just like, for instance, 'Colorless green ideas sleep furiously'.) Given this, consider the only two options to reach the skeptical conclusion: it's either verifiable or it's not. Let's consider each option.

Suppose that C1, i.e., the claim that you can't know how things really are outside of you, is unverifiable. Then, by verificationism, it is meaningless. Since the skeptic won't like this result, she will opt for the alternative, that C1 is verifiable.[4] However, this alternative is equally unattractive. If C1 is verifiable, then, by the definition of "verify," you can *observe* that you can't know how things really are outside of you. But this observation surely amounts to knowledge about how things really are outside of you! So if C1 is verifiable, then there *is* something that you can know about the external world, namely, that you can't know how things really are. A paradox. In brief, if C1 is verifiable, then it is self-refuting.

Putting this all together, we get the following:

Premise 1 If a sentence cannot be verified, it is meaningless. [From verificationism]

Premise 2 C1 (that you can't know how things really are outside of you) is either verifiable or unverifiable.

Premise 3 If C1 is verifiable, then it is self-refuting. [Because if it's verifiable, we can observe something about the external world.]

Premise 4 If C1 is *un*verifiable, then it is meaningless. [Application of P1 to C1]

Conclusion 2 C1 is either self-refuting (by P3) or meaningless (by P4).

This is a very cute little argument. And if it worked, it would certainly make skepticism a nonoption. Unfortunately, the argument has a widely recognized flaw: it rests on verificationism. And there's little reason for the skeptic to accept verificationism. Note first that verificationism—the claim that the meaning of a statement is the observational means of verifying (or falsifying) that statement—is either an empirical claim or it's not. If it *is* empirical, then it begs the question against the skeptic, who is suspicious of all sense-based "evidence" for facts about the world. (Put another way, the antiskeptic likely cannot justify the equation of meaningfulness with "observability" solely on the basis of seemings.) On the other hand, if it's not an empirical claim about the world, it is not verifiable by observation. But then, by its own lights, it runs a serious risk of being meaningless. So verificationism either begs the question against the skeptic or, by its own reckoning, risks meaninglessness. Either way, it leaves skepticism standing.

Still, there may be something to the foregoing objections. Taking a cue from Ludwig Wittgenstein (b. 1889), we might pose the following sort of questions to the skeptic: What would count as knowledge if each case one proposes meets with skeptical doubts? If what I have right now, with my eyes open, wide awake, in good light, etc., isn't knowledge, then what is missing? What would you count as knowledge? Further, if by your lights there aren't any examples of knowledge, is your concept of knowledge really coherent? These are just rhetorical questions, of course, but they are pretty telling. They suggest that, in some sense yet to be elaborated, skepticism really doesn't make any sense. Of course, we want more than this. We want a serious and precise diagnosis of where the skeptic goes wrong, a story that rescues us from the puzzling conclusions. And that is something we don't yet have. But maybe these rhetorical questions are a start.

3 Epilogue: The Gettier "Paradox" and Knowledge as Justified True Belief

To round out this discussion of the nature of knowledge, we should look briefly at a puzzle that has taken its name from the contemporary philosopher Edmund Gettier. We suggested above that, to be an item of knowledge, a proposition must be believed, it must be true, and we must have justification for believing it. And it does seem that all knowledge must meet these three conditions. (To use the traditional jargon: these surely are *necessary* conditions for knowledge.) But are *all* justified true beliefs automatically knowledge? It seems, surprisingly enough, that the answer is "No."

To see this, consider an example. Suppose that Andre believes that his neighbor Samir owns a black Ford. Andre believes this because he has seen a black Ford Mustang parked in Samir's parking spot for the last few weeks. Suppose further that Samir does own a black Ford. Given this, Andre believes (12), (12) is true, and Andre has a good justification for believing (12).

(12) Samir owns a black Ford.

It looks like Andre has satisfied all the conditions for *knowing* that Samir owns a black Ford.

But here's an extra wrinkle: it isn't really Samir's Mustang that is parked in his spot. Several weeks ago, unbeknownst to Andre, Samir rented out his spot to Alicia. And she has been parking her black Ford Mustang there. By coincidence, however, just yesterday Samir inherited his uncle's antique Model T, which, of course, happens to be black. Now, it's still the case that Andre believes (12), (12) is true, and Andre has a good justification for believing (12). But does Andre *know* (12)? Not really.

The problem is, the justification that underwrites Andre's belief— namely, that there has been a black Mustang parked in Samir's spot— isn't actually related to the fact that makes Andre's belief true. (Remember, what makes (12) true is that he inherited a black Model T.)

Nor is this an isolated case. Whenever it happens that the "route of justification" for a belief has nothing to do with what makes the belief true, it seems that the agent doesn't really know the fact in question. Here's another case, for example. Suppose that Andre sees his boss yelling at two employees. They then proceed to empty out their desks and are escorted out of the office by security. Andre thinks (13).

(13) The boss just fired two people.

Suppose further that (13) is true. Now Andre has a belief, it's true, and he has a solid justification for it. Is this enough for Andre to know (13)? Once again, it's not. For suppose that the boss was actually taking part in a "firing drill" with the two people that Andre saw. They weren't really being fired. However, the reason for the drill was that, minutes before Andre arrived and saw the yelling etc., the boss *had* fired two people. There was an awful scene. And precisely to avoid such scenes in the future, the boss, the security forces, and the two volunteers (all seen by Andre) acted out the company's "firing policy." Here Andre does not really know that his boss just fired two people. The reason, once again, appears to be that the events that give Andre his justification aren't appropriately related to the events that make (13) true.

One thing this means is that getting knowledge is even harder than what we made out above. For as these examples show, it's not enough to have a justification for your true belief. To answer the skeptic, then, it won't be enough to show that there are justified true beliefs. Even worse, unfortunately, it isn't clear what more is required. To be sure, it will have *something* to do with justification being of the right sort. But what exactly does that mean? This isn't a question we can address here. In fact, it has occupied epistemologists for several decades. But until that question is answered, it won't be possible to *show* that we have knowledge of the external world.

Study Questions

1. Discuss the difference between knowing something directly and indirectly. What sort of thing, if anything, do humans know directly? Could creatures different from us know things directly that we only know indirectly, or vice versa?

2. What are *modus ponens* and *reductio ad absurdum*? Make up some examples. What is a circular argument? What is begging the question? Give examples of those as well.

3. Contrast skepticism with solipsism. Is solipsism a claim about what we can know or about what there is? That is, is it an epistemological position, or is it more an ontological one, a theory of what exists? (ONTOLOGY is the study of what exists.)

4. Is there any reason to expect the future to be like the past? Discuss some practical implications of a negative answer.

5. Should one accept that the most explanatory theory really is *true*? Is there any alternative to doing so?

6. Consider some of the relationships between ordinary life and philosophical speculation. For example, should you treat your inability to answer skeptical arguments as merely a philosophical puzzle? Or should you allow that inability to alter how you actually live from day to day? Also, is it possible to know that something is a truly paradoxical conclusion that ought not to be accepted as true but should instead be explained away? How can such a case be distinguished from a very surprising conclusion that really is true?

7. What is verificationism? How would it help the antiskeptic if it were true?

8. Describe as many responses to the skeptic about the external world as you can. Which responses, if any, are plausible?

9. Explain the contrast between seeming and being. Can one make safe inferences from "seemings" to the way things really are outside one?

Suggested Further Readings

Ayer 1956 provides a good general introduction to epistemology, as does Hamlyn 1970. See also the references cited in chapter 1, including especially Chisholm 1989, Dancy 1985, Lehrer 1990, Nagel and Brandt 1965, and Russell 1912.

A very good overview of the history of skepticism can be found in Popkin 1964. Some of our discussion is based on Nagel 1987, a very readable book. Specific worries about inferring future patterns from what was observed in the past can be found in Hume 1978 [1739]. A very influential but rather difficult discussion of seemings and of direct versus indirect knowledge can be found in Sellars 1997 [1956]. See also Austin 1962, Ryle 1949 and Wittgenstein 1969 for challenging but rewarding discussions of "direct knowledge of seemings." A clear and accessible introduction to verificationism and its use in philosophy may be found in Ayer 1946. See also Carnap 1932 and Schlick 1932 for early uses of it in philosophy. Verificationism is criticized very effectively in Hempel 1950. (The latter three papers are all reprinted in Ayer 1959.)

The Gettier puzzle was first put forward in Gettier 1963. It is reprinted, with replies and discussion, in Lucey 1996.

Chapter 3

Knowledge of Language

The face of a child can say it all, especially the mouth part of the face.
Jack Handey

This book deals with two general issues: the nature of human knowledge and the nature of the mind, i.e., the thing that *has* the knowledge. Some of the topics we discuss fall squarely under knowledge (e.g., skepticism about the external world); other topics are mostly about the mind (e.g., the relationship between mind and body). Other issues in the text enter both domains.[1] This is true of our next topic, knowledge of language. Though directly an issue of knowledge, it holds important implications for the nature of mind. It would be good to keep this element of overlap in mind as we go through the discussion.

There are many places in which issues about language connect with issues in epistemology and philosophy of mind. Here we will focus on three: what knowledge of language is like, how it is acquired, and the relationship between language and thinking.

Before beginning, a note on how to read this chapter. Many of the ideas introduced are mutually supporting. In fact, you may best be able to understand the parts if you first survey the whole. Thus, it may be best to read through the whole chapter once, not worrying too much about the details, and then reread each section slowly and carefully.

1 The Nature of Linguistic Knowledge

Language has been an object of study for a very long time. Indeed, both Plato and Aristotle (b. ca. 384 B.C.) wrote on language, as did the empiricists Hobbes and Locke. (See the suggested readings for specific sources.) In more recent times, however, there has been a veritable flood of work, especially on knowledge of language. One key figure in this recent theorizing is Noam Chomsky.

Chomsky on Linguistic Competence

Chomsky's first important contribution to this area was an argument to the effect that language theorists must not ignore the internal mental states of agents when trying to account for their "linguistic behavior." He argued that, contrary to what some BEHAVIORISTS claimed, language use is too complex to be described solely in terms of environmental stimuli and habit-based responses. What one must do instead, Chomsky said, is to describe the language spoken by giving a *grammar* of it and then suppose that speakers tacitly know this grammar. It is this internalized information, in the form of a grammar, which allows speakers to use and understand language. It is this move that launches the topic of knowledge of language. And it makes possible our first two questions: What is this knowledge like? How is it acquired?

Of course, speakers only "know" language in a special sense of 'know'. To begin with, as we'll see, much of the knowledge is unconscious. To take one simple example, in some sense all English speakers know that the verbs 'to sing' and 'to bring' have dissimilar past tense conjugations, though neither of them is entirely regular. (Neither is entirely regular because their past tense isn't formed by adding '-ed': one says neither 'bringed' nor 'singed'. But their irregularity is dissimilar because the past tense of 'bring' is 'brought', whereas the past tense of 'sing' is 'sang'.) Yet despite that fact that every speaker knows this, it doesn't follow that any speaker has ever been conscious of it. Besides, it's not clear how the notions of truth and justification apply to language. A person who conjugates 'bring' as 'brang' makes a mistake. But in what sense? Is it the kind of mistake that is rightly called believing a falsehood? Surely not. Or again, is she somehow unjustified?

To sidestep such questions, Chomsky coined some terminology. He suggested that human beings come to have LINGUISTIC COMPETENCE— essentially, they internalize, in some sense of "internalize," a body of linguistic rules—and this linguistic competence contributes to the observed behavioral PERFORMANCE. (Put crudely, linguistic competence is the agent's information about grammar; linguistic performance is what the agent *does* with that information.) He insisted that positing such a competence was necessary to explain the highly sophisticated linguistic performance that we observe: the behaviorist's stimulus and response patterns, which focus solely on performance in the environment, will not do the job. (We discuss BEHAVIORISM in chapter 4.)

Chomsky adds that it is not the case that the linguistic competence in and of itself gives rise to the linguistic performance. Rather, the competence is one causal force among others. For instance, other causally relevant factors include attention, memory, physical tiredness, background beliefs and desires, etc. To take an example: someone may know sentence (1) but may not speak it even when asked because she is too tired or because she believes it would be rude or because she is too interested in other matters or because she stutters, etc.

(1) Peter Piper picked a peck of pickled peppers.

Causes of all these kinds and more can act in concert, interacting with one's linguistic competence, to yield the effect of linguistic performance, i.e., actual speech.

One thing this means for the linguistic *investigator*, i.e., the linguist studying the speaker, is that there is no direct route from the behavior she observes to the nature of the grammar she takes to be "known" by the speaker being observed. The nature of the speaker's competence can only be *inferred* by the linguist, not directly observed. Precisely because speech is the result of interacting causes, what the scientist observes is not solely a reflection of competence—it's a reflection of many factors mixed together. This didn't worry Chomsky, however, since he argued that sciences generally do more than simply make observations and catalogue the results: scientists are always in the business of inferring unobservable causes from observable effects, thereby explaining the observed effects. Hence, here too what the linguists does is to infer the nature of (one of) the unobservable causes (namely, the linguistic competence), on the basis of the observed effects of its interaction with other causes (e.g., tiredness, stuttering, distraction, etc.). The unobserved then explains the observed.

Once we're convinced that linguistic competence exists, even though it cannot be directly observed, the next obvious question is how the competence came to be. And what exactly it looks like. Before turning to these issues, however, it's worth considering an objection that is sometimes made to Chomsky's picture.

An Objection to Chomsky's Notion of Linguistic Competence

Some philosophers, purportedly following Wittgenstein, argue that Chomsky's notion of linguistic competence is founded on a bad picture. We can illustrate this complaint with an example. Suppose that Rudy is going to the store because of his conscious justified true belief that the store is open, sells soda, etc. Once at the store, Rudy says, "I want a soda." What explains this second piece of behavior, i.e., his utterance? Here is what these philosophers call the "bad picture": just as Rudy's going to the store arises from a conscious, justified true belief, so Rudy's *speech* arises from a similar state, albeit unconscious and not quite true or justified. (That is, the speech is produced in part by Rudy's linguistic competence.) The internalized information underlying the production of the words would include things like: the verb 'to want' is conjugated as 'want' in the first person; the indefinite article is 'a', unless the noun begins with a vowel, in which case it is 'an'; articles appear before the noun; the subject precedes the verb; and so on. That is, roughly the same sort of knowledge state yields both kinds of behavior: the trip to the store and the utterance. It has seemed to some, however, that what underlies our observable speech is not *at all* like conscious justified true belief. As far as they are concerned, Rudy's going to the store on the basis of his justified true beliefs is a very bad model to employ when explaining the sounds that Rudy made once he got to the store.

The objection, to repeat, is that Chomsky's notion of linguistic competence is built on a bad picture. Let's spell this out. What Chomsky wants, we saw, is a notion that will help explain people's observable speech. What he proposes, namely linguistic competence, is sort of like conscious justified true belief, but not quite. The 'not quite' consists in doing away with the conscious part and granting that the notions of truth and justification apply at best awkwardly. The complaint being considered is that Chomsky's treatment of linguistic competence as "not quite" ordinary knowledge is not nearly enough of a difference.

But what is the alternative? After all, Chomsky argued that his notion of competence was necessary to explain the highly sophisticated performance that we observe. If we don't have linguistic competence, what explains linguistic behavior? To answer that, we need to contrast two quite different senses of 'know': KNOWLEDGE-THAT and KNOWLEDGE-HOW. Knowledge-that might equally be called propositional knowledge. It's a matter of believing certain truths on the basis of some kind of cognitive learning process. Knowledge-how, on the other hand, is a matter of having certain abilities, e.g., knowing how to swim, catch a ball, or ride a bicycle. Everyone will agree that, in the sense of knowing-how, humans know their languages, that is, they exhibit certain linguistic skills and abilities. We all know how to speak. But this doesn't show that we have propositional knowledge of language, any more than the ability to catch a baseball shows that small children know the differential calculus required to calculate the arc of the ball.

Given this distinction, here is the objection to Chomsky, put in slightly different terms: Some philosophers have been skeptical that knowledge of language should be modeled on propositional knowledge. That is, they would say that Chomsky, in addition to conflating two senses of 'know' in building his construct, has opted for the wrong one. Moreover, once this second variety of knowledge has been explicitly noted, it may seem to provide a perfectly good explanation of linguistic behavior without introducing Chomskyan linguistic competence. To return to our earlier example, what underlies Rudy's utterance of 'I want a soda' is not some complex series of internalized rules but rather knowledge-how: the ability required to produce such words. To see the point more clearly, recall the case of catching the ball. It would seem dead wrong to model ball catching on anything remotely like Rudy's conscious justified true belief that there is soda at the store, that the store is open, etc. Nor would it do to say, "Well, catching a ball isn't *quite* like deciding to go to the store, since it involves unconsciously internalized rules that aren't exactly justified or true." Finally, if an imagined proponent of this unpromising model said, "But something must explain ball-catching behavior," it would seem a perfectly reasonable reply to say that ball catching is an ability, developed through much practice.

A quick review before we proceed. The objection to Chomsky's notion of linguistic competence essentially amounts to the claim that it is modeled on the wrong sort of knowledge. Rather than understanding speech as deriving from a skill (i.e., knowledge-how), it treats speech as arising from *something like* conscious justified belief about some state of affairs (i.e., knowledge-that). The objector's key idea is that whatever produces speech, it's very different from, for instance, the belief that the store is open and that it sells soda.

One reason the two are different we have already noted: the notions of truth and justification apply at best awkwardly to "knowledge of language." Another reason, Chomsky's critics say, is that knowledge of language would have to be unconscious in a very strong sense. This is the point we will now develop in more detail.

You've likely had the experience of a nonnative speaker asking you to explain a rule of English usage (e.g., when to employ 'shall' versus 'will', 'do' versus 'make', etc.). If so, you will realize that you are usually not conscious of the rules—any more than you are conscious of the "rules" you follow when you catch a fly ball or ride a bicycle. Worse, while there are some linguistic rules that you immediately recognize as "what you had in mind" when you are presented with them, this is certainly not always true. So some of the rules we supposedly know need to be *deeply* unconscious. A case in point: do you know what makes (3) peculiar, even though (2) is fine (albeit colloquial)?

(2) Who do you wanna meet? [Grammatical, though "slangy"]

(3) Who do you wanna talk? [Ungrammatical even as slang]

You likely *feel* that the first is okay, while the second is odd. Yet, unless you're a linguist, it's doubtful whether you can state the rule that explains the awkwardness of (3).[2] This shows that linguistic rules are "shallowly" unconscious—we can't easily state the rules when asked. More impressive, however, is that even after the purported rule is explained to you, you're *un*likely to say, "Ah yes, that's the rule I learned!" (If you did respond that way, that would show that the information was only "shallowly unconscious.") Instead, the generalization will probably strike you as unfamiliar and odd. The situation is thus very unlike that of merely *reminding* you of something you know. It qualifies, therefore, as "deeply" unconscious. So, not only aren't the rules immediately available to consciousness, they cannot be easily brought to consciousness. But then, why say that you *know* the rules, in the sense of knowing-that? That is, why introduce linguistic competence, modeled as it is on conscious knowledge? Surely, the objector says, it would be better simply to recognize that linguistic behavior derives from knowledge-how.

Some Replies on Chomsky's Behalf

One might feel tempted to reply, on Chomsky's behalf, that there must be such a thing a linguistic competence, patterned on knowledge that, because linguists can describe it. Indeed, sentences (2) and (3), the very examples used to show that competence would have to be "deeply unconscious," seem equally to show that there *are* rules there to be described. The point is well taken. But it may be overcome if we introduce a bit of philosophical jargon. Philosophers distinguish between being *guided* by a rule and having one's behavior *fit* a rule, i.e., being correctly describable by a rule. Meteors can be said to "fit rules" as they fall from the sky. That means that there are rules, also known as laws, that describe the descent of the meteors. But meteors are not *guided* by these rules: they don't say to themselves, as it were, "I think I should accelerate at 9.8 m/s^2." So an object can have its behavior correctly described by a rule even if the object is not trying to make its behavior fit the rule. Now think again about people and linguistic rules. Maybe what's going on is this: while linguistic behavior may "fit" (i.e., accord with) the complex rules that linguists discover, agents do not *know* these rules in the sense of knowing-that, any more than rocks that accord with the rule that falling objects accelerate at 9.8 m/s^2 know the "rules" of gravitation. Hence there is the illusion of correctly describing linguistic knowledge-that, even though all there really is is knowledge-how.

A different possible reply in defense of linguistic competence runs as follows. Whenever we encounter very complex behavior, which is comparatively "stimulus independent" (i.e., very unlike a reflex), we posit mental states as the intervening cause of the behavior. To give one example, when Weeble the cat jumps off the couch and heads for her food dish in response to certain muffled footsteps, though she has ignored dozens of similar sounds before, one might explain her behavior by saying, "She recognizes Anita's footsteps, realizes that it's late afternoon, and therefore expects food to land in her bowl shortly." On the other hand, should Weeble remain on the couch, it would be explanation enough to note that she did not *want* food right then. Here one has relatively complex behavior, relatively free of stimulus control (notice that Weeble doesn't *invariably* run to her bowl whenever shuffling feet are heard), being explained in mentalistic terms (i.e., recognizing, realizing, wanting, and expecting). Of course, in so far as Weeble's behavior can be treated merely dispositionally, i.e., as a response to a complex stimulus, knowledge-that isn't required, but the more complex her behavior becomes and the more sensitive to other information it is, the more talk of knowing-that becomes appropriate. It goes without saying that the same applies to human behavior. One might explain pulling one's hand away from hot objects in terms of past (negative) stimuli, without calling upon beliefs like "I don't want to get burned," "That object is hot," etc. But when human behavior is not a direct response to stimuli, there seems to be no choice but to appeal to the agent's information.

The general idea, then, is this: If a behavior can be treated as the result of a simple disposition, then knowledge-that need not be invoked, but when such techniques fail, knowledge-that is the explanatory tool of choice. That's because, so this line of defense goes, relatively simple dispositions are all that knowledge-how can handle. Crucially, however, linguistic behavior cannot be accounted for merely dispositionally. It is as flexible, creative, and complex as any behavior known.

But, one might think, wouldn't a speaker be able to state the rules if she really were being guided by them? A partial response would go like this: Especially since Freud (b. 1856), we have taken to explaining complex and stimulus-independent actions in terms of mental states even when the agent does not herself recognize that she is in that state. So, for example, we might account for Mary's rubbing her hands together each time she passes a certain mirror in terms of an apparently forgotten childhood trauma of which she is not conscious. Now, *linguistic* behavior is as complex as can be. In fact, there is a potentially unlimited number of sentences that an agent could speak or understand. What's more, language use is very stimulus-independent. So it makes sense to explain it by appeal to beliefs and such, i.e., knowledge-that. Since, like the case of Mary and the mirror, the knowledge is not conscious, it must be unconscious.

Moreover, Chomsky likes to point out, one can lose all linguistic *abilities* without losing linguistic competence. For instance, consider a person who is comatose. That person cannot speak or understand. And yet if she recovers and immediately starts to use language, it seems most reasonable to say that, while in the coma, she retained her knowledge of language, though she lost her language abilities. So knowledge of language cannot be merely a cluster of capacities.

A natural reply against Chomsky is that one can also have a capacity and yet not be able to exercise it. For instance, Rudy might have the capacity to throw fabulous curve balls, yet have his arms tied behind his back. Here he has the capacity, but he cannot exercise it. And, in response to the claim that knowledge-how can only apply to relatively simple cases, it might be said that capacities can be as complex as you like. Such a use of 'capacity' may be legitimate. What Chomsky will say at this point, however, is that understood in this way, 'John has capacity *x*' has become merely a way of saying 'John has a competence *x*' in his sense. So this way of "objecting" to his view is really a way of granting it.

What Is Competence Like?

The debate continues about whether linguistic competence exists, i.e., whether knowledge-that is the right model for knowledge of language. Going further into it would take us beyond the bounds of this introductory book. Let us therefore take for granted from here on that speakers have such a competence. What is it like? There is a general consensus among linguists that it contains rules for constructing sentences out of minimal parts (called rules of SYNTAX), rules for pronouncing these sentences (called rules of PHONOLOGY) and finally rules, which provide information about what the parts and the constructed wholes mean (SEMANTIC rules). (The terms 'syntax' and 'semantics' will return in an expanded role in chapter 8.) It's also generally agreed that these rules must be PRODUCTIVE. For the moment, this can be understood as meaning that it won't do simply to provide a list of sentences, with the pronunciation and meaning of each. (We'll return to productivity shortly.) The reason is, no list would be long enough. Normal English speakers know not just 10,000 sentences or even 10,000,000. Their linguistic competence enables them to handle an unlimited number of sentences, performance limitations aside. In fact there exist, in *any* natural language, indefinitely many well-formed, fully meaningful expressions. For example, (4) through (6) are all meaningful sentences of English.

(4) a. Phil is sleeping.
  b. John thinks that Phil is sleeping.
  c. Alex surmises that John thinks that Phil is sleeping.
  d. Rudolf fears that Alex surmises that John thinks that Phil is sleeping.
  e. Phil thinks that Rudolf fears that Alex surmises that John thinks that Phil is sleeping.

(5) a. It's cold in Ottawa.
  b. It's really cold in Ottawa.
  c. It's really, really cold in Ottawa.

(6) a. Alice won't be happy until she's earning two million dollars a year.
  b. Alice won't be happy until she's earning three million dollars a year.
  c. Alice won't be happy until she's earning four million dollars a year.

Each list can be extended indefinitely. The first list is extended by putting the last sentence on the list into another sentence. The first list can be extended *indefinitely* because the same names and verbs can be reused; notice, for example, that 'think' and 'Phil' appear twice in (4e). The second list is extended by placing another 'really' after the last 'really'. Again, this can be repeated forever, though admittedly without much point. Finally, the third list is extended by substituting for the numeral in the previous sentence the next highest numeral. And there is no highest numeral.

This fact about languages is sometimes called PRODUCTIVITY. It makes it very plausible that speakers know *rules* rather than lists, i.e., rather than some kind of giant PHRASE BOOK. (A phrase book would be a book of sentences and subsentential units such as phrases and clauses.) After all, phrase books are finite. One can also make the same point without appealing to *unlimited* productivity. Giving a theory of syntax, phonology, and semantics in a phrase book might go like this. The grammarian lists all the words, phrases, and sentences in the language. She says how they sound and what they mean. But how would this go? What is meant by 'all the sentences' in this phrase-book approach? It could only be something like 'all the sentences people have heard, plus all the ones they've thought of'. But everyone can understand expressions that they have never heard, including expressions they've never even previously thought of. Indeed, there are surely expressions that *no one* has ever encountered or thought of but that *would be* understood on first hearing. Consider an example.

(7) In my dream I saw, in the dim light of dawn, six off-white whales in the Carleton University parking lot.

Every English speaker immediately understands this sentence. So the grammar needs to include it. But the phrase-book model would, in all likelihood, leave it off its list simply because, chances are, none of the book's compilers would have encountered this sentence before or even have thought of it. The rule-introducing model, on the other hand, could naturally capture this sentence.

So it seems that the grammatical competence that one ends up with contains rules for building, pronouncing, and interpreting words, phrases, and sentences. That answers, at least tentatively, the question of what knowledge of language is like. But how is this competence acquired? That is our next topic.

2 The Acquisition of Linguistic Knowledge

Recall the debate between empiricists and rationalists. Extreme empiricists maintain that *all* knowledge, including both contents and mechanisms for thinking, comes from sense experience. Extreme rationalists say, to the contrary, that no genuine knowledge comes from sense experience. In between there is a continuum, with more or less emphasis placed on the role of experience. The issue obviously arises for knowledge of language as well. How much of it is derived from experience? Is some of it innate? And so on.

Before providing the arguments, it will be useful to clarify what is and isn't being argued about. The first point is about what the "linguistic rationalists" are *not* committed to. Those who think *some* linguistic knowledge is innate need not maintain that *all* of it is innate. And that's a good thing, for it's perfectly obvious that infants only acquire the language spoken around them, e.g., one never sees a baby, despite living in a unilingual French environment, coming to speak Japanese. That's surely because Japanese, and other human languages, are not innately known *in toto*: clearly, some linguistic knowledge is derived from experience. The question is, is all of it derived from experience? Linguistic rationalists say, "No, not all knowledge of language is based on experience." The second point is about what the "linguistic empiricists" are not committed to. They can happily admit that humans are born with *the capacity to learn language*. This is important, as it's obvious that there is *something* innately different about humans, something that accounts for the fact that in very similar circumstances we learn to speak, though kittens and puppies do not.

One can be even more specific than this: it's not (just) something like our different vocal apparatus that makes us able to acquire language; human *minds* are relevantly different. The linguistic empiricist may allow, for instance, that the human mind is innately smarter than, say, cat minds. What a linguistic empiricist cannot concede is that we are born with *beliefs* about human languages, including beliefs about rules, i.e., that we have innate CONTENTS. Nor can she admit that powerful mental mechanisms for finding structure in the sounds we hear, etc., exist prior to interaction with the environment. In sum, the debate is not about the (absurd) claim that everything we know about our language is innate, nor is it about the (equally absurd) idea that there is nothing innately different about human linguistic competence. Rather, the question is whether there is a significant amount of innate knowledge (i.e., knowledge-that) specific to language.

Nativism Defended

There are many arguments pro and con. Rather than trying to discuss each of them exhaustively, we will simply provide a sampling. This should be sufficient to introduce the debate. Specifically, we will consider arguments from "poverty of the stimulus" and from linguistic universals, plus rebuttals to these.

The POVERTY-OF-STIMULUS ARGUMENT can be quickly summarized like this:

Premise 1 Language users end up with more information about their language than is available to them in their environment.
Premise 2 The best available explanation of this fact is that the "missing" information is innate.
Conclusion The "missing" information is innate.

Notice that this is an *inference to the best explanation*. It has the following form:

p
The best available explanation of *p* is *q*.
Therefore, *q*.

In this case *p* is 'Language users end up with more information about their language than is readily available in their environment' and *q* is 'The missing information is innate'.

This argument form is not deductively valid: the premises can be true while the conclusion is false. That's because something can be the best *available* explanation of a phenomenon and yet still not turn out to be correct. (This happens all the time in science: some very creative theorist comes along, considers a matter in which a good explanation is already accepted, and then produces a still better explanation that displaces the old one.)

Now, despite not being deductively valid, the argument form has real INDUCTIVE MERIT (we introduced induction in chapter 1, section 3); that is, the premises provide significant evidentiary support for the conclusion. If the premises are true, then the foregoing argument for innate knowledge of language is pretty solid. But is it really true that speakers end up knowing things that they couldn't have learned by observation? That's the question that we'll now consider.

First off, notice that the amount of time that first-language learners have available to them and the quality of their "investigative techniques" are quite limited. Children learn their native language in well under five years. Indeed, most children speak in fluent, fully grammatical sentences by age two or three. And they learn mostly by passively listening to what people around them say. They don't, for instance, ask their parents how such and such a verb is conjugated. Worse, they hear a lot of *un*grammatical sentences, which they somehow manage to ignore as misleading evidence. (Put in the terms we encountered above, children hear many errors of *performance*, which obscure the nature of the linguistic *competence* of those around them. Amazingly, they somehow ignore these as not relevant.) So the "situation of inquiry" of a child learning language isn't particularly good: the "stimuli" they have available are "impoverished" and often incorrect. (Hence the name of this argument: the poverty-of-stimulus argument.) Yet, despite these difficulties, children succeed. The best explanation, goes the argument, is that children get some of the information they need, not from what they hear, but from what they innately know.

Here's another way of making the point. Compare the situation of your average infant with that of the whole community of linguists working on the syntax of English. After many years of constant labor by thousands of gifted scientists, who are able not only to listen passively to speech, but also to ask questions and actively perform tests, the linguistic community is just *beginning* to map out English grammar. New discoveries happen all the time; e.g., it was only a short while ago that the contrast between (2) and (3) was first noted and an explanation proposed.

(2) Who do you wanna meet?

(3) Who do you wanna talk?

But wait a second: how can it be that a whole community of Ph.D.s, in a much better learning situation, should be unable to do what any child can do, namely to figure out the grammar of English in a few short years? The answer, it is urged, is that babies "have a head start": they have information at their disposal that, sad to say, is not consciously available to the working scientist. Whereas linguists really do have to figure out the grammar of the languages they study, principally by using the "impoverished stimuli"—hence their painfully slow progress—infants access their innate knowledge of what all human languages have in common, and thereby race ahead.[3]

And this is not the only reason for thinking that language users end up with more information about their language than is readily available in their environment. The more general reason is that while the evidence available to the infant in the environment is of necessity limited, the linguistic competence that the child acquires is unlimited. As we saw above, our grammatical competence cannot be captured by a phrase book. That's not only because there are an unlimited number of sentences but also because, even if there were a finite number, there are ever so many grammatical sentences that no one has ever bothered to use. In contrast, the stimuli available to the child *can* be recorded in a list. A relatively short list, in fact. So how does the child move from the list of words and sentences it has heard to the unlimited grammar it eventually comes to know—a grammar whose rules can create sentences that it *hasn't* heard? Again, the proposed answer is that the child can do this because she makes use of her innate knowledge of how human languages work. (What is input is less than what the system eventually outputs, so there must be something inside, the innate part, that makes up the difference.)

That, in brief, is the poverty-of-stimulus argument. To repeat, the argument only strongly supports its conclusion; it does not definitively establish it, *even if* its premises are true. The reason is that someone could produce another, even better, explanation of how to bridge the gap between experience and the resulting competence. Still, that doesn't make the argument any less good. To the contrary, most arguments in science are inductive in this way. And there's no reason to demand, about the source of linguistic knowledge, more than the kind of highly confirmed hypotheses that one expects from any other science.

The next argument for the claim that some linguistic knowledge is innate is also inductive rather than deductive. Indeed, it's another inference to the best explanation. It goes like this:

Premise 1 Many linguistic rules and principles are universally shared across human languages.
Premise 2 The best available explanation of these shared features is that some linguistic knowledge is innate.
Conclusion Therefore, some linguistic knowledge is innate.

Let's start with the premise that there are language universals. The evidence for this is reasonably good, but it's difficult to present without significant background in linguistics. Here, however, is a simplified example. Imagine that someone says, 'John likes beer and tomato juice. He also likes beer in a wine glass. And he thinks that the Pope likes beer!' Now consider the sentences in (8), given as responses to these surprising statements about John:

(8) a. John likes beer and *what*?
     b. John likes beer in a *what*?
     c. John thinks that *who* likes beer?

Here's an interesting fact: Although all of (8a–c) are grammatical responses in this situation, none of (9a–c) is:

(9) a. What does John like beer and?
     b. What does John like beer in a?
     c. Who does John think that likes beer?

This is interesting because, when a question word (e.g., 'what', 'who', 'where', 'when') occurs inside a sentence, it's often possible to move it to the front. Thus, for example, 'John likes what?' becomes 'What does John like?' and 'John lives where?' becomes 'Where does John live?' But there are restrictions on when the question word can be moved: it's not always possible, for example, to lift the word 'what' from its place inside a sentence, and place it at the beginning. Precisely such restrictions are illustrated by (8) and (9). Now here's the punch line: the restrictions on moving question words around seem to apply not just to English but to all languages. Thus the counterparts of (9), goes the argument, are ungrammatical in Spanish, French, and so on. This general fact about languages is hard to explain unless there is an innately given restriction on the movement of question words. Hence we have an instance of the argument above: there's a universal feature the best explanation for which is innate knowledge of language, so we conclude that such knowledge exists. Provide enough language universals, and this argument starts to look pretty convincing.

Some Antinativist Replies
Now we move to some replies, on behalf of the linguistic empiricist, to these arguments for innate knowledge of language. First reply: the data regarding language remain incomplete. There are thousands of human languages, most of which have hardly been studied at all. And the only languages that have been studied in great detail have tended to belong to the same language family, namely, Indo-European. So it's too early yet to be proclaiming "universals." And it is not so obvious that the experience base available to children is as poor as it's made out to be. In addition, we don't know nearly enough about the brain to be sure that it cannot, without innate contents, extract all the required information about language from the environment. Besides, think back to the previous section on what linguistic knowledge is like. The poverty-of-stimulus argument takes for granted that adults end up with lots of *knowledge-that* about their various languages. The question is then asked, 'How do humans manage to get so much knowledge-that from such a poor data base, in so little time?' But if Chomsky et al. are wrong and knowledge of language is not knowledge-that, then there may be nothing to explain. Or it may be that the best explanation has to do with how the brain gets conditioned, so that we eventually acquire a *skill*. Perhaps the best explanation has nothing to do with information retrieved from the environment getting mixed with information already innately present. In brief, maybe the two phenomena for which an explanation in terms of innateness is given just aren't real: there is no "missing" information to be accounted for, and there aren't really any universals. (This reply denies P1 of the respective arguments.)

The next reply to the NATIVIST (i.e., the person who believes in innate knowledge) applies specifically to the argument from universals. It goes thus: Even if certain attributes really are universal, it isn't true that the best explanation of this is innate knowledge of language. Instead, the best explanation is that certain structures are universal because they are useful (e.g., for communication); others are universal because all human languages share a single common "ancestor," some of whose characteristics have been passed down to all present languages (Putnam 1967, 296). (Notice that this argument attacks P2, rather than P1.) In sum, there probably aren't universals, but even if there were, that wouldn't show that much of linguistic knowledge is innate.

This reply to the nativist—i.e., that even if there are universals, the best explanations are function, on the one hand, and history, on the other—deserves attention. Let's begin with the "history gambit": The idea is to explain linguistic commonalities by appeal to a common ancestor. To the question, Why are languages alike in feature f, the reply comes, 'Because the mother of all languages had property p, and linguistic evolution occurred in manner m. And that resulted in many (all) languages having f'. But this really isn't a complete explanation. It leaves unanswered as many questions as it addresses. Questions like these: Why did the mother language have property p? And why did evolution occur in manner m, so that certain properties like f end up being shared today, while other properties of the mother language are not shared? That is, why has language change been circumscribed in the ways it has? And why *hasn't* it been circumscribed in others? These questions deserve an answer. The answer that comes immediately to mind is, Part of what drives linguistic evolution over time, as well as part of what determined the nature of the mother language, is precisely the innate linguistic knowledge shared by all humans. That is, the explanation falls back on the innateness hypothesis.

But what about function? Couldn't that explain the commonalities? Here's the received view. Functional explanations may be in the offing for certain universals. For example, it comes as no surprise that all natural languages contain proper names (like 'Phil', 'Nancy' or 'Sanjay') precisely because names are enormously useful. But the universals that linguists have pointed to are by no means uniformly useful—things could have been otherwise without decreasing the functionality of language as a whole. For instance, if we think back to the example above, what is *functionally* wrong with moving a question word out of the sentence 'John likes beer and what?' Nothing, so far as we can see.

In sum, it's doubtful that either shared ancestors or functionality can adequately explain the observed universals. And it may be that the best existing explanation of how children cope with their "impoverished stimuli" is innate knowledge-that. In such a case the best explanation right now remains the one favored by the linguistic rationalists: there is innate knowledge of language. This provides serious, though not definitive, support for the rationalist side of the debate, and for the conclusion that some knowledge—specifically, knowledge of language—does not come from the senses.

3   Language and Thought

Sometimes you have to be careful when selecting a new nickname for yourself. For instance, let's say you have chosen the nickname "Fly Head." Normally you would think that "Fly Head" would mean a person who has beautiful swept-back features, as if flying through the air. But think again. Couldn't it also mean "having a head like a fly"? I'm afraid some people might actually think that.
Jack Handey

We've already considered two important connections among language, mind, and knowledge. On the one hand, we saw that human agents know language; on the other, we saw some arguments to the effect that at least some of this knowledge is not acquired by experience but is, rather, innate. The issue in this final section on language is (10):

(10) What is the relationship between language and thought?

This question touches both philosophy of mind and epistemology. Thinking is a mental phenomenon par excellence. Hence it is immediately of interest to philosophers of mind. But thinking—whether it be deductive reasoning, inductive reasoning, creative speculation, learning, or what have you—is also crucial to epistemology because it is by thinking that much of human knowledge is acquired. On the one hand, some knowledge, including very abstract knowledge, seems wholly detached from experience—knowledge in mathematics, for example, seems to come from thinking alone—but even knowledge via observation requires *assimilating* what is observed, and that too requires thinking.[4] Hence the way thought works is bound to interest epistemologists.

Moreover, the role of language in thinking is especially intriguing to epistemologists because it is often supposed that if the answer to (10) is, 'Language and thought are closely related', this would raise many puzzles and problems. For instance, if language and thought are closely related, then maybe language users with dissimilar languages think very differently from one another. And if that's right, who is to say which way of thinking is correct? Or again, if language and thought are closely related, it could be that human language hinders thinking: our thoughts might be forever trapped by faulty language. Nor is it obvious how to evade this trap, for the only escape would seem to involve discovering and repairing the defects of our language, and that's something we could do only from "inside" the language itself.

Now that we have seen why (10) is interesting, the next step would seem to be to answer it. The question as stated, however, suffers from a strange defect: it's too deep, in the sense that the relationships are so many, so subtle, and so diverse that it isn't really possible to answer the question directly and in a satisfyingly clear way. So let's substitute a different question—one that will, we hope, bring out clearly and straightforwardly some of the intriguing links between language and thought while nevertheless retaining the interest of the "too deep" original:

(11) Is thinking just a kind of inner speech?

That is, is all thought a matter of "speaking to oneself," with one's mouth closed as it were? The answer to this question, as we'll see, is pretty clearly, 'No, thought isn't *merely* inner speech'. But arriving at that answer and seeing the attractions of the opposite answer will be a good way of thinking about (10).

First off, it's clear that certain kinds of thoughts are not available to animals and prelinguistic children. For instance, though Weeble the cat may think that someone is coming to the door, and that food is about to arrive in her dish, she couldn't really think that Meera's roommate is arriving at 32 Lisgar Street, Apartment 18, and will soon deposit exactly one quarter cup of Nine Lives in her dish. Or to take another example, Weeble can't think about any person or object that she's never come into contact with. She can't, for instance, wonder about her great-great-grandmother cat on her father's side. Humans, in contrast, can think about people they not only haven't met but couldn't meet: Julius Caesar, Joan of Arc, etc. Indeed, humans can think about people who don't even exist. A person can be searching for "her long lost brother," even if she's an only child. And children think about Santa Claus. It's not plausible that animals share this ability to think of things that they haven't encountered (including things that aren't real).

Why this difference between animals and humans? Here's an obvious answer: Thinking is a matter of inner speech. And a human can think about anything for which a word/sentence exists in their language. Hence the ability to have Santa Claus thoughts and the ability to think about Caesar and Joan—they're possible because English has the names 'Santa Claus', 'Joan of Arc', 'Caesar', etc. As for the complexity and precision of human thought, this is explained by the complexity and precision of sentences. We can contrast 1/4 cup with 5/16 of a cup because we have the right words. Since poor Weeble doesn't know any language, she can't think as humans can. (An aside: Notice also how useful this precision is in scientific inquiry. How far would chemistry or physics get without very accurate and detailed observations involving sophisticated measurements? And just how could this be achieved without language? Or again, consider the accumulation of knowledge over time: how could the results of scientific investigation be passed from generation to generation without language—for instance, just how much analytic chemistry can you capture with a cave drawing? Reflecting upon these points, you can see another reason why theorists of knowledge are interested in the role of language.[5])

There's another feature of thought that the inner-speech story would explain. Thought is productive, in the sense that, our limited lifetime aside, there is no limit to the variety of thoughts we can entertain. And very many of those thoughts are wholly novel, having never been thought before. Now, as we saw in the previous sections, language shares just these features: there are an unlimited number of sentences in any language, very many of them never before used. Given this fact, we can explain the creativity and productivity of thought by supposing that people think by "saying" sentences to themselves internally. Since they have an unlimited number of such sentences, they are able to have an unlimited number of thoughts.

How might one reply? Well, it could be that language helps humans think complicated and novel thoughts without it being the case that thinking is nothing more than speaking to oneself. Put otherwise, language might be a tool for thinking, even if it isn't the vehicle of thought, i.e., the medium in which the thinking occurs. This would equally explain why language users achieve kinds of thoughts, e.g., thoughts about nonexistent things or people who are long dead, that nonlanguage users cannot also achieve. Having the name does help, but not because we think by saying the name to ourselves. (Of course, this leaves open just how the tools do help. To make this response compelling, that blank would have to be filled in.)

Notice also that there's already a possible concession about languageless thought in the foregoing argument. It was allowed that some kinds of thought occurs without language: thus Weeble does expect someone at the door, even if she isn't capable of expecting, at such and such an address, someone she conceives of as Meera's roommate. And that concession, away from an unswerving 'Yes' to (11), is just as well, since human babies presumably can't do all of their thinking in "inner speech." Here's one compelling reason. We saw above that language learning looks like a very difficult cognitive task. But if learning a first language really is a matter of acquiring knowledge-that, then it is a kind of *thinking*. It involves framing generalizations, testing hypotheses, assimilating new data to old, etc. In this case, not all thinking can be a matter of speaking inwardly in one's native tongue. Babies think before they *have* a language to speak—they have to if they are to learn a language.

Before giving up altogether on the idea that thinking is inner speech, consider a possible rebuttal: When people attribute thoughts to cats, dolphins, etc., they are really just unreflectively attributing human features to nonhumans. As when we say to a child, "Look, honey, the dolphin is smiling at you" or "Isn't that sweet, the doggie gave you a kiss." Actually, dolphins don't literally *smile*. And dogs don't really *kiss*. Rather, we interpret certain actions as if they were smiles, kisses, etc., because if *we* did those movements, that's what we would be doing. The same is true, goes this defense of thought as inner speech, for "animal thoughts." We talk as if animals had thoughts, but that's really just ANTHROPOMORPHIZ- ING. Nor is this claim without plausibility. After all, as soon as we try to say precisely what it is that Weeble thinks as she hears the footsteps at the door, we realize that any belief we attribute is probably too precise. For instance, to return to our example, is Weeble expecting a person, a human, a large being, her favorite feeder? Which exactly? There's just no good answer to this. And is she *expecting, anticipating,* or *awaiting* that thing? Again, each of these is too specific.

Don't misunderstand this line of thought. The defender of the inner-speech approach to thought is happy to say that there's *something* going on in Weeble that causes her to run to the door. And she need not deny that dolphins, pigs, etc., demonstrate a *kind* of intelligence. But, says the inner-speech fan, this isn't really *thought*. What lies behind this view is the insight that the single most important piece of evidence for attributing thoughts is linguistic behavior.[6] Without language use, the argument goes, it's just not possible to even guesstimate what an agent might be thinking. Does the agent conceive of the person at the door as a woman, a human, Meera's roommate, Rob's spouse? If we can't ask the agent, there's just no way to tell. None of the necessary evidence is there. But if there isn't *evidence* for such thoughts—because there isn't language use— it can't be rational to *attribute* such thoughts. (This is an application of OCCAM'S RAZOR, named after the medieval English philosopher, William of Occam [b. 1285]. It's the principle, roughly, that we should never posit more than we need to explain the facts. We'll return to it chapter 5. For now, just notice that, on this view, it might be mere faith to assume that cats really have thoughts, since there isn't the right sort of evidence for this conclusion.)

This tactic of denying that animal's mental states really are thoughts raises another interesting point. Those who answer "No" to "Is thinking just a kind of inner speech?" often point to so-called ineffable thoughts— thoughts that cannot be expressed in language. These include thoughts that are hard to put into words and thoughts that aren't just difficult to express but are truly inexpressible. An example of the former is the tip-o'-the-tongue phenomenon, in which you know what you want to say but can't quite find the words to say it. (Anyone who has ever written a poem will have experienced this acutely. Notice how bizarre this phenomenon will seem to a person who insists that having a thought is "saying a sentence internally." If one is saying a particular sentence internally, the objection goes, why on earth is it so hard to produce it externally?) An example of the latter might be complex emotions, which just don't seem to be language-friendly. How do inner-speech advocates accommodate such cases?

Some of them, taking off from the animal-thought cases, simply deny that these are really kinds of thoughts. If the mental states are fuzzy, imprecise, and so on, to the extent that they cannot be expressed in language, then maybe they're not thoughts (though they're mental states of some kind). And what about when we "find" the words for the mental state that was there all along? Perhaps the state only became a thought when the words were found. Before that, it was something, but not a thought. So not only can one deny that animals and babies have inchoate thoughts; one can do the same for adults.

Once we put aside babies, animals, etc., and appeal to fully conscious human thought, the view that thought is inner speech seems to be in good shape. First off, everyone will have had the experience of "hearing" themselves think: you can often actually sense the words passing through your mind. This is even more obvious for bilingual speakers, who will be aware of switching, in their thoughts, from one language to another. A related point. Bilinguals report, very plausibly, that certain information is actually *stored* in one language rather than another. Thus it can happen that phone numbers learned in a French-speaking environment are actually recalled in French, while those learned in, say, a Japanese-speaking environment are remembered in Japanese. Equally striking, bilingual speakers report that they can, for example, do mathematics more easily in one of their languages.

Unsurprisingly, however, INTROSPECTION cuts both ways in this debate. It equally tells us that sometimes adult humans think, not in sentences, but in images. In particular, some famous scientists have reported that their greatest creative leaps involved imaging scenes, like riding on a light wave (Einstein) or watching a ball rolling across the bottom of an indefinitely long basin (Galileo). Or, to return to the phone-number case, there's the opposite phenomenon of not being able to recall a phone number until you try to dial it: here the memory seems distinctly nonlinguistic. Indeed, we might call it "physical memory," the sort of thing that you exhibit when, for example, you find your way around a neighborhood that is only dimly familiar to you, using clues so subtle and unconscious that you couldn't possibly describe them, even to yourself.

Speaking of "physical memory," consider catching a fly ball. Who "hears" inner speech—say about the ball's current trajectory, wind speed, gravitational constants, and differential equations—as the ball descends? In fact, it is generally the case that intelligent action is impeded by thinking things through in language. (Try to type quickly, for example, while describing to yourself exactly what you're doing. It will almost certainly degrade your performance.) Intuitively, then, when we perform some difficult cognitive tasks, sentences don't always go rushing through our minds. So, if image manipulation, "physical memory," and intelligent action count as thinking, there appears to be kinds of thought—ordinary, adult, human thought—that don't occur in language.

4 A Universal Language of Thought (LOT)?

The dispute doesn't end there, however. Those who answer 'Yes' to (11), that thought just is inner speech, have a retort regarding these intuitions of "nonlinguistic thought." What they say is this: The intuitions are misleading, because the "inner speech" is unconscious in these cases. What underlies the conscious experience of image manipulation, for example, is unconscious inner speech; similarly, behind sophisticated motor skills there lies an unconscious body of linguistically couched rules. Now this line of thought hasn't struck people as plausible, where the inner speech is supposed to occur in languages like English or Japanese. But suppose there is a special universal and innate language for thinking. Suppose, in particular, that just as computers have a language of ones and zeroes that underlies all of their programs and applications, there is an equally fundamental language shared by all humans: a LANGUAGE OF THOUGHT (LOT) (see Fodor 1975). Then, just as 3D graphics on a computer screen are realized by behind-the-scenes operations on ones and zeroes, so images in humans are operations on LOT sentences. And just as robotic arms attached to computers get moved by programs, so too do human arms.[7]

One advantage of the LOT move is that it overcomes a number of other problems associated with taking inner speech to occur in publicly spoken languages. For instance, there are ambiguous sentences. And to each such sentence there corresponds more than one thought. But if thinking were having a sentence run through one's head, then where there's only one sentence, there should be just the one thought. (For instance, take the sentence 'Big cats and dogs scare children'. The sentence encodes two distinct thoughts: that *all* dogs scare children and that only big dogs scare children.) However, if the thinking occurs not in English, but in the universal language of thought, then the single sentence could correspond to two sentences in LOT. This would explain why there are two thoughts: because there are two LOT sentences. Another problem about humans thinking in their native tongues is that, on this theory, two people who do not share a language cannot have the same thoughts. Taken to the extreme this seems absurd: can it really be that no unilingual Japanese speaker has ever thought that the sky is blue, just because they don't have access to the English words 'sky' or 'blue'? (Notice that they may have access to translations of these terms, but if what distinguishes one thought from another really is the sentence it is expressed in, then only people who have the exact same sentence available to them can share a thought.) Here again, LOT saves the day. For one can say that the inner speech of Japanese and English speakers both occur in LOT. And by hypothesis, LOT is shared by every human being.

This, of course, leaves us wondering how it is that speakers of English have an easier time thinking about computers, Joan of Arc, corned beef sandwiches, and Santa Claus than speakers of ancient Greek. On the LOT view, all humans think in the same language. If so, it might seem that all humans, across time and place, should be able to think the same thoughts. But, patently, some thoughts, including those just mentioned, are much easier for English speakers. The answer from the LOT camp isn't far to seek, however. Above we said that language can be a tool for thinking, even if it isn't the medium in which one thinks. This lesson might apply here as well: spoken languages are tools for thinking, even though the actual thought occurs in LOT. In particular, it might be that spoken language gives the thinker a means of abbreviating her thoughts: She thinks in LOT but uses, say, English to create shorthand terms. Having such a shorthand allows her to entertain much more complex thoughts than a person who, as it were, has to "spell out" the whole thought each time.

The debate could go on still further, but enough has been said to introduce the topic. And certainly some light has been shed on our original question: how are language and thought related? The answer is, In many, many ways. The next thing you'll want to know is, *Do* people with dissimilar languages think very differently from one another? And *are* human thoughts forever trapped by language-based limitations? Sadly, these are topics you will have to pursue on your own. (See the Suggested Further Readings for some starting points.)

5   Epilogue to Part I: The Nature and Methods of Philosophy

Maybe in order to understand mankind, we have to look at that word itself. MANKIND. *Basically, it's made up of two separate words—"mank" and "ind." What do these words mean? It's a mystery, and that's why so is mankind.*
Jack Handey

At this point we have done enough philosophy that we can stop and reflect upon what exactly "doing philosophy" amounts to. In particular, we are now in a position to ask, What is philosophy? What are its methods? And, what makes it different from other areas of inquiry?

Believe it or not, philosophers don't agree about this. As a matter of fact, the nature of philosophy is itself a philosophical issue. Still, you can get a sense of what philosophy is, and of what philosophers do, by considering some different views on the nature of philosophy. There are, very roughly, two such views.

Some philosophers think philosophy is differentiated by its *topics*. These topics include epistemology and philosophy of mind (the two topics of this book), the nature and existence of God, what is the best political order, and so on. Other philosophers reject this subject-matter characterization of philosophy. First, because the 'and so on' above leaves the boundaries of philosophy too vague. Which questions that we have not listed count as philosophical: are multiculturalism, ecology, and affirmative action philosophical issues or purely social, political, or scientific issues? Second, some reject this way of delimiting philosophy on the grounds that most, if not all, topics of interest to philosophers are also pursued by nonphilosophers. Thus the nature and existence of God is studied by theologians and religious scholars; the source and nature of mind by psychologists; the most effective political system by political scientists and sociologists; and so on. (We will see something of how the topics of this book, knowledge and mind, are studied by other disciplines when we get to chapter 8.)

The truth be told, it becomes difficult to distinguish philosophy from the most theoretical work within science, especially at the speculative frontier of disciplines. Once you go beyond the limit of what has been established by experiments, the only tool you have is your reasoning skills. Thus the most theoretical end of physics, for which we do not yet have concrete data, can look a lot like philosophy. Similarly for the foundations of mathematics or the theoretical groundwork of any area of inquiry: they all can look distinctly philosophical.

True enough, religious scholars, psychologists, sociologists, and physicists may approach their subjects in ways that distinguish their concerns from philosophy. In this sense, their questions are different. To take one example, one might say that religious scholars typically appeal to sacred texts and holy revelation in their studies, whereas philosophers rely on the analysis of concepts, aided by reason. So one might say that religious scholars ask, "What does our tradition say about God?" and that philosophers ask something quite different. Point taken. However, it still won't do to say that philosophy is *the* subject that studies God. For this topic is explored by another discipline, albeit in a different way. Indeed, nowadays it's hard to find *any* topic that is discussed exclusively by philosophers, and if there are any issues that remain the sole property of philosophy, this is likely a temporary accident.

The second account of what differentiates philosophy is this: Philosophers employ different methods from other investigators. It's not (or not just) the kind of questions asked that separates philosophy from other disciplines; rather, it's the way one goes about *answering* those questions. The preferred philosophical method, goes this line, is to think about what is being asked, what theorists actually mean by their terms, which arguments work, and how various theoretical answers relate to one another. That is, philosophers look at questions in disciplines like religious studies, psychology, sociology and so on, and ask questions like these: What precisely are investigators trying to find out here? What would count as giving a good answer to these questions? In contrast, workers within these disciplines just try to answer the questions.

An example may help. A linguist might try to find an answer to (12).

(12) How do children learn language?

A philosopher will ask, What is the meaning of 'How do children learn language?' What would count as a good answer to the question 'How do children learn language?' What does *learn* mean here? (For an example, look back at the very beginning of section 2 of this chapter. We began that section by sorting out what was, and was not, being argued about. On the view of philosophy as methodology, *that* was a prime instance of philosophizing.) Notice that both the linguist and the philosopher are working on the same question. But they are proceeding differently: the linguist is trying to *give an answer* to (12), while the philosopher is asking *about* (12). Or again, when a psychologist asks "How do we learn?" her first impulse is to go out and look: she does experiments with subjects (especially babies); tests, measures, and records their behavior; finds statistically salient regularities; and so on. From this data base, she tries to say how humans in fact learn. When a *philosopher* approaches this question, on the other hand, her *first* step is simply to *think*. In general, the philosopher investigates all the presuppositions and key concepts before she undertakes to answer it. Her job, so understood, is to get a clear view of the overall terrain, as preparation for someone else to dig into the details.

So it might seem that method provides a rather good way of distinguishing philosophy from other forms of intellectual activity. But here again, there are problems. For one thing, getting clear about concepts and presuppositions, before going after the details, is not a uniquely philosophical activity: physicists and pharmacologists and many others do this in their respective domains. Worse, when one tries to get *specific* about what the "philosophical method" really is, it turns out that no satisfactory account of that method is forthcoming. Ask yourself, Does this philosophy-as-a-method story really capture the nature of the discussion of innate knowledge of language, engaged in above, with its appeals to scientific findings about universals, acquisition studies, the brain, and so forth? Many contemporary philosophers would say 'No'. (The issue of method is further discussed in Brook 1999 and in the references he gives there.)

The problem in the end is that philosophy is a very heterogeneous activity: there are so many varieties of philosophy, and so many ways of addressing philosophical problems, that finding *the* philosophical method looks quite unpromising, so much so that our personal suspicion is that no *one* thing ties all of philosophy together. Some rational activities may be considered philosophical solely because of history: long-dead philosophers worried about the issue, so we now call it philosophical. Other activities of reason are philosophical because they are second order: they involve thinking about the tools of thinking: concepts, ways of explaining things, good evidence, etc. Still others are philosophical because of the methods employed. (For example, analytic philosophers thinking about issues such as knowledge and mind tend to rely heavily on THOUGHT EXPERIMENTS and ANALOGIES.) In the end, it may be that philosophy hangs together only loosely. If so, the best approach to answering "What is philosophy?" is to keep *doing* philosophy by working on some central problems. With any luck, by the end you will "know it when you see it." (We will return to this issue briefly at the end of the final chapter.)

Time to sum up. We have tried to give you some sense of what philosophy itself is. To that end, we considered two views on the nature of philosophy: that it is distinguished by its *subject matter*, and that it is distinguished by its *method*. Neither view looks ultimately satisfactory, but the foregoing discussion of them should give you at least a feel for what philosophy is.

Study Questions

1. Contrast competence and performance. Why can't we directly observe someone else's competence? How does performance provide evidence about competence?

2. Give examples, other than those in the text, of knowing-how and knowing-that. Into which category would you place knowledge of language? Why?

3. Explain the difference between rule-fitting and rule-guided behavior. Give an example in which a person is clearly guided by a rule. What distinguishes this example from cases where it's less clear whether rule guidance is present?

4. When one talks of "knowledge of language," is one attributing beliefs to speakers? Are those beliefs justified and true? If not, is there any point in calling what the speaker has 'knowledge'? Given that Chomsky's notion of linguistic competence is modeled on knowledge-that, could one develop a different notion of competence?

5. Review both of the arguments given in this chapter to the effect that much of linguistic knowledge is innate. What social consequences, if any, would follow from linguistic nativism?

6. We said, when discussing animal thoughts, that one ought not believe in things for which one has no evidence whatsoever because that would be to posit the existence of something for which one has no evidence (Occam's razor). Explain this principle, and give an example. What distinguishes this from the view that one should not believe in things for which one lacks a definitive *proof*?

7. We discussed two ways of distinguishing philosophy from other disciplines: by its topics and by its methods. Explain each. How would you characterize philosophy?

Suggested Further Readings

The key Platonic dialogue on language is the *Cratylus*. Aristotle writes on language in a number of places, but see especially *De Interpretatione* and the *Categories* on language and logic; also, see the *Poetics* on metaphor, among other topics. (These are available in many editions.) Descartes discusses the creativity and flexibility of human language use in his 1931 [1637] work. See also "The Port Royal Grammar" by his followers Antoine Arnauld and Claude Lancelot (1975 [1660]) and Chomsky's (1966) commentary thereon. Key empiricist writings include Book III of Locke 1965 [1685], which proposes that words only get meaning by being (ultimately) paired with material received from the senses, and Hobbes 1996 [1668], which explicitly discusses the idea that thought is "mental discourse." For an excellent survey of the history of philosophical speculation on language, see Harris and Taylor 1989.

For general introductions to contemporary philosophical issues about language, see any of Alston 1964, Blackburn 1984, Davis 1976, Devitt and Sterelny 1987, Martin 1987 and Stainton 1996. Fromkin and Rodman 1993 is a good introduction to linguistics. In particular, it introduces phonology, syntax, and semantics.

On Chomskyan themes—e.g., competence/performance, critiques of behaviorism, innateness, etc.—start with some of his own writings. Parts of Chomsky 1959, 1965, 1969, 1986, 1993 can be read even by beginners, but Chomsky 1975, 1980, 1988, 1990 are specifically intended to introduce Chomsky's views to nonspecialists. On innateness in particular, we suggest any of the following collections: Block 1981, Hook 1968, Piatelli-Palmarini 1980, Stich 1975. For a critique of Chomsky on innateness, see Putnam 1967.

The most famous proponent of the view that the public language one speaks greatly shapes the way one thinks is Whorf (1956). His views are critically discussed in Pinker 1994 and Pullum 1989, among other places. Speaking of Pinker, his 1994 is a very accessible, lively introduction to many issues surrounding language, including nativism, the influence of spoken language on thought, and Fodor's (1975, 1987) LOT hypothesis. Fodor's views are discussed in Churchland and Churchland 1983 and Dennett 1975, 1977. Davidson (1975) defends the idea that, when all is said and done, all thought is really inner speech in a public language. Dennett 1995 contains an entertaining discussion of the difference that language makes to minds. Finally, a general discussion of the parallels between language and thought may be found in Vendler 1972 and Fodor 1978. Both are quite challenging.

PART II
Mind

Chapter 4

Mind and Body:
The Metaphysics of Mind

1 Introduction: Conflicting Visions of the Mind

We have been considering questions of EPISTEMOLOGY, that is, questions of knowledge (recall that the Greek word for 'knowledge' is 'episteme'). The questions that we now turn to are questions in METAPHYSICS, also known as ONTOLOGY. Metaphysical/ontological questions are questions not about knowledge but about the nature of things, questions so general and so basic that it is difficult to find any way for simple "physics" (or any other science) to tackle them. Thus, metaphysical questions are questions beyond physics ('meta' means *beyond*). The metaphysical questions that we will take up concern (a) the nature of the mind and its relation to the brain (especially the part of the brain that is crucial for perception, thinking, consciousness, etc.), and (b) one of the mind's most important abilities, the ability to make choices. (The first question will be addressed here and in chapter 5; the latter in chapter 6.)

A number of different terms are used for what we want to talk about in these chapters, including the following:

(1) a. Mind
     b. Cognitive system
     c. System of mental states and events
     d. Psyche
     e. Soul
     f. Ego

We don't want to say that these terms all mean exactly the same thing. Indeed, the exact meaning of some of them is not very clear. To simplify our task, however, we will take there to be enough overlap in what they are all talking about for us to use the term 'mind' in place of all of them. (We will have occasion to return to the term 'cognitive system', however.)

As we noted in chapter 1, there are two main positions on the nature of the mind and its relation to the brain. They are known as DUALISM and MATERIALISM. As we will soon see, each position comes in many different varieties but the general idea is this. For the dualist, the mind (or the mental) and the brain (or the neural) are two radically different things. They may be in the closest relationship with one another, but they are still two things, not one. For the materialist, by contrast, the mind simply *is* the brain (or some aspect of the brain or the brain plus something else— at any rate, nothing but processes of matter). There is no question of the mind being one thing, the brain another; the mind is simply processes of matter. Here is how to think of the difference.

Compare the statements '*A* causes *B*' and '*A* is *B*' (heat causes water to boil; water is H_2O). In the first relationship, *A* causes *B*, *A* and *B* are different things (or different states and events), one of which causes the other. The dualist thinks that the mental and the nonmental are in this relationship (except that most dualists think that the causal connection runs both ways): two different things, each causally affecting the other. In the second relationship, there are not two things, just one—one thing described in two different ways. Though not always accepting that the mind exactly *is* the brain, as we will see, all materialists accept the idea that the mind is nothing more than a material system (the brain or the brain plus something more, like social institutions or the physical world). There may be a number of ways to describe this system ('mind' and 'brain' being the two most obvious), but there is only one thing.

Before we explain the two positions more fully, we should try to head off two potential problems with terminology. First, the term 'materialist' has a number of meanings. For example, Madonna sang about the "material girl." Historians talk about a "materialist theory of history." We say that someone who wants more and more goods is very materialistic. None of these uses of the term 'materialist' has much to do with the one that we are using here. Here 'materialist' simply means a person who believes that the mind is made out of matter.

Second, there is a huge and vitally important disagreement within the materialist camp about the material system that constitutes the mind. The older view is that the mind is nothing but the brain, though exactly *how* minds are "realized" in brains has been a matter of debate. More recently, some have come to think that brains get to be minds only if brains are related to something else. Here there are two main candidates: a stable social setting and a physical world. We will discuss this newer view when we get to the doctrine called EXTERNALISM in chapter 8. For the time being, it is enough to note that there are these two fundamentally different approaches *within* materialism to what material system is relevant. To mark the two sides of this debate, we will sometimes talk about brains and BRAINS PLUS, where the 'plus' refers to whatever else besides a brain might be needed for a material system to constitute a mind.[1]

To explain dualism and materialism further, let's start with some analogies. Dualism can be compared to the relationship of the heart and the lungs. The heart and the lungs work in the closest association, yet they are still entirely different things: you can take one out and leave the other, for example. This is not a perfect analogy, as we will see, because the dualist wants to say that the mind is far more different from the brain than the heart is from the lungs. Let us define dualism as follows:

(2) *Dualism* The mind is something radically different from anything made out of matter.

Contrast materialism:

(3) *Materialism* The mind is complex processes of matter.

For the materialist, the mind and the brain are like water and the elements oxygen and hydrogen, (4), or like a calculator and the arithmetic we use it to do, (5):

(4) Water and H_2O

(5) Arithmetic and activity in a calculator

Water and arithmetic have many complicated and important characteristics (water can remove our thirst and cool us down, arithmetic can determine how big our tax refund should be). Nonetheless, (pure) water is now understood to be nothing other than a combination of hydrogen and oxygen, specifically, the combination described by the formula 'H_2O'. Likewise, the arithmetic that the calculator does is not something different from the calculator. It is just the activity of the calculator (specifically, the opening and closing of various logic gates to shunt the flow of electrons in certain directions and not others). Indeed, doing arithmetic is not a "thing" at all; it is an activity (this distinction will become important in a moment). In short, water and H_2O are not two different things. And the activity of the calculator and the arithmetic thereby done are not two different things. In both cases we are dealing with only one thing, one thing described in two different ways, but still one thing. There is also an important difference between these two analogies, as we will see.

So the question is this:

The mind-body question Is the relation of the mind and the brain like the relation of the heart and the lungs, only with an even bigger difference, or is it like the "relation" of water and H_2O or the "relation" of the arithmetic and the activity in the calculator?

We put the word 'relation' in *scare quotes* (sometimes called 'shudder quotes') because we want to emphasize that we are talking about an unusual kind of relationship, or perhaps two unusual kinds of relationships. A relationship is usually between two things. Yet with water and H_2O and the calculator and the arithmetic done using it, we have only one thing. To the extent that we are talking about a relationship at all, we are talking about a relationship of the thing to itself, an unusual kind of relationship. As the example of water and H_2O illustrates, odd relationships of the first kind have played a big role in science—a lot of science involves the search for them. Both kinds of "relationships" play a big role in materialist theories of the mind and brain.

As we've said, the unusual "relationship" comes in two forms. Our two examples illustrate them. Again compare (4) to (5).

Pure water simply *is* H_2O. By contrast, the arithmetic is *not* simply the calculator or some activity in the calculator. For one thing, the same arithmetic can be done in many other ways: in the head, on paper, on an abacus, and so on. Likewise, the calculator can do many other things besides this piece of arithmetic. So what is the difference?

The difference is something like this: water and H_2O are the same thing—the same thing under two different descriptions but still the same thing; by contrast, the arithmetic done by the current activities of the calculator is no thing separate from the calculator (it is, after all, done on the calculator), yet it is *not the same thing as* the calculator either.

Philosophers call the first relationship *identity*, as in 'The evening star is identical to the planet Venus'. (The evening star is the first heavenly body to appear in the sky at night, in the northern hemisphere at any rate. It is not really a *star*, of course. It's the planet Venus.) When a kind of thing described in one way, e.g., as 'water', is shown to amount to some single kind of thing described in some deeper and more general way, in this case, H_2O, we say that the first has been *reduced* to the second. The deeper and more general description is usually one derived from some broad scientific theory of the world as a whole, in this case the atomic theory of matter.

(6) *Reduction* One kind of thing is reduced to another when the first
   kind described in one way is shown to consist in some single kind of
   thing described in some deeper and more general way in all or
   virtually all cases.

One of the big questions about the mind is whether it will over time be
reduced to the brain.

There is less agreement about what to call the second relationship, the
one between the calculator and the arithmetic done on it. One approach is
to say that the calculator *implements* or *realizes* the arithmetic. For present purposes, exactly how we label the difference between identity and this
other relationship does not matter. What matters is that they *are* different.

The difference between these curious "relationships" matters because
very different varieties of materialism derive from each. The theory that
the mind is *identical* to the brain in that each kind of state or event
described in mental language will eventually be reduced to, understood to
be, some kind of state or event in the brain is called, not surprisingly, the
IDENTITY THEORY.

(7) *Identity theory* Every mental state and every mental event of a given
   kind is (is identical to, is one and the same thing as) some brain state
   or some brain event of a given kind.[2]

The view that the mind *is implemented in* or *realized by* the brain but is
not, strictly speaking, identical to the brain is called 'FUNCTIONALISM'.
Here's a first pass at a definition of 'functionalism':

(8) *Functionalism* The mind is certain functions of a complex system: a
   brain or a brain plus other systems.

Defined this generally, identity theory and functionalism would be
compatible with one another. We will tighten up the definitions and lay
out exactly where these two variants of materialism disagree more clearly
later. For now, let us note just two things.

First, even though both identity theorists and functionalists think that
the mind is *nothing more than* matter, identity theorists *assert* that the
mind can be reduced to the brain and functionalists *deny* that the mind
can be reduced to the brain (or brain plus), even though they both insist
that the mind simply is processes of matter. This is a neat balancing act
on the part of functionalism. The basic idea is this: even though mental
activities are activities in matter (mainly the brain), mental activities
cannot be understood if they are *described* as activities of the brain
(or brain plus other material processes). Mental activity needs its own

language. Again, computers provide an analogy: even though the arithmetic that my computer is doing is simply an activity of the computer, we need to use the language of arithmetic to understand it (the language of plus and minus, etc.). We cannot understand what the computer is doing if we restrict ourselves to the language of electron flows, etc.

Second, the word 'identity' has many different uses. What it is used to talk about in psychology is very different from what it is used to talk about in mathematics; the way it is usually used in everyday life is different from both; and what philosophers use it to talk about is different from all three. Psychologists talk about things like identity crises. Mathematicians talk about an expression and a transformed version of it as being identical. In everyday life, we say that two things that are exactly similar are identical. (For example, we say that this chair is *identical* to that one. The phrase 'identical twins' is another example.) Philosophers (and sometimes scientists) talk about water being identical to H_2O. All this is confusing: it is too bad that the little word 'identity' has come to name so many different things in modern thought, and that these various things are so unlike one another.

All we need to remember for purposes of the mind/body problem is that here 'identity' means *being one and the same thing*, with two (or more) very different ways of describing the thing in question. Thus there aren't two things, the evening star and Venus. There's only one thing, named or described in two different ways. Note that this is quite different from the everyday sense of 'identity'. When we speak of "identical twins," we have two objects in mind: twins are two people, not one. When philosophers talk of identity, however, they mean being one and the same thing. That's the sense of 'identity' at work in the identity theory.

Having introduced two versions of materialism, namely, identity theory and functionalism, we turn now to the contrast between dualism and all forms of materialism. The two visions of the mind contained in dualism and materialism could hardly be more different. Recall the definition of 'dualism': the mind is something radically different from anything made out of matter. Many dualists maintain that whatever the mind consists of has no weight and no shape. Many dualists also think that how mind works is special. They may believe that the mind relates to the body and the world around it in a straightforward cause-and-effect way,[3] but, many of them urge, its internal states and events do not relate to *one another* in a straightforward cause-and-effect way. Rather, the mind's states and events relate to one another by various of these states and events *implying* other states and events, in roughly the way that the premises of an argument relate to one another and to their conclusion. As we have seen over and over in this book, premises imply their conclusion (in a valid argument). When they do, such premises do not *cause* their conclusion. Let us explore this alleged difference between the relationship of implication and the relationship of cause and effect.

When we examined how arguments work in chapter 1, we were exploring one of the ways in which one thing, the premises, imply another thing, the conclusion. For instance, suppose that you engage in the following reasoning:

Premise 1 I'd like to get a good mark in this course.
Premise 2 If I'd like to get a good mark in this course, then I should understand the positions and arguments discussed in this book.
Conclusion Therefore, I should understand the positions and arguments discussed in this book.

Now consider the relationship between the premises and the conclusion. You reached the conclusion because that is what the premises *implied*. Put another way, if you accepted the premises as true *and you are rational*, then you have to accept the conclusion. Now ask a different question: did your accepting the premises *cause* you to accept the conclusion? Many dualists would say that it did not. Here's why. If you had not been rational, had not been able to recognize and follow an implication, you would *not* have reached the conclusion. Therefore, though the premises *implied* the conclusion, your acceptance of them did not *cause you to reach* the conclusion. From this, says the dualist, we can see that how the mind works is very different from the usual cause-and-effect pattern.

Of course, a safer conclusion here would be that the premises were at most only *a part* of the cause. For there is a more complicated causal question that we could ask here: did the *whole process* of premises, your ability to recognize an implication, your generally good level of rationality, etc., cause you to reach the conclusion you reached? This question is beyond our scope here; indeed, it is beyond the scope of this book. All we are trying to do is to illustrate how dualists use special features of the mind's abilities, in this case the mind's ability to follow an argument, to urge that mental states enter into relationships that are very different from the relationships that states and events in the brain or anything else made of "mere matter" seem to be able to enter into. (Of course, appearances may be misleading on the brain side too: how can dualists be so sure that states and events in the brain cannot enter into relationships of implication with other things in the brain? We will return to this set of issues in chapter 8, where it will become a major theme.)

Now recall the definition of 'materialism': the mind is complex processes of matter. For materialists, minds *are* matter, namely, the matter of the brain (or brain plus). If so, in contrast to dualism, minds *are* made of something that has precise shape, etc., namely, the brain, and they clearly operate according to ordinary processes of cause and effect.

As we said, there are important divergences within materialism. Indeed, on one issue, namely whether the mind *is a thing at all*, dualism and the identity theory actually agree: the mind is a thing (an immaterial thing for dualists, a material thing for identity theorists). On this issue, they both disagree with functionalism, which sees the mind as merely a system of functions. Nevertheless, the dualist and all materialist visions of the mind fundamentally conflict. There is no possibility of them both being true; if one of them is true, the other has to be false. To bring out the size of the conflict, let's explore the very different implications that they seem to have for two issues of vital practical importance to us.

Immortality

I hope that after I die, people will say of me: "That guy sure owed me a lot of money."

Jack Handey

Immortality is the idea of surviving after death here on earth. (Strictly speaking, immortality is the idea of living *forever*—being *nonmortal*—but we will concentrate on surviving the death of the body for any period of time.) Can we look forward to continuing on after earthly death? If dualism is true, there is at least the possibility that the mind (the soul, the psyche—some crucial part of the person) could live on after earthly death: the body could die; the mind live on. If materialism is true and the mind simply *is* the brain, on the other hand, then it would seem difficult to argue that when the brain dies, the mind can nevertheless continue to function. The only possibility would be for the body as well (or at least the brain) to live on, or perhaps to come back to life some time after death. But it is hard to make sense of the *brain* surviving earthly death or of the brain and body coming *back into* existence. The only way we know of is to suppose that bodily resurrection or something like it occurs. This is a tenet of certain faiths, but it is part of this idea that a Deity must intervene to achieve it. We will stick to means of survival that would not require divine intervention.

After the brain dies, *something* about the body continues on, of course. For example, the molecules that make up my body continue to exist and so does the energy they contained. The energy is immediately dispersed, though, and so eventually are the molecules (as the body decays and its matter is absorbed by other matter such as worms and plants).[4] But what we care about with respect to immortality is not whether *something or other* related to me will go on. What each of us cares about is whether *I* will go on, the very person that I am now. What would be involved in *you* continuing to exist after your body dies? Start here: each of us is one and the same person throughout bodily life, or at least through long stretches of it.[5] We all change over time, of course: in early life we get bigger, stronger, smarter, etc., then later in life we lose muscle mass, often gain weight, and suffer bodily and even mental deterioration. Nevertheless, we also continue to exist as the same person throughout at least many changes of this kind. (We say "at least many" because there may be some changes so massive that the person ends even if the body continues to live. See note 5.) Philosophers have a name for this continued existence: PERSONAL IDENTITY.

(9) *Personal identity* Being one and the same person over a period of time.

Personal identity is fundamental to human life as we know it. The notion is fundamental to personal relationships. If Louise loves Petra and Petra has to go away for six months, it is Petra that Louise wants to see again. If Petra does not appear when the six months are over, it would not remove Louise's disappointment if someone came along and said, "Oh, that's OK. Petra had an identical twin, and she is still here." Moreover, the same person can persist through a host of changes. Louise can love Petra as the same person even though Petra has cut her hair, has had an accident and lost a limb, has matured, etc. Petra is still one and the same person, Petra. Our legal system is also based on the idea of a person persisting as the same person over time: you are responsible for what your earlier self did. Equally, the idea of one and the same person is fundamental to property and inheritance. If Karl bought a property ten years ago and hasn't sold it or given it away, then Karl is the owner of it now; no one else owns it. This is true even if, for instance, Karl has changed his taste in music or has had plastic surgery or what have you. And if Maria was named in a will ten years ago, Maria is the only person who has a legal right to that inheritance—again, whatever changes she may undergo in the meantime.

Now we can formulate the idea of immortality more precisely. The idea of immortality is simply the idea that one can continue as the same person after bodily death, that someone can go on *as the very person that she is now*, after her body dies.

(10) *Personal immortality* A person will continue to survive *as the person she is now* after the death of the body.

That is to say, your identity as you is not destroyed when your body dies.

As we said, whether one can survive the death of the body is an important issue, and we will return to it at the end of chapter 5. For now, all we want to show is that dualism seems to offer the best hope of life after death. If materialism is true, it is very difficult to see how immortality is possible. (Again, for present purposes, we put resurrection aside.)

Free Will
Think again of how dualism differs from materialism. This difference has also been thought to have important implications for the existence of freedom of choice, or freedom of the will. You have free will when you have alternative choices available to you and nothing forces you to pick one of them; rather, you pick the one you do by your own unimpeded inclinations and deliberations. What is needed for a choice to be free in this way is controversial (we will examine the issue in chapter 6). One common idea is that for you to have free choice, the selection that you made must not be the only selection that you could have made.

Now how does the difference between dualism and materialism enter in? As follows. Many philosophers, political theorists, theologians, and others have thought that if we are *caused* to select the beliefs, actions, etc., that we select, then those selections could never be free, could never be real *choices* at all. (If a selection is not made with freedom of choice or free will, then it was not really a choice, as we are using the word 'choice'.) Why would a selection's being caused remove the possibility of its being free? Because if there were sufficient causes to bring about the selection, that's the only selection that could have been made by that person in those circumstances.

Now, on the materialist picture of the mind, there are sufficient causes for everything that happens in the mind. Thus, these theorists conclude, if the materialist picture of the mind is correct, no one ever has a choice about what he or she selects, and there is no free will. With dualism, on the other hand, the prospects for free will appear to be better. Dualists, most of them anyway, allow that in addition to (or perhaps even instead of) the mind's containing patterns of cause and effect, it contains a different kind of pattern, a pattern, as we said above, that is more like the relationship of the premises and conclusion of an argument than the relationship of a cause to its effect. If so, then dualism contains the possibility of our selecting our beliefs and actions on some basis other than being caused. Dualism thus seems to contain the possibility of our having a choice about what we select, of our being free.

Unlike the situation with immortality, where most philosophers agree that if materialism is true, then immortality of any significant kind does not exist, there is a lot of disagreement about free will. Some philosophers still believe in the stark alternatives we've just outlined: if materialism is true, there is no free will; dualism is the only hope. Other philosophers believe that, far from free will being *ruled out* by causality, free will *is just a particular kind* of causality. That is to say, a choice's being free is quite *compatible* with its being caused, if it is caused in the right way. (This theory is called COMPATIBILISM, not surprisingly.)

As we said, we will examine the whole issue of free will in chapter 6. For now it is enough to note that the position you accept on the nature of the mind and its relation to the brain can have profound implications for what you can believe about other major issues such as immortality and freedom of the will. In philosophy, as in other academic disciplines that are concerned with building and assessing big theories, everything connects. What you say on one issue holds implications for what you can say on others. That's what makes theory building so interesting.

2   What Makes Something Mental?

When we first introduced philosophical questions about the mind in chapter 1, we said that one of the two main questions about the mind is, What is it like? Before we examine the various theories of how the mind relates to the brain in any further detail, it would be well to get a firmer grip on what we are talking about when we talk about the mind. What is characteristic of minds?

We will look at this question in the form 'What marks off the mental from everything else?' As the Austrian philosopher Franz Brentano (b. 1838) put it, what is the mark of the mental? Here is one reason why the question is important. The issue we are exploring is whether the mind is simply processes of matter or something different from processes of matter. To settle this question, we need to know what we are talking about when we talk about the mind. More generally, for any type of object, x, to ask whether every x is a y, we need to know what xs are.

This requirement is more important for dualists than it is for materialists. For materialists, the mind is merely processes in matter. If so, the mental and the nonmental are all the same kind of stuff, matter, and it is not urgent to pin down exactly which aspects of matter are which. (Some materialists do not even believe that there are any minds, as we will see later in this chapter.) The dualist, however, holds that the brain is one kind of thing, the mind is a radically different kind of thing. With two such radically different kinds of thing, it is extremely unlikely that there will be any grey area, any borderline cases, between them. Much more likely, there will be a clear boundary, a clear place where the mind stops and the nonmental starts. And the dualist will lack clarity about what she means by 'mind' unless she has a clear idea of what would put something on one side of this boundary and what would put it on the other.

Our question is, What makes something mental and something else nonmental? First, notice how we ask the question. We do not ask, What makes something mental, something else *physical*. For the materialist, the mind is processes of matter, so the mental *is* physical. Thus, to ask what distinguishes the mental from the physical would already be to BEG THE QUESTION against the materialist. For the materialist, the question is, What distinguishes the part of the physical realm that is mental from the part that is not? We need to ask the question in a way that is *neutral*, that is to say, does not beg the question against either position. 'What distinguishes the mental from the nonmental?' is neutral in this way.

Next we will introduce a new term, CRITERION. Exactly what a criterion is has been a matter of great controversy. For our purposes, let us define the phrase 'criterion of A' as follows:

(11) *Criterion of A* A feature or group of features that are central to all and only things of type A.

Now we can say that what we are seeking is a *criterion* of the mental.

At least four things have been suggested as the criterion for something's being mental. Though philosophers have been trying to characterize what we mean by 'the mind' (or some cognate concept) at least since the time of Plato and Aristotle, it was Descartes who first articulated the modern conception of the mind, and the proposed criteria of the mental that we will consider are derived from his work. The four things are these:

- Nonspatiality
- Intentionality
- Special access
- Consciousness

We need to clarify these suggested criteria and assess their adequacy.

Nonspatiality

Nonspatiality is the idea that the mind, the mental, does not have a *precise* locus, in the sense of having a clear shape, precise location, etc. Descartes firmly believed this. (Indeed, he seems to have believed that the mind is not spatial at all, though it is not clear what he meant by this.) It is easy to think of things that do not have precise spatial location. Suppose I throw a rock in the ocean. What is the precise boundary of the ensuing ripples? They don't have any, because they go on indefinitely, though getting smaller and smaller the further away they are.

Similarly, one might think, with respect to the mind. I have a thought. Where is it located? "Well," you might reply, "in your head." Ah, but where in my head? One inch down, two inches in from the left, $2\frac{1}{2}$ inches in back of my forehead? This feels peculiar: thoughts don't seem to be things that have a precise location in this way. (Some philosophers call the idea that thoughts have a precise location a CATEGORY MISTAKE, like saying that the square root of the number two is purple. A category mistake attempts to combine two types of concepts, for example a mathematic concept and a color concept, that make no sense together.)

Let's suppose that it is true that thoughts do not have a precise location. Would that be enough to make nonspatiality (in the sense of not having a precise location) a criterion of the mental? No. Some purely physical things, like ripples, also lack precise location; as we saw, they have the same degree of nonspatiality. On to the next proposed criterion of the mental.

Intentionality

The term 'INTENTIONALITY' is a word invented by philosophers to describe states and events of certain kinds that have the interesting characteristic of being *about* something. This has come to be called the aboutness relationship and is found in most mental states. A belief is about whatever is believed. A perception is about whatever is perceived. A fear is about whatever is feared. And so on. It is important to keep in mind that 'intentionality' is an invented term. It has no close relationship to any word of ordinary English. In particular, it is not talking about intentions (though intentions are one of the many kinds of states and events that have intentionality—just to complicate things). The notion of intentionality has played very diverse roles in recent philosophy of mind, and we will say more about the concept later in this chapter. For now, our question is simply this: is intentionality a criterion of the mental? At first glance, it certainly seems to be. Indeed, what could be more central to being mental than being about something? But we need to look more closely.

An adequate criterion of the mental must have at least two features: it must not be too *broad*, and it must not be too *narrow*. A suggested criterion is too broad if it applies to more than the kind of thing under consideration. For example, as a criterion of being a chair, having a seat would be too broad because other things besides chairs have seats. (That was the trouble with nonspatiality; it was too broad—it applied to things, like ripples, that had nothing to do with the mental.) A suggested criterion is too narrow if it does not apply to everything that it would need to apply to. For example, as a criterion of being a chair, having legs would be too narrow because there are perfectly good chairs that do not have legs, chairs made out of a single shaped piece of plywood, for example. It was this notion of being neither too broad nor too narrow that we were trying to express when we spoke in (11) of a criterion of *A* as true of *all and only* things of type *A*. 'All' expresses the idea of not being too narrow; 'only' the idea of not being too broad. Now, what about intentionality? Is intentionality too broad or too narrow?

It may be too narrow. There are some kinds of states and events in us that do not seem to have intentionality, yet seem to be candidates for being part of the mind. Two in particular stand out, bodily sensations and mood states. By 'bodily sensations', we mean things like pains, tickles, feelings of warmth or cold, and so on. Suppose I feel a jolt of pain. What is that pain about? It does not seem to be about anything. If my skin hurts because I got too much sun, what is that hurting about? Again, it seems that the answer is, 'Nothing'. (It is very important not to confuse what a state or event is *about* with its *cause*. If materialism is true, every state and event will have a cause, including those that are not about anything.)

How some people respond to this argument, remarkably enough, is to *deny* that pains, tickles, etc., are mental. These people allow that these states and events certainly *seem* to be mental, but then too, tomatoes *seem* to be vegetables, yet they are not (tomatoes are a fruit). These people make this move to rescue intentionality as the criterion of mentality; if the supposed counterexamples—pain, tickles, etc.—are *not* mental, then they are not counterexamples to intentionality as a criterion of the mental.

Unfortunately, and this often happens in philosophy, it would seem that to answer this challenge, we need precisely what we are looking for, namely, an adequate criterion of the mental. How else can we decide whether pains, tickles, etc., are mental or not? And away we go, around and around in a tight little circle. But maybe we can find another strategy. Maybe there are states or events that are so obviously mental that no one could reasonably doubt it, yet that do not have intentionality, not always at least.

This is where mood states enter in. By mood states, we mean states like anxiety, depression, elation, contentment, and so on. The nice thing about these states for our purposes is that sometimes they are about something, sometimes they are not. Compare anxiety *about an exam* to the kind of free-floating anxiety that some people feel *about nothing in particular*. The first sort of anxiety is clearly about something and therefore has intentionality, but the second sort of anxiety does not seems to be *about* anything. (Feeling tense because of tiredness would be an example.) If this is correct, the feeling of free-floating anxiety does not have intentionality. That there are two kinds of anxiety is bad news for intentionality as a criterion of the mental: if intentionality is a criterion of the mental, then the same kind of mood state, i.e., anxiety, would then sometimes be mental, sometimes not, which would be very odd. This suggests that intentionality is not the criterion of the mental that we are seeking.

Some have thought that intentionality may also be too broad to be a criterion of the mental. Pictures and words are about something and therefore have intentionality. So do diagrams and semaphore flags and a host of other things. Yet pictures, words, etc., are not mental states. From this direction too, then, intentionality would appear to be ruled out as the criterion of the mental. Perhaps the "too broad" objection can be answered: the intentionality of pictures, etc., is derived. Some mind gives it to them. By contrast, our intentionality is not given to us by another mind and so to that extent is original with us.[6] However, the "too narrow" objections would still stand. This negative conclusion is surprising; intentionality is such a prominent feature of our minds. What this shows is that something can be very important to something else, as intentionality is to the mind, and yet not be a criterion of it, i.e., not satisfy (11).

Special Access and Consciousness

Special access and consciousness are the final candidates for the criterion of the mental, and they can be considered together. 'Special access' names the idea that I have a kind of access to some of my states and events that I do not have to yours and you do not have to mine. I am directly aware of some of my states and doings on the basis merely of having and paying attention to them, whereas I must infer yours from your behavior, etc., and you must do the same with mine. (Special access thus defined used to be called 'privileged access'. That is not a good term, because it suggests that others do not have *any* access, i.e., that the states and events in question are not knowable by others. As we will see in more detail in chapter 7, this is a hard position to maintain.)

The reason that we can consider special access and consciousness together is that special access *simply is* one kind of consciousness; it is, roughly, introspectibility (see INTROSPECTION). And being introspectible is what is meant by saying that something is conscious, in the sense of 'conscious' at work here. (There are other senses of 'consciousness', too. For example, sometimes 'conscious' means 'sentient', as in 'She has regained consciousness'. Here 'consciousness' refers to regained access to the world around her, not or not just to access to herself.)

So the question is, Is special access or introspectibility a criterion of the mental? This suggestion certainly needs to be supplemented, but when we do so, it does seem to mark out approximately what we mean when we talk about the mental. That is to say, it includes all and only the kinds of states and events that we consider to be mental, i.e., all and only aspects of what we take the mind to be. If so, it is neither too broad or too narrow.

The supplement goes like this. By the mental, we don't just mean states and events that we could introspect by choosing to do so. We mean all mental states and events, and most people now think that many of them are unconscious, i.e., they exist but are not introspectible. Can we supplement the idea of special access to take account of them? Start with states and events like the perceptions and feelings that you are aware of having right now; these you can introspect without any difficulty. Then there are things like your memories. You are not introspectively aware of most of them right now, but you could introspect them at will, any time you want to. ("What did you do last Sunday?" "Oh, I went hiking." Even though you might not have been thinking of that hiking trip, you recall it as soon as you are asked.) Finally, there are the truly unconscious states, such as the rules we are using to interpret the syntax of sentences, repressed memories of terribly painful experiences (if such things exist), and so on.

For these genuinely unconscious states, you are not introspectively aware of them right now, and you could not become introspectively aware of them even if you tried. But *were* you to become aware of them, (directly aware of them, not aware of them by inferring them from behavior or something else), it *would be* by becoming able to introspect them. This assumes that one can be directly aware of mental states and events that one has only by introspection. If we accept that assumption (and it is plausible), we have the supplement to the idea of special access that we need to allow it to cover everything that we intuitively want to include in the mind.

Any states or events that clearly fall within what we intuitively want to call the mind seem to have special access as thus modified. That is to say, special access seems to be neither too broad nor too narrow. If so, it is the criterion of the mental that we have been seeking. It has one further virtue as a criterion: since it is about how we gain access to the states and events, not a feature of the states or events themselves, it is guaranteed to be *neutral* with respect to whether the states or events it picks out as mental are also physical or not. We have found our criterion of the mental.

We have been assuming for the sake of the current argument that genuinely unconscious states exist. If they do not, so much the better, so far as our search for a criterion of the mental is concerned. Without them, the overall search for a criterion of the mental would become that much easier; we would not need the supplement to special access that we have just laboriously developed.

3   A Wealth of Positions

Now that we have some idea of what we are talking about when we talk about the mind, namely, states and events of which we could become directly aware only by introspection, let's turn to the various theories of how this mind relates to the brain or brain plus. We have already met the two main contending theories: dualism and materialism. Both dualism and materialism come in a number of different forms.

The first thing to notice is that the dualism/materialism distinction is not the most basic distinction in the field. The most basic distinction is between dualism and all forms of what philosophers call MONISM. The term 'dualism' is derived from the term 'duality', which means two. 'Monism', as the term is used in philosophy, means one. Hence:

(12) *Dualism* There are two radically different kinds of thing—either in general or in the human person.

(13) *Monism* Everything is, or is made up of, one kind of stuff.

(We say "is, or is made up of" because, as we saw earlier, there is a sense in which such things as acts of doing arithmetic on a calculator are not *the same thing as* the calculator doing something, but they are made up of the calculator doing something, and there is no other kind of thing involved.)

The kind of stuff that present-day monists immediately think of is matter. But that has not always been so. Prior to the rise of modern science four or five hundred years ago and even long after its rise, many philosophers thought that the basic stuff of the universe was not matter but something idealike or mindlike, some sort of "mind stuff." This view is called IDEALISM.

Earlier we tried to head off a problem about the term 'materialism'. The same kind of problem arises about the term 'idealism'. There is a common use of the term to refer to someone with high principles, as in 'Mother Teresa was filled with idealism'. That use of the term has very little to do with the use we are making of it. As we use the term 'idealism' here, it simply means the view that everything in the universe is like ideas or minds in important ways.

In addition to monism (all one kind of thing) and dualism (two kinds of things), why not also triadism or quadralism, etc.? Let us call the idea that the human person is even more than two fundamental kinds of thing PLURALISM.

(14) *Pluralism* There are more than two fundamentally different kinds of thing, either in general or in the human person.

Pluralism is certainly a possible position. A few theorists in Europe and North America, as well as some Oriental and aboriginal theorists, have advocated the view. But it has played little role in contemporary Western theorizing about the mind. In our tradition, the fundamental division has always been between mind stuff and body stuff. There are some further things to be said about this division. First, as feminist writers have urged, this division has tended to go with a division between rationality and emotion, between "higher" parts of life such as thinking and imagining and "lower" parts of life such as sexual desire and the body in general. Some writers maintain that the division has played an unhealthy role as a result. Second, some theorists believe that there are also abstract entities that are neither mental nor material. Numbers are their most common example. We will not go into that issue here, because we are restricting ourselves to "concrete" entities: entities made out of matter, entities that have consciousness and personalities and interact with other entities, and so on. Anyway, the only division in the human person that has impressed itself on theorists in the Western tradition is the division between mind and body.

To sum up, when theorists believe that the body is one kind of thing and the mind is another, radically different kind of thing, their view is called dualism. When theorists believe that the mind is simply an aspect of the brain or brain plus, their view is called materialism. We will now explore some of the widely different forms that each view can take. Dualism often does not get the attention it deserves nowadays, so we will start with dualism.

Dualism

As table 4.1 reminds us, the basic division is between dualist and monist models of mind. Three main kinds of dualism need to be distinguished: substance dualism, property dualism and explanatory dualism. We begin with SUBSTANCE DUALISM:

(15) *Substance dualism* The human person is made up of two distinct substances: a material body and an immaterial mind.

Table 4.1
Positions on the mind/body problem

Dualism

> Substance dualism: A person is two kinds of thing—immaterial mind and material body (Descartes).
> Property dualism: A person has two kinds of properties (Strawson).
> Explanatory dualism: We need two kind of explanation—mechanistic explanation and psychological explanation—to explain the human person (Fodor).

Monism

> Idealism
>> Subjective idealism: Everything is a representation in me (Berkeley?).
>> "Absolute" idealism: The world is states in some conscious being (Hegel).
> Materialism
>> The mind exists.
>>> Identity theory (now a minority view)
>>> Functionalism (one living position)
>> The mind is a myth.
>>> Behaviorism
>>> Neurophilosophy (the other living position)

This is the classic form of dualism. It sees the human person as made up of two distinct substances: a material body and an immaterial mind. The two substances are in some sort of relationship to each other, but they are two things, not one. Moreover, as the substance dualist sees it, they are totally different from one another. One is made up of atoms and molecules, creates waste, reacts chemically with other objects, can have its tissue damaged and repaired, and so on. On the other hand, it feels nothing, thinks nothing—it is merely fancy clockwork, to use an image of Descartes's. The other "substance" is not made of matter, has no weight, cannot have its substance damaged (not in the usual ways at any rate), has no chemistry, and so on. On the other hand, this object does feel, think, and perceive, and it is conscious. Descartes's way of putting the distinction was to say that the body occupies space (*res extensa*), while the mind does not occupy space but is a thing that thinks (*res cogitans*). (For Descartes, "thinking" included perceiving, being conscious, and so on). These two different substances are in a tightly coordinated relationship.

The second major variety of dualist theory is PROPERTY DUALISM. To understand this view, we need to introduce a new distinction. The distinction is between objects and properties. Take the chair that you are sitting on. It *is* an object, and it *has* various properties. Its properties include being made out of wood, being three feet high, being painted brown, and so on. Or again, the monitor on a computer *is* an object, and it too *has* properties. It is a color monitor, its screen has shape, it has controls below the screen, and so on.

In rough terms, the difference between an object and a property is this: a given object can have many properties, and a property can be shared by (or be instantiated in) many objects, but a property does not "have" objects, nor is an object "shared by" (or "instantiated in") many properties. For example, this chair can have many properties—in addition to being brown, it has four legs and a back, is made out of wood, and so forth. Equally, there may be many other objects that share certain of these properties with it: think of a pencil, which shares the property of being made of wood with the chair. But brown doesn't have the chair. Nor is the chair shared by being made of wood. (Indeed, those sentences don't even make sense.) Or again, to give a related general feature of the contrast, objects are individual things, which occupy *one certain place*, while properties can be instantiated in *many different places* at once. Thus the *brown color* of this chair also exists on the chair across the room, six more in the next room, and so on. But the chair itself, the object, can have only one location. Further examples of objects include Weeble, Rob's salt shaker, Canada, the moon, the book in your hand, and so on. Further examples of properties, which objects have, are being pink, smelling like chicken, being made of glass, being large, being round, etc.

Given this contrast between objects and properties, we can introduce property dualism.

(16) *Property dualism* The human person is a single, unified object, but that object has two radically different kinds of properties: mental properties and material properties.

Substance dualism, which we just discussed, maintains that the human person consists of two kinds of objects, two *substances*. Property dualism by contrast maintains that the human person is only one thing—one object, one substance—but that it has two radically different kinds of *properties*. Let us call this one object the mind/brain, so as not to assume in the very way we describe it that it is one or the other or both (such an assumption would be begging the question). The two kinds of properties are *mental properties* and *bodily properties*. Thus, for example, the mind/ brain has thought properties, and it has neural properties, but for the property dualist, neural properties are not thought properties, and vice versa. No matter how we try, we will never understand either kind of property in terms of the other.

Property dualism may seem far-fetched, but it has real attractions. Things having two (or more) kinds of properties are as common as could be. Take a book. It has both a color and a shape: one object, two kinds of properties. Moreover, the two kinds of property, i.e., color and shape, are as different from one another as property dualists think that thoughts and neurons are. Colors cannot be understood as combinations of shapes (obviously!) and shapes are definitely not combinations of colors. One object, two completely independent kinds of properties. This is exactly what property dualists want to say about the person, and it is a nice balancing act. On the one hand, they genuinely mean it when they say that the human person is all one thing. On the other hand, they also mean it when they say that this one thing has radically independent kinds of properties.

One of the important implications of property dualism is that, even though the human person is one thing, we will always need two very different kinds of explanation to explain a person, one to explain neural properties and another to explain cognitive properties like thinking and perceiving. This brings us to a third kind of dualism, EXPLANATORY DUALISM:

(17) *Explanatory dualism* To understand ourselves, we need two very
    different kinds of explanation, PSYCHOLOGICAL EXPLANATIONS and
    MECHANISTIC EXPLANATIONS.

To appreciate the difference between mechanistic explanation and psychological explanation, let's start with an example. Suppose that our
friend Pavritra has just walked down the hall and poured coffee into her
cup. We can think of two very different ways in which we might explain
Pavritra's behavior. One would be to say (18). The other would be to say
(19).

(18) Pavritra walked down the hall because her brain sent certain signals
    to her leg muscles, her leg muscles contracted and relaxed in a
    certain highly coordinated way around her knees and ankles and
    toes, and so on.

(19) Pavritra walked down the hall because she wanted a cup of coffee
    and thought that there might still be some coffee left in the pot in
    the coffee room.

In (18) we have an example of *mechanistic explanation*. It is the kind of
explanation at work when we explain something by causes (here muscle
movements, changes in brain chemistry, etc.). In (19) we have an example
of *psychological explanation*. Here we explain not just Pavritra's bodily
movements but also the action she performed by making them. We do so
by referring to her *reasons* for doing what she did: what she wanted, what
she believed about how she could satisfy her want, etc.

The basic idea behind mechanistic explanation will be familiar to most
people. We use it to explain why the car won't start, why it will rain later
today, etc. By contrast, the structure of psychological explanation is far
from familiar, even though we all give and receive psychological explanations every day. (Here are some everyday examples: "Why did you
change the channel?" "Because I was bored with this show and wanted to
see what else was on." "Why did you leave in such a rush?" "Because I
couldn't be late for that class and I suddenly remembered that they had
changed the bus schedule.") To show what psychological explanation is
like, we need to return to a notion we introduced earlier, intentionality.

Intentionality, as we said, is aboutness. Let us look at some examples.
Suppose that Andy is walking down a street, a dog starts barking at him,
and he feels afraid. What is he afraid of? That the dog will attack him.
The relationship between his fear and what his fear is about, the danger of
the dog attacking, is what philosophers call intentionality.

(20) *Intentionality* The property of something being about something
else.

Let's look at some more examples of intentionality. Suppose that Bjorn
wants a cup of coffee. What is his desire about? That he have a cup of
coffee. Suppose that Bjorn imagines owning a new car. What is his imagining about? That he own a new car. Suppose that he sees his good friend
Carlos coming down the hall. What is his seeing about? Carlos coming
down the hall. And so on. That's intentionality.

Now contrast some states that do not have intentionality. Suppose that
Andy's hair is brown. What is it brown about? Well, *nothing*. Brownness
of hair does not have intentionality. Suppose that Andy can run a mile
in four minutes. (Yeah, right.) What is his running the four-minute mile
about? Again, *nothing*.

States with intentionality always have two elements: the state and what
the state is about. What the state is about is often called the *intentional
object*, but there is a problem with that term. Mental states are almost
always about some object's *doing* or *being* something. That is, they are not
about an object all on its own, but about an object's having a property—
what we might call a SITUATION or STATE OF AFFAIRS. Thus, my desire was
about my having a cup of coffee, my seeing was about Carlos's coming
down the hall, and so on.

Intentional states and events have a number of fascinating features.
Perhaps the most fascinating is that intentional objects—that is to say, the
object that an intentional state or event is about—need not be real. They
are real in one sense, of course: they are one aspect of a representation.
But what they describe need not correspond to the external world.
(Compare: a drawing is a real entity, but the situation that it depicts may
not really exist.) In fact, there are two ways in which an intentional object
can fail to correspond to reality. One is when the things in the believed/
imagined/desired situation exist, but they are not doing what the intentional state or event has them doing. (For example, suppose that Carlos
does exist, but he isn't coming down the hall. Then the *participant* in the
intentional object, i.e., Carlos, is real enough, but the situation as a whole
that Bjorn allegedly saw is not.) The other way in which intentional objects
can fail to correspond to the real world is when *the things described* by the
situation do not even exist. (For example, Joey can hope that Santa will
bring him lots of presents. The intentional object here is that Santa will
bring Joey presents. But in fact, not only does this *situation* not correspond to reality, one *entity* in the situation, namely Santa, isn't real: sad
to say, there is no such jolly old man.)

That we can represent intentional objects that are not the case is very important. Indeed, it is what makes all theoretical and creative thought possible. To build theories, we must think up hypotheses without knowing whether they say what is the case or not. We then test them and discover that some do and some do not. Novels are simply a vast exercise in thinking up intentional objects that are not the case (the characters, scenes, locations, etc., of the novel). And so on. Without the possibility of intentional objects that are not the case, there would be no thought or creativity as we know them.

The most common place to find intentionality is in REPRESENTATIONS. To understand what a representation is like, think of a picture. A picture is an ordinary physical object, made up of paper or canvas or whatever and having an array of colors and shapes on its surface. But a picture also has a special feature: it is a picture *of* some situation. Or think of a use of a word (more exactly, a TOKEN of a word, one particular *occurrence* of it. We'll discuss this notion of a token and its relationship to something called the type/token distinction in more detail later.) So think of a token of the word 'dog'. A word token is a physical object, just as a picture is. And it also has the special additional property that a picture has: it is *about* something. In this case, the word 'dog' is the name of friendly little beasts that like people and attract fleas.

Most mental states and events are like pictures and words in this respect: mental states and events too are about something. When a mental state or event is about something, it is called a representation. Representations are things like thoughts, imaginings, and perceptions: states and events that picture or present states of affairs. Representations, then, have intentionality.

The term 'intentionality' was introduced into contemporary philosophy by Brentano; few terms have played a larger role in recent philosophy of mind. The intentionality of some of our states and events has been used as a mark of the mental, as we saw, and as an argument for one kind of dualism, as we will see in chapter 5. It has also been used to anchor a theory of free will (chapter 6). And, to return at last to our topic, intentionality is what makes *psychological explanation* possible.

Recall mechanistic explanation and contrast it with psychological explanation. Mechanistic explanation explains by reference to causes, such as chemical changes, muscle movements, etc. Psychological explanations explain in a quite different way. They explain, as we said, by finding a person's *reasons* for what he or she did and what those reasons were about. In short, psychological explanation appeals to states that have intentionality.

Some philosophers have argued that a person's reasons for doing something are not a cause of her doing it, but this does not seem right: a desire for *x* seems to be a perfectly good cause of my going to get *x*. Rather, the difference between the two kinds of explanation goes like this. Think again of (18) and (19), the two ways of explaining Pavritra's action of walking down the hall to the coffee room. When we give Pavritra's reasons for doing the action, what does the explanation in terms of her reasons do for us? They explain the action by telling us *why* she did it. By showing us what motivated her to do the action, they make sense of her doing it. By contrast, an explanation in terms of brain states, muscle contraction, etc., may tell us *how* the action came about, but it would not tell us anything about *why* the person did it. Both of these two types of explanation are fundamental to our understanding of ourselves and others, and they both probably involve cause-and-effect relationships, but they are otherwise very different from one another.

It is important to note that both kinds of explanation could be correct; they do not contradict or even necessarily compete with one another. Explanatory dualism is not the same thing as explanatory conflict. Indeed, to know the *whole* story about Pavritra's little walk, for example, we need to have both kinds of explanation of it; each explains a different aspect of her walk. Roughly speaking, as we said, mechanistic explanations explain *how* she did it, and psychological explanations explain *why* she did it. The two explanations are complementary.[7]

To summarize so far, after distinguishing *dualism* from all forms of *monism*, we then explored three varieties of dualism. They were these:

- *Substance dualism* The mind is one thing, the brain is another; they may interact but they are two entirely different things.
- *Property dualism* Though the mind/brain is all one system, it has two fundamentally independent kinds of properties: mental properties (like experiencing thoughts and desires) and nonmental properties (like having circuits in the brain).
- *Explanatory dualism* Whether the mind is two things or has two irreducible kinds of properties, we have two distinct and equally valuable ways of explaining human behavior, only one of which appeals to intentionality.

As we will see, explanatory dualism is a very important notion. Many positions on the nature of the mind and its relationship to the body can be distinguished according to their attitude to explanatory dualism. Before we can see how that works, however, we need to lay out the monistic alternatives in more detail. We will start with idealism.

Idealism

Monism, as we said, comes in two varieties: idealism and materialism. The two main variants of idealism, in turn, are SUBJECTIVE IDEALISM and ABSOLUTE IDEALISM (see table 4.1 again).

(21) *Subjective idealism* The view that everything that exists is either myself and my states or constructs out of myself and my states.

(22) *Absolute idealism* The view that the whole universe is one vast mind and that everything in it is a state of this one universal mind, including all states of what we call matter.

Subjective idealism is often associated with the English philosopher Bishop George Berkeley (b. 1685), though he himself actually tried to avoid it. Subjective idealism sounds pretty peculiar to us now but was once taken extremely seriously in the particular brand of empiricist philosophy that developed in England. It tends to collapse into solipsism or at least extreme skepticism and is no longer held by many philosophers. Absolute idealism is associated with Georg W. F. Hegel.

The difference between these varieties of idealism is simple: for a subjective idealist, everything that exists is mindlike because nothing exists but me and states of me. For the absolute idealist, by contrast, there is the full range of objects that we all accept—solar systems and marbles and minds and so forth—but all these things and everything else that exists are states of some vast supermind. Nowadays even fewer philosophers take absolute idealism seriously than take subjective idealism seriously.

It does not automatically follow that the current lack of respect for idealism in either of its forms is justified, of course. That is a separate question. Indeed, an awkward little conceptual puzzle rears its head here: how can we even *distinguish* one "Everything is *x*" view from another? Start with the claim of idealism, "Everything is idea." Well, if *everything* is idea, then what is being denied? The claim certainly seems to deny something, namely, that something is not idea. But if *everything* is idea, what would a nonidea thing be *like* for an idealist? Similarly for materialism. If everything is made of matter, then what would a nonmaterial thing be *like* for a materialist? Fortunately, there may be a way to resolve this puzzle.

If the world is simply matter, then everything should conform to the cause-and-effect relationships that one finds in matter. If, on the other hand, the universe is one vast mind, then one would expect to find relationships of the kind characteristic of minds throughout the universe. One of the things characteristic of minds is to relate things rationally—to move to a later position, for example, because it is *implied* by an earlier one. Thus one move open to the idealist is to say that the whole universe is a realm of rationality. It seems that Hegel did indeed believe that the world is just that, a realm of rationality, indeed, that it is becoming progressively more rational (what exactly he meant by 'rationality' is a major issue in interpreting his philosophy, however).

Given this contrast, we can then choose between all-inclusive materialism and all-inclusive idealism. All we need to do is to ask, Is there evidence that everything is governed by rationality? If the evidence suggests that nothing beyond the bounds of ordinary minds is governed by rationality, then the evidence would be against idealism (at least the brand of idealism that we are sketching or perhaps caricaturing here) and in favor of materialism. And that does seem to be the direction in which the evidence points.

There is an additional possibility that we should at least mention, however: what if our conception of matter were to radically change? Until a century or so ago, we had a nice, clean picture of matter: matter is extended in space, has mass, and so on. More recent discoveries have greatly complicated that picture, however. We now have chaos and quarks and antimatter and quantum states and causation that takes place faster than light can travel. Plus there are, we're told, material things that have no precise location, or have only charge but no mass. One might well ask, therefore, If matter is this weird, what does the assertion that everything is made out of matter amount to? In particular, what does 'Everything is matter' *exclude*? An extreme case in point: suppose twenty-third century physicists conclude that there is something they call Cartesian matter, a kind of matter with all the features that Descartes ascribed to mental substance. Would this vindicate materialism? Idealism? Dualism? Maybe the best answer is that it would vindicate none of them, because if our notion of matter ever expanded to include what idealists and dualists meant by mind, the whole debate would become pointless.

Fortunately for assessing the fortunes of dualism versus monism, we do not need to decide what the final, ultimate monist picture will look like. All we need to be able to do is to assess whether minds and brains (or mental properties and neural properties) are fundamentally different from one another or not. What exactly the stuff of the brain will turn out to be is a separate question—a profoundly interesting question, but still a separate question. For simplicity, we will refer to the dominant monist position as 'materialism'. It would be well to keep in mind, however, that matter—and therefore materialism—might turn out to be quite different in the end from how we now think of them.

Materialism

I hope some animal never bores a hole in my head and lays its eggs in my brain, because later you might think you're having a good idea but it's just eggs hatching.
Jack Handey

As table 4.1 makes clear, just as idealism has taken a number of forms historically, so has materialism. (Table 4.1 mentions only materialist theories *of the mind*, but there are also materialist theories of the world as a whole: theories that everything whatsoever is made of matter, including purportedly abstract objects like numbers. We will restrict ourselves to the mind and not discuss these larger metaphysical theories.) Materialist theories of mind take at least four forms.

To understand the differences among them, we need to introduce a new distinction: that between materialist theories of mind that *assert* that minds exist, holding them to be one aspect or another of the brain or brain plus, and materialist theories of mind that *deny* that minds exist. It is important to grasp this distinction clearly because it is all too easy, but extremely wrong, to think that when materialists say that the mind is the brain, they are thereby denying that there is any such thing as the mind. Some materialists say this, but some definitely do not. As table 4.1 illustrates, two of the materialist theories of mind that we will consider insist that the mind exists and say that it is the brain. The other two deny that there is any such thing as minds.

Minds do exist First, materialist theories that *do* accept that minds exist. These theories maintain that the mind, which indisputably exists, will turn out to be the brain (or the brain plus something else material, like the environment or social institutions) when we finally understand what the mind is. The theorists who accept this kind of materialist theory have in mind cases like that of water. Water indisputably exists, but when we discovered what it is, it turned out to be hydrogen and oxygen. Does this mean that there really isn't any water? No, of course not. Similarly for the materialists that we will now consider, the fact that the mind may turn out to be the brain does not mean that there are no minds. For these theorists, minds do exist; they are brains.

The two varieties of materialism that we introduced earlier in this chapter, namely, identity theory and functionalism, both hold that there is such a thing as the mind and that it is the brain. Recall how we defined 'identity theory': every kind of mental state and every kind of mental event is (is identical to, is one and the same thing as) some kind of brain state or some kind of brain event. Keep in mind that we are using a precise notion of 'identity theory' here. The most general notion would simply be that the mind and the brain are, in some sense, a single thing. But functionalists also believe this, so it is too general to pick out where identity theorists and functionalists disagree. On our more precise definition, where they disagree soon becomes clear.

Brain states are things like neural circuits, and brain events are things like patterns of firings in neural circuits. Here is one of the simplest and oldest examples of what identity theorists have in mind: pain is C-fiber stimulation. (C-fibers are the type of nerves that carry signals important for sensations of pain from the various regions of the body to the brain.) It turned out that this identity picture is much too simple even for pains, for pain is not one simple kind of nerve activity.[8] The idea behind it, however, had some appeal: in the same way that water and H_2O are the same thing, it was hoped that each kind of mental state or event and some complex kind of nerve activity would turn out to be the same thing.

Unfortunately, it is impossible to identify many, probably most, kinds of mental states and events with any single kind of brain state or event, no matter how complex. There are various difficulties with trying to do so, but here we will discuss just one: the problem called MULTIPLE REALIZABILITY. Multiple realizability is the idea that a given function, for example thinking about the weather, can be performed in many different ways and by differing circuits in the brain. An analogy will help to make the point clear.

Think of clocks. What makes something a clock? Simply that it has the function of telling the time. Next, think of the range of devices that can be used to tell time: sun dials, hour glasses, water clocks, weight driven clocks, spring driven clocks, quartz clocks, atomic clocks—all these are clocks and can be very good clocks. Now the crucial question: what do all these devices have in common? Only one thing: they can all be used to tell the time. Otherwise, they have nothing in common whatsoever. If so, there can be no "identity theory" of clocks: there is no kind of thing, no kind of material object or state(s) of a material object, with which all and only activities of telling the time can be identified. Nor are clocks in any way unusual in this respect. Think of all the different things that count as vehicles. Or radios. Or flower holders. Or chairs. Etc. The list could go on forever.

One more example of multiple realizability, particularly relevant to minds and brains, is the computer and its functions. Think of a fairly powerful computer with a big active memory performing a calculation. Sometimes it will use one part of active memory, sometimes another, depending on what else is going on it in. Or think of the same program being run on a Mac and on a PC. If the same computational activity can be done in very different computers, or in different ways by the same computer, there can be no "identity theory" tying a particular kind of calculation that a computer performs to one kind of computer or one kind of state or event in a computer.

Now an important question: does multiple realizability get in the way of understanding the relationship between computers on the one hand and the software and computations that we run on computers on the other? No, it just makes the issue complicated. Now, mental activities can also be performed by various sorts of physical things. Take seeing. In addition to humans, word has it that cats, computer vision systems, and, for all we know, Martians can see. Next, problem solving. In addition to the human brain, computers and chimpanzees can solve some kinds of problems. And so on. That is, functions of minds can be realized in multiple ways, just like functions of computers. And we suspect that multiple realizability will get in the way of understanding the relationship of the mind to the brain just as much as it gets in the way of understanding the relationship of computational activities and computers—not very much.

Multiple realizability entails that the identity theory is too simple to be the correct theory of either relationship. If simply identifying mind types with brain types is too simple, what is the alternative? The most important alternative to date is FUNCTIONALISM. Recall our first-pass definition of this view: the mind is certain functions of a complex system, the brain. Taking her lead from computers, the functionalist says that the way to understand the mind is not to see it as particular parts of the brain or even as particular kinds of brain circuits. What makes some process in a computer a computation? Well, what the computer *does*. Where the computer does it and even how the computer does it do not matter. Similarly, the way to think of the mind is as *what the brain does*.

What gives something a mind, on this view, is its being able to do certain things. If something can perceive, achieve consciousness, think about its world and itself, plan courses of action, make decisions, etc., then it has a mind. That is what having a mind consists in, and that is all that is necessary for having a mind. How the thing is built and even how it is "engineered" to perform these tasks do not matter. What matters are the tasks performed, how one task relates to another, and so on. Sometimes the brain may use one set of circuits, sometimes another, but as long as the resulting state or event *does* the same thing, it is the same mental state or event.[9]

The crucial idea behind functionalism, the idea that sets it irretrievably apart from the identity theory of the mind, is the notion we just introduced: multiple realizability. Says the functionalist, there will almost always be a number of *different* ways of performing each task, and different brains may do the same task differently. This is multiple realizability: the same task can be implemented or *realized* in different ways in different brains (not to mention other information-processing systems, such as computers). Each time each function is performed, its performance is some state or event in the brain, but the same type of function can be performed by different kinds of brain circuits and different patterns of activities in brain circuits when it is performed in different brains (and perhaps even on different occasions in the same brain). The options would be multiplied if how the brain is hooked up to the world makes a difference, as in the brain-plus story. So, says the functionalist, the idea that each *type* of mental state or event is identical to a single *type* of brain state or event is far too simple.

Here's a way to illustrate the functionalists' point. If functionalists are right, there may be far less to "read off" of the brain about what is going on in the mind than some theorists have hoped. Moreover, we cannot automatically go in the opposite direction and make inferences about the nature of the brain from what the mind is doing. The "material realizer" could be neurons, silicon chips, or green cheese—so long as the system performs the appropriate tasks, it has a mind. If functionalism is the correct view, the relation between the mind and the brain—between the tasks performed and the system that performs them—will be very complicated. We will not be able to tell how a function is realized by looking at the function alone. Nor will be able to tell what function is being performed by studying only the brain.

We can make the distinction between the identity theory and functionalism more precise if we introduce a couple of new terms: TYPE IDENTITY and TOKEN IDENTITY. A type is just what it says: a type of thing (chairs, convertibles, ideas). A token is one occurrence of a type (the armchair over there, my ancient silver Chevrolet convertible, the new idea that just popped into my head). This distinction allows us to see clearly the difference between identity theorists and functionalists. Identity theorists say that every *type* of mental state or event is (is identical to, is one and the same as) some *type* of brain state or event: think of the example of pain and C-fibre stimulation. (Hence, mental types can be *reduced* to brain types, in the sense of (6).) Functionalists, on the other hand, deny that types of mental states and events can be identified with types of brain states and events; for example, the single type of mental state, belief that it's raining, can take the form of many different kinds of brain states. Yet, they maintain, *each and every particular mental state or event* is *some particular brain state or event*; for example, each particular belief token is some state or other of the brain. (Recall the case of clocks: Each particular clock is a material thing. None is made of mysterious "clock-stuff." And yet what clocks have in common is their function, i.e., telling time, not their material makeup. So the type clock is not identical to any one type of physical stuff.)

Let us add this new point about functionalism to (8) on page 67:

(23) *Functionalism* The mind is certain functions of a complex system—
     a brain and perhaps other systems—*and* each and every particular
     mental state or event is some event in such a system.

The rejection of type-type identities frees functionalists from the impossible task of trying to find some single type of brain state or event to correspond to each type of mental state or event, while allowing them nevertheless to remain good materialists. In short, identity theorists believe in type-type identities between mental states and events and brain states and events. Functionalists aren't any less materialists than identity theorists, but they believe in token-token identities, not type-type identities.

Most functionalists believe one further thing about the mind, something that will become important when we take up forms of materialism that deny that minds exist. If mental kinds are irreducible to brain kinds, then it is unlikely (to say the least!) that the terms that explain kinds of brain states and processes will also explain mental kinds. If one set of terms worked for both, why wouldn't we be able to reduce the one to the other? If we can't, then we need one vocabulary to explain the kinds of states and processes that the language of neuroscience captures, and we need another vocabulary to capture and explain states and processes described in cognitive terms. What two vocabularies? Recall the notion of explanatory dualism. For most functionalists, the appropriate language for the mental is the language of intentionality, the language of reasons for actions. And the language and style of explanation for the brain is the mechanistic language of neuroscience.

Next, notice that the two kinds of language go together with the two kinds of explanation described earlier. The language of intentionality goes with, indeed may well be required for, psychological explanation (though many functionalists would want to supplement the former in various ways), and the language of neuroscience goes with mechanistic explanation.

Given all this, we need to add yet another element to our definition of functionalism. We now need to add the idea that to capture and explain mental phenomena, we have to use the language and explanatory style of psychological explanation:

(24) *Functionalism*: The mind is certain functions of a complex system, a brain and perhaps other systems, *and* each and every particular mental state or event is some state or event of such a system, *and* we have to use the language and explanatory style of psychological explanation to capture and explain mental states and events.

With this we finally have a fairly adequate definition of functionalism. So let us turn to the alternative approach, the view that minds do not exist. It too comes in two forms.

Minds do not exist   We turn now to the varieties of materialism that deny that the mind exists. These views are initially less plausible than views that hold that minds exist, but they have played an important role in twentieth-century intellectual life and deserve some attention.

Two theories have denied that there is any such thing as minds, BEHAVIORISM and the position that we will call NEUROPHILOSOPHY.[10] The best-known version of behaviorism, and the one that we will consider, is the one associated with B. F. Skinner. This theory asserts that there is only behavior and the organism's DISPOSITIONS to behave. There is no such thing as the mind.[11] (Dispositions are tendencies to react in a certain way in the face of certain inputs. Thus, glass has a *disposition* to break when hit, but steel does not. Dispositions can be part of how something is built, or they can be induced into something through training, experience, etc.)

The idea behind this radical form of behaviorism is something like this. Suppose that you hear someone say something and, as we would naturally put it, you think hard about how to respond. According to radical behaviorism, what is really going on in you is that the incoming sentence has set off a complex pattern of dispositions, including dispositions for selecting from other dispositions the ones best suited, according to your conditioning, to respond to the situation. When these best dispositions are selected, you respond. And what about what we call thinking? Well, "thinking" is merely how that train of interlocking dispositions plays out.

Behaviorism was a worthy scientific attempt at REDUCTION as defined in (6) on p. 67. Behaviorists tried to reduce incredibly complex cognitive phenomena such as perceiving, remembering, and thinking to simple building blocks, namely, stimulus-response correlations and a capacity to be conditioned into new correlations (new dispositions to respond to stimuli). Unfortunately, the building blocks were too simple. Too much processing goes on between stimulus and response for behaviorism to be true. As a result, very few theorists any longer accept behaviorism in this extreme form. (See note 10 for less extreme forms.)

A trendy new successor to behaviorism appeared about two decades ago, largely through the efforts of two contemporary philosophers, Paul and Patricia Churchland. Originally, the view took the form of ELIMINATIVE MATERIALISM. Eliminative materialists, like behaviorists, just urged that there is nothing remotely like the mind in the traditional sense. More recently, eliminative materialism has transformed into a broader theory that many now call *neurophilosophy*, after the 1986 book of that name by Patricia Churchland. With neurophilosophy a positive theory of what the processes in us *are* like has been developed. With this positive account, eliminative materialism becomes neurophilosophy. The negative claim first.

For eliminative materialists, the idea that people have minds is a theory, just as much a theory as the theory that certain women (whom we now think of as schizophrenic or even just aggressive advocates of heretical ideas) were witches possessed by Satan—and just as false. Say these theorists, all the other theories with which we first tried to explain ourselves and our world turned out to be false and have died out. Why not the theory that we have something called a mind? The universe did not turn out to be giant sphere, as Aristotle believed. The world is not organized in a great chain of being, with levels and levels of ever-increasing reality, as some medieval scientists believed. The earth is not the center of the solar system, as most theorists believed up to about 400 years ago. Troubled or challenging women are not witches possessed by Satan, as was believed in the Middle Ages and after. And so on. Why should we expect our first psychological theory, the theory that people have minds, to turn out any better, even though we cherish the idea that we really have beliefs and desires and hopes and fears?

The argument they mounted against the idea that minds exist is complex but was based on one essential point. We have been trying to come up with good explanations of ourselves based on the idea that we have minds for at least 2,500 years, since the time of the Greeks. We are not any better at it than they were. That suggests that we have been barking up the wrong tree.

The problem, said eliminative materialists, runs as deep as the idea that we have minds at all. The view that we have minds is the view that we have beliefs, desires, emotions, values, and other states and events like them. This view of the human person has been given a rather dismissive name; it is called FOLK PSYCHOLOGY. According to eliminative materialism, we have to get beyond this traditional folk psychology just as we have got beyond folk physics (for example, we no longer believe that cannon balls fall faster than feathers in a vacuum), folk cosmology (we no longer believe that the earth is flat), and folk psychiatry (we no longer believe that troubled people are possessed by demons). Put a bit more precisely and in the jargon we introduced earlier, what eliminative materialists denied was that there is anything in us that corresponds at all closely to our notion of states and processes that have *intentionality*. The language of beliefs, desires, emotions, etc., they say, is a language of snares and delusions, in the end no more about anything real than the language of the starry sphere or demon-possessed witches.

One natural reaction to these claims is astonished disbelief: "The language of thinking and feeling and doing things for a reason is not about anything real or important? How could that be?" In this reaction we see just how much eliminative materialists want to eliminate. What kind of understanding of ourselves would it be that made no reference to why we do what we do? Of course, eliminative materialists had reasons for what they said. In particular, as they saw it, folk psychology and mentalistic talk are infected with many weaknesses. Here we will mention just three.

First, the states and events that intentional language describes can only be measured in a very general way, if they can be measured at all. We might be able to say that one desire is stronger than another, but how much stronger? 1.26 times? 27.8 times? There is no way to make sense of such comparisons. Since all truly scientific language is about events that can be measured with some precision, this failing alone ensures that folk psychology will never develop into a scientific psychology.

Second, folk psychology cannot even begin to explain a great deal that is obvious and central to mental life, everything from why we need sleep to why we do certain kinds of reasoning well and others quite badly to what causes some minds to misfunction in dramatic ways.

The third argument is a bit more complicated, so let's lay it out formally:

Premise 1 Folk psychology is a radically false theory.
Premise 2 The key terms of radically false theories do not stand for anything real.
Conclusion The key terms of folk psychology (e.g. 'belief', 'desire', 'pain') do not stand for anything real.

Other theorists have tried to answer these objections, of course. One response points to the crucial role of P2. If this premise is false, then the fact that folk psychology is limited and/or contains false views would contain no implications for the existence of the states and events that folk psychology talks about. We cannot go into that issue here (see Stich 1996 for a good discussion).

Eliminative materialists did not just reject and criticize. They also have a positive proposal. Their proposal can be summed up in one word: neuroscience. They urge that to understand ourselves at any depth, we need to replace the theory that we have something called the mind with theories about what unquestionably does exist, namely the brain and its environment. And we need to approach the brain in the language appropriate to it, the language of extremely complex patterns of hookups among neurons, not the traditional language of intentionality. Eliminative materialism has become neurophilosophy (see chapter 5, section 5).

At this point some people may be wondering exactly how functionalism and eliminative materialism disagree. Supposedly, functionalism maintains that minds exist, while neurophilosophy denies that minds exist. Yet both sides hold that the mind (in the case of neurophilsophy, what we are really talking about when we talk about the mind) is *a system of the brain*. Where's the disagreement?

Recall the third clause of (24): we have to use the language and explanatory style of psychological explanation to capture and explain mental states and events. Here's the disagreement: while functionalists believe that we must use the language of intentionality and psychological explanation if we are to understand ourselves, eliminative materialists believe that this language and style of explanation may be fine in everyday practical life, but they get us nowhere at the level of developing deep, explanatory theories of ourselves. That's a substantial disagreement.

Indeed, we can capture the differences among most of the positions we have been examining by looking at the attitude they take to psychological explanation and explanatory dualism in general. (Explanatory dualism, recall, is the view that we need at least two radically different kinds of explanation to explain ourselves completely.) Dualists mostly accept explanatory dualism. And why not? For them, *explanatory* dualism just reflects the *metaphysical* dualism of the human person: each kind of explanation deals with one side of the metaphysical split. Functionalists also accept explanatory dualism, as we just saw. Since they *reject* metaphysical dualism, however, their reason is different from the reason that dualists give. For functionalists, the human person is a *single* system, but we still need to use *two* kinds of explanation to explain it adequately, one to deal with its reasons for what it does, the other to deal with the causal processes that realize (or otherwise underlay) these reasons.[12] Reasons and other mental states are real. We just need a second kind of explanation to explain them adequately. Finally, identity theorists and eliminative materialists reject explanatory dualism, identity theorists because all psychological explanations will eventually reduce to mechanistic ones, eliminative materialists because the states and processes referred to in psychological explanations do not exist, not in anything like the form supposed in these explanations, at any rate.

To summarize, having laid out identity theory, functionalism, behaviorism, and eliminative materialism, and what eliminative materialism has evolved into, namely neurophilosophy, we can now see what is living and what is dead in materialist positions on the mind and attach some rough dates (see table 4.2). Behaviorism is dead. Identity theory is mostly dead. Eliminative materialism has morphed into neurophilosophy. What is living are functionalism and neurophilosophy.

We now turn to the question of what should we believe. Dualism? If so, what variety of dualism? Materialism? If so, what variety of materialism?

Table 4.2
What is living and what is dead in materialist views of the mind

Materialism from 1900 to the 1960s (dead)
Identity theory (replaced by functionalism)
Behaviorism (replaced by neurophilosophy)
Materialism since the 1970s (living)
Functionalism (mind consists in functions of the brain)
Neurophilosophy (mind not important; only neurons are)

Study Questions

1. Can any *two* things ever be identical in the sense of 'identity' that philosophers use? In what nonphilosophical sense can two things be identical? For example, what do we mean by terms like 'identical twins'?

2. What is a criterion? Why do we need a criterion of the mental before we can resolve the debate between dualists and materialists?

3. Explain each of the proposed criteria for mentality: nonspatiality, intentionality, consciousness, and special access. Which is best?

4. It might be objected, to the special-access criterion, that there are mental states that we can never know introspectively. Look very carefully at the criterion as stated, and see whether this objection really poses a problem.

5. What is monism? What is materialism? Why is the latter only one of the possible monist theories of mind?

6. Describe each of the three kinds of dualism noted above: substance, property, and explanatory dualism. Some people think that explanatory dualism isn't really a kind of dualism at all. Why might they think this? Are they right?

7. Contrast functionalism with the identity theory. In what sense are both functionalists and identity theorists committed to the existence of minds? In what sense are both camps materialist nonetheless? (Hint: review the difference between token identity and type identity.)

8. Explain what is meant by folk psychology. How do historical parallels suggest that folk psychology may be radically false, and hence that beliefs, desires, etc., may not really exist?

9. What is eliminative materialism? How did eliminative materialism evolve into neurophilosophy?

10. Contrast functionalism with eliminative materialism.

Suggested Further Readings

There is a discussion of the mark of the mental in Kim 1996. It is an accessible summary of an inaccessible older article of his.

Classic statements of dualism include Descartes 1931 [1641] and Plato 1981 [ca. 390 B.C.]. Among the few early statements of materialism, Hobbes 1996 [1668] and La Mettrie 1994 [1748] are especially important. See the Introduction to Haugeland 1997 for more on materialism versus dualism. Property dualism in contemporary philosophy has been championed by Peter Strawson (chapter 3 of 1959), whereas substance dualism is closely associated with Descartes (see especially his 1931 [1641] work).

Frege 1892 is a classic, albeit difficult, paper on the "relation" of identity. Armstrong 1968, Place 1956, and Smart 1962 are foundational treatments of the identity theory. See Fodor 1983 for a defense of functionalism and P. M. Churchland 1984, Dennett 1978b, and Flanagan 1984 for more on behaviorism. Chomsky 1959 is a famous critique of behaviorist approaches to the human mind.

There are numerous anthologies of seminal articles on issues in philosophy of mind. We recommend any of Block 1981, Geirsson and Losonsky 1996, Lycan

1990, Morton 1997, and Rosenthal 1991. P. M. Churchland 1984, Flanagan 1984, Jacquette 1994, and Kim 1996 are good, more advanced overviews. Taylor 1963 is an old but very fine introduction.

See P. S. Churchland 1986 for an extended discussion of neurophilosophy and the issues surrounding eliminative materialism and Stich 1996 for a deep critique of eliminative materialism. One of the best presentations of the details of neurophilosophy is Churchland and Sejnowski 1992.

A good anthology on personal identity is Kolak and Martin 1991. See also Parfit 1984. Perry 1978 is a delightful, accessible, and short discussion of personal identity and how it relates to the possibility of surviving death. See also T. Nagel 1987 on life after death.

On the vicissitudes of introspection, see Armstrong 1963; also Shoemaker 1963, selections from which are reprinted in Rosenthal 1991. Another important source on this issue is Sellars 1997 [1956]. See also Rorty 1979 and Ryle's (1949) attack on "the given."

The key works on intentionality are Brentano 1995 [1874] (especially book 2, chapter 1) and Chisholm 1955. Cummins 1989 provides an excellent account of issues about meaning and mental representation.

A great deal of work has been done on the nature and value of psychological explanation and the status of the states and events that it talks about, e.g., beliefs and desires. Donald Davidson (1980) did a lot of the original work, and it was developed in a most interesting direction by Daniel Dennett (1987). Jerry Fodor (1975, 1981) has made a heroic attempt to combine psychological explanation with realism about mental states and events, i.e., with the view that mental states and events really exist and are not merely "useful fictions." For a readable view of the current attitude of neurophilosophy, see P. M. Churchland 1995.

Chapter 5

Mind and Body:
What Should We Believe?

Midterm review. On the mind/body problem we have so far done the following:

- Introduced the two basic positions: dualism and materialism
- Briefly sketched the implications of each for immortality and free will
- Examined whether there is a criterion of the mental
- Laid out the main varieties of dualism
- Taken a brief look at idealism
- Sketched the main varieties of materialism, looking in some detail at functionalism and neurophilosophy

The previous chapter gives us a fairly complete survey of dualist and monist positions on the mind. Now we come to the key question: Of the range of different positions, which should we believe? Which has the greatest likelihood of being true? That is the topic of this chapter.

1 Why Has Dualism Had Such a Strong Appeal?

Before we turn to that question, let's stand back for a minute and survey the scene as a whole. For the past fifty years or so, most philosophers of mind, psychologists, and other researchers working on the mind have been materialists of one stripe or another. (Indeed, the vast majority of them have held the variety of materialism we earlier called FUNCTIONALISM, a view to which we will return.) Indeed, materialism is so widely believed nowadays that dualism is often not even taken seriously. This simple faith in materialism makes it easy for those who hold it to forget that things have not always been thus. Indeed, up until about 100 years ago, it seemed clear to most people that some form of dualism had to be true, anyone who thought otherwise was simply ignoring some obvious facts. Any view that seemed so obviously true to so many highly educated and intelligent philosophers and psychologists is not a mere silly, simple-minded mistake. It may (or may not) be wrong, but it is not silly or simple-minded.

In fact, dualism was so dominant prior to about 1900 that theorists of any enduring influence who were materialists can be counted on one hand: the Greek philosopher Democritus (b. ca. 460 B.C.), the Roman philosopher Lucretius (b. ca. 94 B.C.), the English philosopher Hobbes, a few French philosophers such as de la Mettrie (b. 1709) and Condillac (b. 1715), and that's about it. Until very recently, almost all the most intelligent people in the world believed in dualism. The most significant exception, actually, consisted not of materialists but IDEALISTS. (We discussed them in the last chapter.) A theory that seemed so obviously true to so many intelligent people for so many centuries is not to be lightly dismissed. What is it about the mind that made dualism seem so compelling to so many people for so long?

Two answers are often given, but they are both too simple. The first oversimple answer: until very recently, most philosophers were religious; religious people believe in immortality; but (barring bodily resurrection, which many found too mysterious) it is difficult to believe in immortality unless you believe in dualism; so philosophers believed in dualism. This answer is a bit insulting. It suggests that some of the greatest minds who ever lived let their religious convictions control their theory of mind. Anyway, it is not true. Descartes, the philosopher who invented the dualist picture of the mind as we know it, had doubts about many important aspects of religion, yet dualism still seemed to him to be true. Indeed, he thought that he had a number of absolutely airtight arguments to show that it is true.

The second oversimple answer: INTROSPECTION, not religious faith, is what made dualism seem plausible. When philosophy and psychology replaced introspection with something better about 1900, dualism soon lost its appeal. This answer is a lot better than the first one. Indeed, it has an element of truth to it. One of the reasons why it has seemed to many people that the mind is something different from the brain is indeed the way in which we appear to ourselves in introspection. Introspection is the awareness we have of ourselves "from the inside." It's the awareness you have of your thoughts, feelings, etc., just by having and paying attention to them. By contrast, if you want to become aware of someone else's thoughts, feelings, etc., you have to observe their bodily movements, listen to what they say, etc.; in short, you have to pay attention to how their thoughts and feelings are manifesting themselves on the surface of the

body. This contrast between awareness of one's own thoughts and awareness of the thoughts of others is one of the main sources of the PROBLEM
OF OTHER MINDS, and we will explore it in more detail in chapter 7. Now,
many philosophers and psychologists have held that when they "look into
themselves," the self that they find is utterly different from anything that
could be made out of matter, including the matter of the brain. This is
what Wittgenstein described as the feeling of an "unbridgeable gulf
between consciousness and brain process" (1953, §412). As we appear to
ourselves in introspection, we appear to be something quite different from
anything made out of nerve cells or anything else made out of matter.

So introspection has been one of the sources of the appeal of dualism.
Unfortunately, introspection has turned out to be not a good method for
uncovering the nature of the mind. With the creation of laboratories for
studying human behavior in Germany, the United States, and Russia
toward the end of the nineteenth century and with the (re)discovery by
Freud that a great deal of human mental activity is not open to introspection (is *unconscious*, in one of the meanings of the word 'unconscious'), theorists came to see that there is a great deal that introspection
cannot tell us about the mind. Introspection is central to self-knowledge
in everyday life—without introspection, we would not be aware of ourselves and this would be as good as being dead—but having a crucial role
in everyday life is not the same thing as being a good tool for discovering
what we are really like. In addition to not giving us any access to the
many things in the mind not open to introspection, introspection also
suffers from being unverifiable and inconstant from person to person:

• *Unverifiable* How can anyone else check your introspections? Worse,
how can even you compare how your mind seems to you with how your
mind actually is?
• *Poor intersubject reliability* How one person seems to herself is very
often different from how another person seems to himself, even concerning the same issue.

Finally, it turned out that introspection is often easily fooled. As Freud
and others showed us, we distort our awareness of ourselves in all sorts of
ways. Indeed, as later theorists have shown, we can even make things up
in introspection (this is called CONFABULATION). In short, introspection is a
thoroughly unreliable tool for studying the mind and it was abandoned in
favor of laboratory experiments and other methods around 1900.

Whatever the problems facing introspection, was it the main basis on
which people were led to accept dualism? Not in our view. Introspection

was one thing that made dualism seem plausible, but we believe that another thing played an even larger role in its acceptance.

Before we look further into what gave dualism its appeal, let us introduce a second issue to see if we can't deal with the two of them together. If we want to understand what it is about the mind that gives dualism its appeal to some people, we also want to know what it is about the mind that makes materialism seem just as obviously true to other people. What is it about this thing called the mind that makes two such totally different conceptions, dualism and materialism, so attractive to different people?

The distinction between dualism and materialism is just one reflection, in our view, of a vast, deep distinction between two ways of viewing human beings. Let us call these two ways of viewing people two *images* of the person, a term coined by the contemporary American philosopher Wilfrid Sellars. One image of the person is related to relationships, responsibility, social groupings—in short, to everyday life, to how people appear in our ordinary dealings with them. The other image is more scientific. Sellars called the former the MANIFEST IMAGE and the latter the SCIENTIFIC IMAGE. We can define the two images as follows:

(1) *Manifest image* The image of the person as a single, unified center of consciousness and decision making.

This is the image of the person that we find in ordinary moral, social, and interpersonal life. Here we view the person, this center of consciousness and decision making, as a being that can focus attention on things; take account of reasons for doing this or believing that; make decisions in a unified, focused way; govern him- or herself by freely chosen standards; and so on. (Sellars choose the term 'manifest image' because this is the way we manifest ourselves to ourselves in everyday life.)

(2) *Scientific image* The image of the person as a vast assemblage of cells tied together into a complex system.

This is the image of the person as an organism, a middle-sized mammal in a world of similar creatures—a mammal that is, for example, closely related to chimpanzees, gorillas, and other primates. Here we view the person as we view other organisms: as a huge mass of neurons and other cells linked in complex cause-and-effect relationships. (In fact, there is more than one scientific image of the person alive in our culture currently: in addition to the organic, neurological image just sketched, there is also the picture of the person as a complex information-processing system.)

Now, the manifest and the scientific image do not contradict one another. They are simply two alternative ways of looking at one and the same thing, in this case, the human person. However, for some people, the manifest image seems to be the better picture, i.e., the picture that is truest to our real nature. As we said, it emphasizes the conscious, reasoning, unified aspect of people, and for some people, these properties are the heart of the matter. On the other hand, for other people, the scientific image seems to offer the best hope of generating a complete, detailed, deep theory of persons, it being the image of the person as an incredibly complex biological or information-processing system.

People who are most at home in the manifest image will also tend to think that the scientific image can never capture important elements of what a person is. For these people, dualism will be very attractive: it may appear to be the only theory that offers any hope of capturing those aspects of people that, as it seems to them, the scientific image cannot capture. On the other hand, people who expect that the scientific image will eventually explain everything essential about the human person tend to find materialism more appealing.[1]

This distinction between the manifest and scientific images also explains the difference between what most people believed prior to 1900 and what most researchers on the mind believe now. Prior to 1900, for most people the *only* image of the person was the manifest image. As Descartes put it, the mind is "a thing which thinks" (1931 [1641]), where by 'thinking' he meant all the features of the manifest image: unified consciousness, focused decision making, governing oneself by freely chosen standards, etc. The idea that people might be nothing more than complex organisms did not take hold until after Darwin (b. 1809) late in nineteenth century. Before then, dualism seemed obviously true.

By contrast, for most theorists now, it is some version of the scientific image that seems to tell the fullest story about people: people are complex organisms, or perhaps complex information-processing systems, but at any rate complex *natural* systems, part of the material universe, like other animals and objects in general. People for whom the scientific image is dominant will be drawn to materialism.

We now have a picture of the background against which dualism looked obviously true to most people and materialism looked equally obvious to a few. The vast divide between the manifest and the scientific images of the person is what mainly accounts for these phenomena. So let's turn to the big question: which view should we believe (if either)? Because the dualist side is often slighted by contemporary theorists, we will begin by examining arguments for dualism. Some of them are very interesting.

2   Four Arguments for Dualism

Here is the big question put more precisely: is the mind (as delineated in chapter 4) an aspect of the brain (or brain plus), or is it something different from the brain? That is the big question if we are considering substance dualism. If we are considering property dualism, the big question is this: is the mind simply neural properties of the brain, or is it made up of properties that are radically independent of neural properties? Put yet one more way, is the mind a thing separate and apart from the brain, though in close association with it (substance dualism); is it a set of properties that share a single mind/brain unit with other, purely neural properties (property dualism); or is it simply an aspect of the brain (materialism)? Which view should we accept?

As we just saw, some form of dualism seemed obviously true to most thinkers for virtually the whole of human history up until about one hundred years ago. It is unlikely that a view that was believed that widely has nothing going for it. Many arguments have been advanced by philosophers in support of dualism. They generally have the same structure: Find some property of people (or minds) that no material object could have or that is not a material property of any object. Infer that people (or the business part of people, i.e., minds) are neither material objects nor made up of material properties.

We will consider four such arguments. These four are not by any means all of the arguments advanced on behalf of dualism. They just strike us as four of the most interesting ones. They all derive in one way or another from Descartes, though the form in which we will consider them is sometimes quite different from the form they took in Descartes's writings. They can be grouped into two sets of two (see table 5.1). The horizontal distinction is in terms of the kind of dualism argued for. Two of the argu-

Table 5.1
Four arguments for dualism

	Property dualism	Substance dualism
Introspection	Mental state vs. brain state	Conceivability
Nonintrospection	Intentionality	Indivisibility

ments aim to prove property dualism, two of them aim to prove substance dualism. The vertical distinction needs a word of explanation.

Earlier in this chapter, we mentioned that one of the perennial reasons why people believe in dualism is how we appear to ourselves when we introspect ourselves. We just appear to be something very different from any brain process. And it is certainly true that a number of the most influential arguments for dualism have made exactly this kind of appeal to introspection. Consider this statement of Descartes's: "When I consider the mind, that is to say, myself inasmuch as I am a thinking being,..." (1931 [1641]). Notice the move: to examine the *mind*, Descartes looks into *himself*—he appeals to introspection. Descartes simply assumes that the best way to find out what the mind is, is to look into his own self. It would be hard to imagine any theorist making that move now. Nowadays theorists would be much more likely to set up an experiment. (We looked briefly at why introspection was abandoned as a research tool in the earlier discussion.)

If introspection has been one basis for arguing for dualism, however, it has certainly not been the only one. The simple-minded picture of why people believed in dualism prior to this century is too simple. Of the four arguments named in table 5.1, two of them appeal to introspection, but, as we will see, two do not, certainly not in any obvious way. Nor should we leave the impression that Descartes used only arguments from introspection. In fact, he mounted arguments for dualism of both the kinds we are distinguishing here.

It is time now to see how these arguments go. Let's first take a look at the two arguments for property dualism. Property dualism, recall, is the idea that mental properties are utterly independent of neural properties, even if I, the thing that has both kinds of properties, am one single thing.

Mental-State-versus-Brain-State Argument

The mental-state-versus-brain-state argument is simple. Its simplicity notwithstanding, it is probably the source of a lot of the appeal of dualism. Imagine a tasty, tempting meal. Form a really clear image of it. Now pay attention to that image. If that image is a brain state, it should have the properties of brain states. It should be made out of millions of tiny gray or white units, it should be soaked in blood and other liquids, it should be in total darkness—in short, it should be like a brain state.

But the image that I am introspecting has none of those features, so the argument goes: it is a single image, not an assembly of millions of units; it is not gray or white like brain cells are—in short, it is nothing like a state of a brain. Conclusion: mental states like images are totally different from states of the brain.

Argument from Intentionality

Next, our old friend intentionality. As we said in chapter 4 when we considered it as a criterion of the mental, intentionality enters into philosophy of mind in numerous places. There it was offered as a criterion of the mental. We will now examine the use philosophers have made of it to argue for property dualism.

The argument is deceptively simple:

Premise 1 States and events that have intentionality can be false as well as true, inaccurate as well as accurate.

(Example: Compare 'I believe that rocks are hard' and 'I believe that the Tooth Fairy will give Rob $1 tonight'. The first belief is true, the second is false (or else Rob is in for a *big* surprise!). Yet both beliefs have intentionality, i.e., are about something. Being about something in this way is what makes perception, thought, science, literature, and all the other products of the human mind possible.)

Premise 2 To be false is to represent what is not.
Premise 3 The material world cannot have to do with what is not.
Conclusion Therefore, states and events that have intentionality cannot be states of matter or events in matter.

Many philosophers have accepted some form of this argument, including Russell (1912).

Conceivability Argument

Now substance dualism. The conceivability argument is the first of two arguments that we will examine for substance dualism, the idea that the mind and the brain are two different things. We have derived the conceivability argument from an argument that Descartes (1931 [1641]) mounts in his Second Meditation, but we will give it our own form. It goes like this:

Premise 1 I can conceive of myself without a body.
Premise 2 If I can conceive of myself without a body, then it is possible for me to be without a body.
Conclusion 1 Therefore, it is possible for me to be without a body.
Premise 3 But if C1, then I am something more than a body.
Conclusion 2 Therefore, I am something more than a body.

This is a very nice argument from a number of points of view. First, it looks to be *valid*. It appears to have the following form:

P1 *A*
P2 If *A*, then *B*
C1 *B*
P3 If *B*, then *C*
C2 *C*

This is clearly a valid form of argument: it is just two applications of *modus ponens*. Of course, we need to make sure that the argument *really does* have this form. If it does, then attention turns to its premises. Is P1 true? Is P2 true? Is P3 true? For if the conceivability argument is valid and the answer to these three questions are all 'Yes', then the argument is also *sound*—and that means that dualism is true. We will try to answer these questions, but before we do, we need to lay out the fourth argument.

Indivisibility Argument
The indivisibility argument, also derived from Descartes, is extremely simple. To our minds, it is also extremely powerful. Indeed, we think that it proves a form of dualism. (Whether it is the form of dualism that Descartes and other dualists wanted is another question.) Here is how it goes:

Premise 1 The mind cannot be divided.
Premise 2 All material objects, including the brain, can be divided.
Conclusion Therefore, the mind is not the brain (or any other material object).

Notice that the term 'divided' could mean a number of different things. We will return to this issue.

3   Assessment of the Arguments

How well do these four arguments for dualism stand up to critical evaluation?

Mental-State-versus-Brain-State Argument
At first glance, the mental-state-versus-brain-state argument looks pretty solid: as we are aware of mental states, they do indeed seem to be nothing at all like brain states. We need to ask, however, whether what mental states *seem to us* to be like is necessarily a good indication of what they

are like. Could appearances be deceiving here? Many things do not appear to be as they are.

Consider a lowly table. Modern science tells us that a table is mostly empty space. Indeed, well over 99 percent of it is empty space. It is made up of atoms and molecules, and atoms and molecules consist of a small number of extremely tiny electrons circling at a vast distance, relative to their size, from an only somewhat larger nucleus. There is nothing in the space between them. If so, tables are mostly empty space.

Yet they do not appear to be mostly empty space. They appear to be completely solid. Perhaps the same is true of mental images: perhaps they appear to be very different from brain states yet are brain states.

The analogy with a table can be put another way. Ask yourself, "How would a table that was mostly empty space appear to us?" Answer: "As a solid table." For that is how mostly empty space containing a bunch of nuclei and electrons appears to us: as solid. Now ask, "How would a complex circuit in the brain appear to us in introspection?" Perhaps the answer is "As a mental image." What else would you expect a brain state to appear as?

In short, the mental-state-versus-brain-state argument does not work. We have found an analogous case, a case that seems indeed to be completely analogous in the relevant respect, and it has revealed a flaw in the original argument. The argument depends on an inference principle that we considered in chapter 2: the way things seem → way things are. And we saw that this principle is not always reliable. A stick in water *seems* to be bent, but for all that, it is not bent. The inference from how mental states seem to us to how they are may be no more reliable than the chapter 2 example of an inference from how the stick seems to us to how the stick is.

Before we move on, note something important: we have not shown that mental states *are* brain states (or that mental events are brain events). All we have shown is that an argument that they are *not* does not work. But, as we will try to show in the next section, that may be enough. On to the second argument.

Argument from Intentionality

Is having intentionality enough to show that something cannot be made out of matter? Possible counterexamples immediately come to mind: photographs and sentences in a book. They are clearly made out of matter, yet they are about something and can be false and inaccurate as well as true and accurate. If so, having intentionality does not stand in the way of something being made out of matter. However, as we said in chapter 4, sentences and such may derive their intentionality from elsewhere, so they are not a clearcut counterexample. The real problem is that we do not understand intentionality well enough to say with any confidence *what* it implies for the mind/body problem. For this reason, it cannot be used as an argument for anything.

Again, it is important that we are not arguing that intentional states *are* brain states; we are merely urging that an argument that they are not does not work.

That brings us to the arguments for substance dualism, the idea that the mind and the brain are two different things.

Conceivability Argument

We said that *if* the conceivability argument is valid and *if* the premises are true, the argument is sound and dualism is true. It is now time to examine those two big *if*s. First, premise 1: I can conceive of myself without a body. Is this true? *Can* I conceive of myself without a body? It is in fact far from clear that I can. Perhaps I can form some vague idea of being without a body, but whether I can form a clear, complete picture of myself without a body is another question. (I can also form a vague idea of a round square, but just try to form a clear image of one.) Indeed, there is a risk that P1 is *begging the question*, already assuming, that is, that dualism is already true—just what the argument is trying to prove. For if I *am* my body—and that possibility has to remain open till the conclusion is reached—then for the argument not to beg the question, to conceive of myself without a body I would have to conceive of myself without *myself*. In short, P1 is far from clearly true and also seems to beg the question.

Next, is the conceivability argument valid? One requirement for an argument to be valid is that all the key words in the argument are used with the same meaning throughout. Changing the meaning of key terms is called the FALLACY OF EQUIVOCATION and ruins an argument. Here is an example of an argument that clearly fails because of equivocation:

Premise 1 Happiness is the end of life.
Premise 2 The end of life is death.
Conclusion Therefore, happiness is death.

(The problem, of course, is with the word 'end': in P1 it means goal; in P2 it means termination.)

Compare P1 (I can conceive of myself without a body), and P2 (If I can conceive of myself without a body, then it is possible for me to be without a body). To have a chance of being true, P1 has to be using 'conceive' in a very weak, "form a vague idea of" sense (see the example of the round square just above). But P2 requires the much stronger sense of 'conceivable' at work in this inference principle:

(3) *The principle of conceivability* What is conceivable is possible.

Showing that something is conceivable in *this* way is enough to show that it is possible. This sense of 'conceive' is stronger than the one used in P1 because conceiving of a round square in that former sense emphatically does *not* show that round squares are possible. If P1 and P2 are using the word 'conceive' in two different senses, then the argument suffers from a fallacy of equivocation, and P1 and P2 together do not entail C1.

Interestingly enough, the move that many people object to immediately, the move made by P3, may be alright. P3 depends on the following inference principle:

(4) *Inference principle* If it is so much as possible for *me* to be without *a body*, then this *me* is something more than the body.

And (4) seems alright: If *I* could exist without *a body*, then it would seem that this I does indeed have to be more than the body. Yet because of the problems already found with P1 and P2, it does not matter whether P3 is true or not, and we won't examine it further.

To summarize, even if P3 is all right, the argument as a whole is not. First, P1 may beg the question it is supposed to help settle. Second, the move from P1 to P2 seems to suffer from equivocation. If so, the conceivability argument is not valid, and even it is were, it would not be sound.

Indivisibility Argument
The indivisibility argument goes as follows:

Premise 1 The mind cannot be divided.
Premise 2 All material objects including the brain can be divided.
Conclusion Therefore, the mind is not the brain (or any other material object).

To assess it, the first thing we have to do is to get clearer about what is meant by saying that the mind is indivisible. There are two ways in which it might be impossible to divide something:

• Into two or more whole examples of the thing
• Into parts

When Descartes said that the mind is indivisible, he may have thought that both kinds of dividing are impossible. It now seems likely that he would have been wrong about splitting a mind into two or more whole minds. The evidence is difficult to assess, but consider cases of dissociative identity disorder (what used to be called 'multiple personality disorder') and patients who have had brain bisection operations (more properly known as hemispherectomies). In both kinds of cases, it could be argued that one mind has split into two (or more) minds. (See the Suggested Further Readings for more information about multiple personality and hemispherectomy). If so, both kinds of cases at minimum put pressure on the idea that the mind cannot split into two or more whole minds. Because the possibilities concerning the division of minds into two or more *whole* minds are at best unclear, we will focus on P1':

Premise 1' The mind cannot be divided into parts.

Here is an argument for P1': A chair can be divided into parts. When we do so, the various parts are separated from the object (and from one another) but continue to have the properties that they contributed to the object when they were joined to it.

(5) *A part of x* Something that can be separated from x and yet retain its integrity as a distinct unit whose role in the original system remains clear.

Now, the parts of a mind would presumably be things like the thinking apparatus, the emotions, the language-processing unit, perhaps the sense of humor, and so on. And the suggestion is that these cannot be separated from the whole mind and yet retain their integrity as distinct units. Why? If any of the mind's aspects were to be taken from it, *that aspect would cease to exist; it would have no existence apart from the mind.* Think of such aspects as a sense of humor, an ability to think through hard problems, memory, imagination—none of these could exist apart from the mind of which they are an aspect. By contrast, a leg separated from a chair does continue to be a distinct unit, namely, a chair leg. Therefore, aspects of mind are not parts, not in the sense that legs are parts of a chair.

P2' is straightforward:

Premise 2' The brain can be divided into parts.

P2' also seems to be true. Items in the brain can be separated from it and yet retain their integrity as distinct units with the properties that gave them their roles in the original system (this happens in neuroanatomy laboratories every day). The conclusion would then follow:

Conclusion Minds are not brains.

So far so good, but perhaps 'so good' is not quite good enough. Rather than looking further into whether P1′ and P2′ are true and whether C follows from them, let us accept C for the sake of argument and ask a different question: So what if C is true? Would that give substance dualists what they want?

We think not. Here's the problem. Descartes and others like him want not only dualism but also *immaterialism*—that the mind and brain are not just distinct things (which we are granting for the sake of argument) but also that the mind is *not made out of matter*. It is the latter that is not at all established by this argument. Moreover, many dualists want *separability*—they want to show that the mind could go on separated from the body after death. That is to say, they want the mind to come out as not only an object distinct from the brain but also as an immaterial and separable object. This stronger conclusion is needed if there is to be any serious hope of immortality, and grounding at least a possibility of immortality has been an objective of most substance dualists (see section 6). Thus, even if the mind cannot be divided into parts, that would not be enough to prove that it is immaterial or that it is separable from the body.

Indeed, the (limited) kind of dualism proved by the indivisibility argument is found in all sorts of things that are obviously completely material. Think of radios. We cannot break a radio's functions into separate parts existing apart from the rest of the radio. If you try to separate out these functions, they cease to exist: if we remove the ability of a radio to pick out individual stations, for example, that tuning ability does not continue on outside the radio, pulling in our favorite stations. Similarly with computers. If we remove a computer's ability to check spelling, that function does not continue on somewhere outside the computer. If so, a radio and a computer are different from the hardware that makes them up, and we have just proved dualism for radios and computers! However, it is not a form of dualism of any interest to traditional substance dualists, because none of the "objects" in question can exist outside the matter that makes them up. In this sort of dualism, nothing need be either immaterial or separable.

The reason that radios, computers, etc., are more than the hardware out of which they are made is that to be a radio or a computer, a thing must have certain *functions*. That is true of many kinds of things; for many kinds of objects, to be an object of that kind, something must have certain functions. Such functions cannot be separated from hardware as computer chips, dials, drives, etc., can be, yet they are still crucial to the object's being the kind of object it is. That is what explains our dualism, not any immateriality in the units.

Minds and brains are exactly parallel. Minds are more than the "wetware" of the brain; they also consist in certain functions. That is why minds cannot be split into parts, while brains can. It has nothing to do with minds being made out of anything immaterial. Curiously enough, the indivisibility argument, which philosophers accepted for hundreds of years as one of the most profound and convincing arguments for dualism and immaterialism, turns out, when closely examined, to be really a new argument for functionalism!

4   What Should We Believe?

If none of the arguments for dualism works, i.e., if none of them gives us any reason to believe that the mind is different from the brain or that mental states and events are different from brain states and events, what should we believe? There is a way of settling the question that will look very dubious to some people at first but seems to us entirely valid and also very powerful. This is the notion of BURDEN OF PROOF.

In some cases in philosophy it is important to know who has the burden of proof and the dualism/materialism debate is one of those cases. The idea of burden of proof can most easily be illustrated by reference to criminal and civil law. In criminal law, the burden of proof is on the prosecutor. The prosecution must prove the defendant guilty (beyond a reasonable doubt). The defendant, by contrast, does not need to do *anything* to establish his or her innocence. Indeed, if a defense lawyer thinks that the prosecution has not proven its case, the defense can ask for the case to be dismissed without presenting any evidence. The burden of proof is on the prosecution. In a civil case, by contrast, the burden of proof is equally on both parties. A balance of probability is all that is required to win or lose a case. The side most likely to be right on the balance of probabilities wins the case.[2]

Where does the burden of proof lie in the dualism/materialism debate? To answer this question, we need to bring back OCCAM'S RAZOR, which we first introduced in chapter 3. Occam's razor is the principle that we should not multiply entities needlessly. What this means, in more straightforward terms, is that you should not believe in something unless you have *some reason* to believe it.

Let us give an example. Suppose that Rob walks into a room and says, "Are those leprechauns ever lively!" Andy says, "I don't see any leprechauns." "Ah," says Rob, "leprechauns are not the kind of thing you can see." So Andy gets a very fine screen and passes it over every cubic inch of the room. He says, "The screen didn't touch anything, so there can't be any leprechauns in the room." Guess what Rob will say: "Ah, but leprechauns can't be detected with a screen." And so on. It won't take you long to conclude that Rob has no evidence of any kind for there being leprechauns in the room. And from this you will quite rightly infer that neither Rob nor anyone else should believe that any leprechauns exist in the room. Why? The operative principle is this:

(6) Excellent evidence that something does not exist is a complete lack of evidence that it does exist.

Now apply Occam's razor in the same way to dualism. Materialists and dualists agree that matter exists, so we don't need any argument for that. The dualist wants to maintain, however, that something else exists, too: something immaterial or some kind of nonneural property. The burden is on the dualist to produce some reasons for believing that this something else also exists. If we can find no evidence for anything more than matter, the only rational thing to believe is that nothing exists except matter, which is the materialist's position.

So what should we believe? For anyone who accepts Occam's razor and also finds that none of the arguments for dualism gives us any evidence that persons are made up of something more than matter, the answer is obvious: we should believe materialism. We have lots of reason to believe that we are *at least* material objects, so if none of the arguments gives us any reason to believe that we are made up of *anything more* than matter, we should believe that we are simply made up of matter, that we have no immaterial element.

That leaves us with one last question: which form of *materialism* should we believe? The two options remaining from our discussion in chapter 4 were functionalism and neurophilosophy. Obviously, functionalism is the more immediately plausible of the two, but plausibility is not enough. What we need is something that determines which is more likely to be true, not merely which is initially more plausible.

Here Occam's razor is of no use to us. Both parties believe in the same number of kinds of stuff, namely one, matter, and both parties agree that every mental event is also an event in the brain: there is no multiplying of substances *or* properties in either theory. What separates functionalism from neurophilosophy is that functionalists believe that this mind/brain is a bunch of symbol-manipulating powers that have intentionality, and neurophilosophers deny these claims. Having intentionality is one more property than neurophilosophers want to allow, but it is not clear that Occam's razor counts against positing this property. Anyway, functionalists think they have good reasons to posit the property of intentionality, and Occam's razor gets a start only if there is *no* argument or evidence for something. If so, Occam's razor is not going to help us here. In fact, it may very well be the case (and this is a crucial point) that there is nothing distinctively *philosophical* about the disagreement between the two theories at all. The disagreement may be a straightforwardly EMPIRICAL QUESTION:

(7) An *empirical question* is a question that requires evidence from
    observation and experimentation and cannot be answered by
    argument or analysis alone.

In the case of functionalism and neurophilosophy, the most important "evidence from observation and experimentation" that we need is evidence about which approach will result in the most comprehensive, satisfactory theory of what we currently call the human mind.

Such facts as we currently have available pull in both directions. Cognitive psychology, indeed cognitive science generally, generally uses the language of intentionality. Functionalism advocates using the language of intentionality to do psychology, while neurophilosophy rejects as it as useless. So the huge success of cognitive psychology provides some support for functionalism. On the other hand, the neurosciences have leapt forward in the past decade, generating new discoveries by the hundreds every week. To the extent that the success of this work is leading theoreticians away from the traditional conception of the mind as a system best described using the language of intentionality, this success lends support to neurophilosophy. In our view, this is as far as we can go at the present time. Which picture of the mind is the best one is an issue, we think, that cannot be settled by philosophical analysis and argumentation. We will return to this issue in chapter 8.

Just to complicate matters even more, we should recall once again the issue of our ever changing and ever more complicated conception of matter. As we argued at the end of section 3 of chapter 4, a *sufficiently large* change in our understanding of what matter is like could conceivably cause us to rethink the materialist conception of the mind from the ground up, especially if the new conception of matter turns out to be more like the classical dualist and idealist conception of mind than our current conception of matter. If that happens, who knows whether any of our current ideas about functionalism and neurophilosophy would survive.

5 Is the Mind Fundamentally a Symbol Processor?

One thing a computer can do that most humans can't is be sealed up in a cardboard box and sit in a warehouse.
Jack Handey

Recently a new, deep-running issue has appeared that opens the chasm between functionalism and neurophilosophy even wider. Recall that eliminative materialism started off as essentially a critique of folk psychology and a recommendation to look to neuroscience. The move to the deeper issue that we are about to introduce is a large part of what the transformation of eliminative materialism into neurophilosophy has consisted in.

The new issue is nothing less than the fundamental nature of the human cognitive system. (The COGNITIVE SYSTEM is the system that processes information about the world, itself, one's body, etc. 'Cognitive system' is the successor term in contemporary cognitive research for what used to be called 'the mind'.) As we saw, functionalists ground their model of the mind in information-processing functions described and explained using the concepts of "folk psychology," i.e., concepts that attribute intentionality. Most functionalists hold that these functions that make up the mind are primarily symbolic processes. A SYMBOLIC PROCESS is one that starts with strings of symbols—strings of words structured by the syntax of a language, for example—and transforms these strings of symbols into other strings of symbols according to rules. This is very much the way traditional computers work; the COMPUTER METAPHOR plays a considerable role in contemporary functionalism.

The idea that the mind is a symbol-processing system is not the only possibility, however. Neurophilosophers tend to hold that the mind does its cognitive processing nonsymbolically. Symbols only appear at the end of the process: we translate cognitive results into symbols when we want to communicate them to others in speech or preserve the results in written form.

This new debate, about whether the human cognitive system is fundamentally a symbol-processing system or not, has been added to the old debate about the scientific usefulness of folk psychology. Functionalists urge that cognitive activity is symbol manipulation a long way down. There is nothing more basic than symbol manipulation (except implementation in assemblies of nerves). Neurophilosophers reject this idea and claim instead that the actual processes that perform cognitive tasks do not use symbols; symbols enter only after the information-processing is over, at the stage, as we said, when we want to write the results of the processing down or when we want to communicate them to others.

This disagreement leads to a deeper form of the old disagreement over whether such a thing as a mind exists. Both parties start from a common conception of what a mind would have to be like: it would have to be a symbol processor. If so, then if human cognitive systems are symbolic almost all the way down, minds exist. If, on the other hand, cognitive activity is fundamentally non-symbolic, with symbols entering only at a late-stage translation process, then the human cognitive system is not at all like what we normally think of as minds, and it would be clearer and more precise simply to say either that minds do not exist or that the mind, in the traditional sense, only enters as a late, superficial aspect of human cognition.

If most of the activities of the human cognitive system are not transformations of strings of symbols into other strings of symbols, then what are they like? We can only touch on this big question. But the basic idea runs as follows (see Churchland and Sejnowski 1992). The fundamental role of cognition, say the neurophilosophers, is to turn the input of the senses into control of motor output: to turn perception of food into actions to get the food, perception of a tiger into actions to avoid the tiger, and so on. Now, when someone sees a ball coming at her head and ducks, it is very unlikely that it is *strings of symbols* or *rules for transforming symbols* that transform the information from her eyes into the contracting and stretching of her muscles. For one thing, simpler animals like mice are very good at ducking, avoiding danger, etc., yet they very likely have no strings of symbols in their brains at all. Next, they point out, language and all other activities that have a *clear* symbolic structure are late arrivals on the evolutionary scene; perception and motor control arrive far earlier. Indeed, few animals even have a structured symbolic system like language. But the bulk of human cognition is likely to be similar to cognition in other animals. If so, it is likely that the bulk of human cognition is nonsymbolic and that symbolic processing is merely a late evolutionary addition stacked on top of an already-existing nonsymbolic system. (If this sounds like a replay of the debate in chapter 3 over whether thought is inner speech, well, it is. What neurophilosophers add is that, because "thought" *isn't* inner speech, not even inner speech couched in the language of thought, minds as we usually conceive of them do not exist.)

Of course, language and other symbolic processes turned out to be absolutely crucial to human development. If we had no language, then we would have no books, no bridges, no science, no modern medicine—and no philosophy texts. In short, we would have no life as we know it. That would explain why theorists have emphasized language to the virtual exclusion of everything else in their models of the mind. But it does not follow from this that they are right. For all its importance to us, symbolic processes may indeed be merely a superficial layer in our cognitive processing. That is the challenge with which neurophilosophy confronts our orthodoxies, and it is one of the great intellectual challenges facing current research on the mind.

In the mid 1980s, theorists devised a new model for how nonsymbolic processing might work. They called such systems CONNECTIONIST SYSTEMS or NEURAL NETWORKS. Unlike traditional serial computers and traditional models of cognition, connectionist systems do not contain discrete, separate symbols. Nor do they contain explicitly represented rules for transforming symbols. Yet they can do highly significant cognitive work.

The difference between the connectionist picture and the traditional symbolic picture is very deep. For connectionists, thinking is fundamentally a process of associating properties with other properties, much like the old empiricist idea of the mind as a vast system of associations (introduced in chapter 2). On the symbolic picture, the mind works by following out the implications of sentences and sentencelike structures. This is closer to the old rationalist picture (also introduced in chapter 2), though with more room left for the input of the senses. One of the crucial questions for connectionism is, Can connectionism model language? Recall our discussion of the relationship between language and thought (chapter 3). Even if a lot of thought is nonsymbolic, as neurophilosophers maintain, language is still central to some of the most important kinds of thinking. So if connectionism cannot give us an account of language, then connectionism cannot be the whole story about the human mind. (For more on this fascinating new debate, see Rumelhart and McClelland 1986, where it all started, Fodor and Pylyshyn 1988, Clark 1989, and Horgan and Tienson 1996.)

Time to sum up. Like the general question of whether functionalism or neurophilosophy as a whole is a better picture of human cognition, the specific question of whether the symbolic or nonsymbolic picture of human cognition is the better one is in the end an EMPIRICAL QUESTION, and we do not yet have the facts we need to settle it.

However the symbolic/nonsymbolic debate turns out, it is one of the most interesting examples of how philosophical work on cognition is being penetrated and informed by work from other cognitive disciplines. Left to themselves, it is unlikely that philosophers would ever have invented connectionist models at all or seen more than a tiny fraction of what is built into the debate about the mind as a symbol processor. This new meeting of "minds" (how else can we put it?) between philosophical and other approaches to cognition will be a main theme of chapter 8. When we return to the issue of functionalism versus neurophilosophy there, we will tip the scales very tentatively and very slightly in favor of functionalism.

6   Do We Need to Study the Brain?

I think a good movie would be about a guy who's a brain scientist, but he gets hit on the head and it damages the part of the brain that makes you want to study the brain.

Jack Handey

The debate between functionalism and neurophilosophy raises a further issue that we haven't examined yet: do we need to study the brain to understand the mind? Even if the rational thing to do is to accept some form of the materialist theory of mind, the two leading forms of materialism, functionalist and neurophilosophy, tend to differ strongly over the importance of studying the brain. Here's why.

If, as functionalists maintain, types of mental states and events can never be identified with, or reduced to, types of brain states and events (in the sense of (6) on p. 67), then it would seem that so far as understanding cognitive function is concerned, it should not matter whether we know much about how the brain is built or not. That was indeed what functionalists thought for many years: in principle, they held, we can understand the mind while knowing virtually nothing about the brain. One of the slogans of functionalism is that function does not determine form—a given function can be performed by many different kinds of systems. The job is to understand the functions that make up the mind. The details of the particular apparatus performing them (brain, computer, whatever) do not matter. A cognitive-psychologist friend of ours recently put it this way: "I don't care whether cognitive functioning is done in the brain or the liver!" This view or one like it was held by many theorists in the heyday of classical ARTIFICIAL INTELLIGENCE, when researchers believed that we would soon have computers that could perform mind functions nearly as well as we can. Such optimism about how quickly we would understand cognition proved to be wildly exaggerated, be it artificial cognition or "natural" cognition (natural cognition, in case you are wondering, is us).

Neurophilosophers and their scientific fellow travelers took exactly the opposite view, of course. Since study of the brain using the language and techniques of neuroscience is the *only* way to understand what we now misleadingly call "the mind," study of the brain is absolutely crucial. And neurophilosophers follow their own advice. Many of the great centers of cognitive studies in Europe and the United States have affiliated themselves with neuroscience research centers.

More recently, functionalist philosophers of mind have also started to change their minds on the issue of whether the study of cognition (cognitive science) can be done without studying the brain (neuroscience). For one thing, *how* a task is performed tells us a great deal about precisely *what* task is being performed. Nevertheless, a great deal of the work on cognitive functions in cognitive psychology and linguistics still takes place with very little knowledge of the brain.

7   Why Isn't Functionalism Just Good Old Dualism in New Clothes?

Let's close this discussion of functionalism and neurophilosophy with a question that will have occurred to many readers: Why is functionalism a *materialist* theory? Why isn't it just property dualism in a new guise? (If it were and if no arguments for dualism are sound, then we would have to reject functionalism too, of course.) Let us come at this question by once again turning to *psychological explanation.*

Neurophilosophers reject psychological explanation—the search for reasons, goals, purposes, etc.—as a dead end. They want us to focus on mechanistic explanations of how the brain works. Functionalists, by contrast, embrace psychological explanation, as we saw. Indeed, the central figure of contemporary functionalism, Jerry Fodor (1975 and elsewhere), argues that psychological explanation is currently the only game in town. That is to say, the only way we have to explain ourselves and others currently is in terms of beliefs and desires, in terms of our reasons for doing what we do. And the only way to describe our reasons for what we do is in the language of intentionality that neurophilosophy wants to dismiss as scientifically useless.

If this is what functionalists believe, how exactly do functionalists and property dualists differ? The obvious answer is that functionalists hold that there are token-token mind/brain identities. That is to say, even though they deny that any *type* of mental state or event (e.g., all beliefs about the wetness of water) can be identified with, reduced to, any *type* of brain state or event (e.g., circuits of such and such type), they hold that every *token* (or occurrence) of a mental state (or event) is nothing more nor less than some brain state (or event). Thus, even though they do not believe in the identity theory of the mind/brain (as defined in (7) on page 67), they are still materialists. So they say. But what kind of materialism is it that insists that the types of states and events that make up the mind can never be identified with types of states or events in the brain (or even the brain plus)? This looks suspiciously like some kind of mind-brain dualism.

If functionalism looks suspiciously like a form of dualism, what form of dualism? Certainly not *substance* dualism. The substance dualist believes that persons are made up of two very different kinds of things. No functionalist believes that. Functionalists believe that the mind/brain is one single system. At the other end, functionalism *embraces* explanatory dualism, so it definitely is this form of dualism, but explanatory dualism is also compatible with materialism, so there is no risk to functionalism as a form of materialism from that direction. The only form of dualism left is property dualism, so what the question boils down to is this: is functionalism just a new form of property dualism?

Let us come at this question via explanatory dualism. Explanatory dualism does not maintain that the *mind* is a duality of any kind. It maintains only that we have a duality in the *explanations* that we can give of the mind. This is why explanatory dualism is entirely compatible with materialism. Now, it is hard to see why the need for two kinds of *explanation* would force us to postulate that minds have two kinds of *properties*. Consider some analogies. To explain the growth of plants, we need explanations of both how they get water and how they photosynthesize carbon, yet no one advocates a "property dualism" for plants of any philosophically interesting kind. Similarly, many linguists hold that we need a different kind of theory to explain the syntax of a sentence from what we need to explain the semantics, the meaning, of a sentence, yet there is only one language being explained. (These comparisons are a nice example of the way analogies work in philosophy, by the way.) Thus, from the fact that we have two ways of explaining human behavior, it does not automatically follow that human beings have two radically different kinds of *properties*. And similarly with functionalism.

Even though functionalists insist that kinds of mental event cannot be identified with or reduced to kinds of events in the brain, they still insist that every mental event is some brain event. In the jargon we introduced earlier, they reject type-type identities but insist upon token-token identities. Property dualists, by contrast, hold that mental events are not neural events at all; the properties of the mind/brain that are mental are completely independent of physical properties of the mind/brain. Thus functionalism is not property dualism.

This difference between the materialism of functionalists and the dualism of property dualists tends to go with a deep disagreement about the nature of mental properties. Functionalists view them as perfectly straightforward properties of the world, open to scientific exploration and explanation like any other. We may need to use a special kind of explanation to understand them, namely psychological explanation (as described in chapter 4 and discussed above), but many kinds of phenomena that cannot be easily reduced to brain states need their own kind of explanation: color vision and phonetic processing are two examples. By contrast, property dualists tend to think of mental properties as deeply mysterious in nature, certainly not the sort of thing that could be studied scientifically. Indeed, many property dualists think that the only way to observe mental properties is by introspection. As we saw earlier in this chapter, however, most scientific-minded theorists reject introspection as a viable way to study the mind. In short, for all their superficial similarity, the differences between functionalists and property dualists run very deep.

8   Immortality Again: Can We Look Forward to Life after Death?

Sometimes I think I'd be better off dead. No, wait. Not me, you.
Jack Handey

We've spent a lot of time talking about the nature of mind and its relation to matter. We will end this chapter by considering an issue that motivates many people to *care* about whether the mind is or is not simply processes in matter. The issue is immortality; we introduced it near the beginning of chapter 4.

(8) Can (and will) we continue to exist after the death of the body?

More specifically, the issue is PERSONAL IMMORTALITY, which holds that a person will continue to survive *as the person she is now* after the death of her body. So the specific question of interest is (9):

(9) Can (and will) I continue to exist *as me* after the death of my body?

One of our two conclusions will be that there's little evidence that the answer is 'Yes', little evidence for an afterlife. Our other conclusion (you might call it our big conclusion) will be that, surprisingly, having little hope of a life after the death of our body shouldn't be very upsetting.

Here's the plan. We will present two different arguments, each of which tries to show that there is life after death. Neither of these arguments works very well. Since those who endorse life after death have the burden of proof, i.e., they need to give some *reason* for their view, those who don't believe in the afterlife have the most rational position if no other positive arguments are forthcoming. But things are worse than that for the afterlife proponent. For there are several compelling reasons for thinking that there is no life after death. (Each of these anti-immortality arguments harks back to the foregoing discussion of dualism and materialism.) The overall conclusion, then, is that the mind probably ceases to exist when the body dies. Having reached this conclusion, we will consider whether it is really so distressing.

One argument that you sometimes hear in favor of the afterlife is this:

Premise 1 If life truly ends at death, then life ultimately has no meaning.
Premise 2 It would be awful if life ultimately had no meaning.
Conclusion Therefore, life does not end at death.

This argument suffers from two very serious flaws. First off, it's merely *an argument from hope*. Sadly, arguments from hope are, well, hopeless. Specifically, they are invalid: the conclusion can be false while the premises are true. To see this, compare the following: Andy and Rob really wish they had a million dollars each; therefore, Rob and Andy do have a million dollars each. The premise of this parallel argument is true: we certainly *wish* we were millionaires. But, we can assure you, the conclusion is false. So, insofar as this is just an argument from hope, i.e., insofar as the arguer is merely *wishing* that the conclusion were true, it cannot succeed.[3] Besides, there's a second flaw in the argument. Though P1 may look plausible at first glance, in the end it's not obvious at all. To see this, ask yourself *why* exactly must life continue to exist after the death of the body if it is to have any meaning. Couldn't life's meaning derive from the 75-odd years that the body is alive? Or couldn't the source of meaning be one's fellows and one's achievements during this life? Unless there's a good answer to these questions, P1 is also questionable. If so, this first argument, though quite familiar, is not very promising.

Here's a less familiar, but more intriguing, argument for life after death.[4]

Premise 1 If you cannot even imagine something, then it doesn't really exist.
Premise 2 You cannot even imagine the death of your own mind.
Conclusion Therefore, your mind never dies.

The argument's form is fairly simple. But the premises need to be explained.

P1 basically joins together two logical principles: first, that if you cannot imagine something, then it's not *possible*, and second, that if something is not possible, then it isn't *actual*, i.e., it doesn't in fact exist. (We saw the converse of this argument above: the existence of mind without body was said to be conceivable, and hence possible.) A parallel example may help here. You cannot even imagine a colorless red ball. That's because it's *impossible* for something to be both red and colorless. Now, given that colorless red balls are impossible, it's no surprise that there aren't any to be found in your closet. In fact, there aren't any to be found *anywhere*: impossible things, since they *cannot* exist, clearly *do not* exist. (Notice, in contrast, that certain things that do not exist are nonetheless possible things: Weeble has no offspring, so "Weeble's black kitten" isn't a real object; it is nevertheless a possible object. That is to say, Weeble might have had a black kitten.) Now P2 says, of your mind's death, that you cannot imagine it. Hence, by P1, there's no such thing as the death of your mind. This is a convoluted way of saying that you must continue to live after the death of your body.

Even if we grant P1, what supports P2? Essentially this: that whenever you try to imagine your absolute nonexistence, you fail. That is, your mind's death is wholly and utterly unfathomable. That's because you have absolutely no idea of—you cannot experience, even in your own imagination—your own total annihilation. To put it metaphorically: each time you try to imagine, from the inside as it were, what it feels like to not be, *you* are there. Hence what you imagine is not a situation in which your mind has really ceased to exist.

But this argument doesn't support P2, as T. Nagel shows. If it did, we could argue that because "you can't conceive of what it would be like to be completely unconscious, even temporarily" (Nagel 1987, 88), therefore you will never be unconscious. And that's absurd. You do become unconscious, every night. Again, you can't experience, even in your own mind, total unconsciousness. That wouldn't *feel like* anything. But this cannot demonstrate that you will never be completely unconscious.

The argument is built on a fallacy of equivocation. It equivocates on 'imaginable' (recall the related problem with 'conceivable' in the conceivability argument). In one sense, you clearly *can* imagine yourself being unconscious. That is, you can think of yourself, from the outside, lying motionless on the street, having been knocked out. What you cannot do is *simulate* the sensation of unconsciousness. That's because there is no such sensation. Here's a comparison. Suppose that someone says, "Imagine riding a raft down that river." You can do this in two ways: by "experiencing the ride" from a rider's point of view, but without actually taking the plunge, or by picturing yourself, i.e., your body, on the raft, bolting down the rapids. In the case of consciousness, only the second kind of imagining is possible. That's because there is no *sensation* of unconsciousness, no "way that it feels." So in the first sense of 'Imagine yourself being unconscious', you can't do it. But, crucially, unimaginability *in this sense alone* doesn't show that people are never unconscious. To show this, being unconscious would need to be *wholly* unimaginable, which it clearly isn't.

Similarly, it is perfectly possible to imagine the nonexistence of your mind, in the sense of thinking of your lifeless body, from the outside (e.g., it's certainly possible to imagine your own funeral), though there's another sense of imaginable, the one where you "take on" the agent's point of view, in which you can't imagine what it's like for your mind not to exist. The question is, which sense of "imaginability" is at work in P1? Presumably, it's not just the restricted sense of 'imagine' in which 'Imagine that you're *x*' requires "experiencing" what it's like to be *x*, without actually being *x*. 'Imagine' in P1 is being used in the broad sense. But, if we read 'imagine' in this broad sense, P2 is just plain false, however initially appealing and intuitive the premise may be on a weaker reading of 'imagine'. Hence this argument for an afterlife also fails.

Remember the lesson drawn about the invisible leprechauns: someone who posits something needs to provide some reason for believing in it (Occam's razor). Thus, when no reasons are forthcoming, one may rationally reject the proposed entity without argument. So, as we saw, if there's no grounds whatever for believing in both mind and body, then the materialist (who believes in body only) wins. Similarly here: unless there is some reason (however minimal) to believe in the afterlife, the afterlife skeptic triumphs. Put otherwise, if neither side presents arguments, the result is *not* a tie: the person who makes the claim about the extra kind of existence to the effect that there is an afterlife (who makes the EXISTENTIAL CLAIM, as philosophers call it) loses. Still, winning by appeal to burden of proof isn't very satisfying, so let's see if there are any arguments against an afterlife.

We will consider two arguments for the conclusion that death really is the end. The first is one that we have already introduced, in the first section of chapter 4: in the absence of a being with godlike powers able to reassemble and reanimate long-dead bodies (bodily resurrection), life after death requires, though it is not guaranteed by, dualism. If dualism is true, we can understand how life after death might be possible. On the other hand, if dualism is false and the mind is just the brain, then the mind clearly cannot exist when the body is dead (again, in the absence of miraculous intervention). The trouble is, as was argued above, dualism is likely not true. Even worse, though the truth of dualism seems like a *necessary* condition for life after death, it isn't a *sufficient* condition. Recall, for example, property dualism: here the continued existence of the nonmaterial mental properties clearly *requires* a body. For it is the body that houses the mental properties. Hence, for property dualists, if there's no body, there's no mind, i.e., when the body dies, so does the mind. Nor is it only the property dualist who will think that the continuation of the mind is body-dependent.

Consider this: the mind, even for the substance dualist, gets most of its stimulation from the body. Furthermore, the mind acts via the body. Given that so much of mental activity arises from bodily stimulation and so much of it is designed to contribute to bodily movement, some philosophers have concluded that the human mind is *essentially* embodied. That is, the human mind is radically unlike, say, the mind of pure intellect that some theorists would assign to God. Taking this seriously, however, it seems that the *human* mind could not exist without a body, even if the mind is a distinct substance. An afterlife hopeful might say, "Well, the mind would undoubtedly undergo changes once it lost all sensory input and once it ceased to have behavioral effects in a physical world, but it would still exist." This is a fair point. However, it raises an uncomfortable question: if your mind, considered as a separate substance that merely accompanies the body, changes *very* radically after death, would it be appropriate to say that *you* survive the death of the body? On this hypothesis it's true that *something* would still exist after your body died, something associated with your body. But being so drastically different from who you are now—i.e., an embodied, worldly, sensual being—

would that "something" be you? If the answer is 'No', then once again it turns out that the continued existence of you requires a body, *even if dualism is true.*

The argument as a whole may be summarized as follows:

Premise 1 If dualism is false, then there is no life after death.
Premise 2 If dualism is true but the continued existence of the mind requires a body, then there is no life after death.
Premise 3 Either dualism is true, but the continued existence of the mind requires a body, or dualism is false.
Conclusion Therefore, there is no life after death.[5]

The argument is valid. But is it sound? For instance, someone might well say, "There can be an afterlife, even if the existence of the mind requires a body, because we could continue to exist in *another* body." Indeed, functionalism—as we have said repeatedly, a version of materialism— presumably permits this: if the mind is just a set of functions, a kind of program running on the brain, then your "program" could plausibly be transferred to another brain, or to a silicon-based computer for that matter. So it seems that some varieties of materialism are consistent with life after death. In which case, P1 is just false.

The afterlife skeptic won't give up this easily, however. First, while functionalism apparently makes the after-death existence of the mind *possible* even without dualism, it doesn't make it *actual.* In the world as it actually is, death is the end, because our "programs" *aren't* stored elsewhere, not even by reincarnation; death occurs before the mind is "backed up" onto another physical medium. Materialism requires that there *always* be a physical medium. So the idea of your mind "passing into" another body, far away and years later, just isn't credible. Besides, suppose your program *were* restarted in another body. Would this really be a matter of *you* surviving? It may seem that the answer would be 'Yes'. But consider the following sort of case.

Imagine that you've gone into the Eternal Life Center to have your body rejuvenated and your mind transferred into the fixed-up body. You climb onto the table, hear some whirring sounds, and then the lights go out. As you descend the table, an embarrassed attendant explains that there's been a slight glitch. He tells you, "The way the technology normally works is this: a new body is created, the information from your brain is put into its brain, and your old body is then destroyed. The problem is, though a new body was created and your program was put into it, the power unfortunately went out before the old body (i.e., you!)

could be atomized." Now, they can't let two of you leave the center. So the attendant makes a simple request: "Please return to the table, so we can destroy the old body."

Many people would resist this request. And yet purportedly (the rejuvenated) "you" is already in another room, so "you" will still be alive after the troublesome old body is gone. Why not agree, then, if transferring your "program" is sufficient to achieve continued life? The answer seems to be that having your mind "moved" to another body may, despite initial appearances, actually be a way of *dying*, not a way of continuing to live. In that case, P1 really is true: without substance dualism, there can be no life after death. Since substance dualism likely isn't true, it seems probable that the mind dies when the body does. (Puzzles such as this, about what philosophers call *personal identity* are well discussed in Parfit 1984.)

We end by considering whether this is such an awful conclusion. First, an obvious point: it might be *boring* to live forever. Even if you would like to live longer than the usual 75 years, you probably would not want to *never* die. Also, death sometimes ends great suffering, whether physical pain or mental depression or something else. So death is not always, no matter what the circumstances, bad. On the other hand, is death *as it usually occurs* good? After all, as a matter of fact it does not typically cut off extreme pain or boredom. On the contrary, the deceased typically misses out on good things (or, more precisely, things which *would* have been good). And death ordinarily comes long before extreme boredom sets in. So death isn't usually a good thing, though there are circumstances in which it might be good. Instead, death, by depriving us of continued enjoyment of life, is usually an unwelcome fate.

Some people go further than that, however. Some people think that death is *really* bad. Indeed, they find the prospect of dying to be absolutely terrifying. Is this a reasonable attitude? By dying, one is likely to miss out on some pleasures, and this may be a bad thing. But death should not be *scary*. This for two reasons. First, "the time after life" is just like the time before birth, on the assumption that there is no afterlife. But the time before birth was not awful. So, because the "beforelife" and the afterlife are basically the same, you should not expect the time after death to be awful. Indeed, death, we are supposing, is the end: there is nothing left after the body dies. But you cannot reasonably be afraid of *nothing*. There is no pleasure, it's true. But there's also no pain, no suffering, indeed, no displeasure of any kind. Hence there is nothing to be afraid of.

As Nagel (1987) says, death is something to be afraid of only if we will survive it.

The overall conclusion, then, is that there is insufficient evidence to justify belief in an afterlife. Hence we should not believe in it. But this should not frighten or depress us, because, though death is a little bad (the good times stop), it is not *really* bad.

Study Questions

1. Contrast the manifest image and the scientific image. Why does the manifest image point to dualism and the scientific image to materialism? Could they be combined? If so, how?

2. Are there problems with introspection that make it a poor source of information to use in science? If so, what are they? If not, why not. (It certainly appears that there are problems!)

3. Explain each of the four arguments for dualism given. Which ones use introspection? Which don't?

4. Do you think that any of the arguments for dualism work (that is, do they prove dualism)? If so, which one, and why? (If not, skip this question and go on to the next one.)

5. Outline the responses to these four arguments given in the text. Do you think that the dualist has any effective response to any of the reasons given for rejecting the arguments for dualism?

6. Can you think of any arguments for dualism of your own? How would a materialist argue against you?

7. How does the notion of "burden of proof" play a role in the dualist-materialist debate? What is Occam's razor? How deeply does it cut against certain claims?

8. Why is functionalism a version of materialism, while property dualism is not?

9. What sort of life changes would result in a loss of personal identity over time? Wouldn't death count, if anything does? If that's right, what would it be for anyone to survive death as the same person?

10. Why is it harder to believe in life after death if you are a materialist? Are explanatory dualists and property dualists any better off than materialists in this regard? Explain.

Suggested Further Readings

As we noted at the end of chapter 4, arguments for dualism may be found in Descartes 1931 [1641], property dualism is defended in Strawson 1959, and Hobbes 1996 [1668] and La Mettrie 1994 [1748] are especially important early (and rare) statements of materialism. Sellars 1997 [1956] introduced the distinction between the manifest image and the scientific image. P. M. Churchland 1984, Flanagan 1984, Jacquette 1994, and Kim 1996 are good overviews of the dualism-materialism debates. Jacquette 1994 espouses property dualism.

An interesting paper that both reviews the phenomena associated with brain-bisection operations (hemispherectomies) and discusses the problem of how to think about these phenomena is Nagel 1971. Marks 1980 is a short book entirely devoted to the topic. A long, controversial, but very readable account of dissociative identity disorder (what used to be called 'multiple personality disorder') can be found in Hacking 1995.

The new debate over connectionism can be followed in Rumelhart and McClelland 1986, Fodor and Pylyshyn 1988, Clark 1989, and Horgan and Tienson 1996.

For more recommendations, see the Suggested Further Readings at the end of chapter 4.

Chapter 6

Free Choice

I wish I would have a real tragic love affair and get so bummed out that I'd just quit my job and become a bum for a few years, because I was thinking about doing that anyway.

Jack Handey

In chapters 4 and 5 we examined big metaphysical questions about the nature of the mind and its relationship to the brain. In this chapter we turn to a different metaphysical question, this one about a most important power of the mind, the power to make decisions and control actions. Here the crucial question is, Do we have the power to make our decisions freely, or do we have no freedom over the courses of action that we take? This is one of the most profound and difficult questions about the human mind that there is. (Because of its difficulty, we again recommend that you read through the whole chapter once or twice, to get the general shape of the topic, then go back and focus on anything that remains unclear. With free will, it is easy, as the old saying puts it, to lose the forest for the trees.)

The usual name for this topic is FREE WILL but we prefer the name FREEDOM OF CHOICE. The reason is this: the notion of free will involves the notion of the will, and it is not too clear what a "will" is supposed to be. Is it our desires? Is it our power to identify and assess our desires, selecting some to act on, rejecting others? What exactly is the "will" supposed to be? Since the notion of the will is very murky and we all know what it is to make a choice (or to seem to make a choice: whether we ever do make free choices is a main issue of this chapter), we prefer the term 'freedom of choice'.

There is a terminological issue that we need to clear up right away. Recall the discussion of the terms 'choice' and 'selection' near the beginning of chapter 4. As we said there, it is part of the very *idea* of a choice that it is made freely—an unfree choice would be a contradiction in terms. So when we speak of a *choice,* we will always mean a free choice. Sometimes we will say "free choice" to emphasize the point, even though the term is a PLEONASM (a phrase in which one part is redundant). When we want to be neutral as to whether an act was free or not, we will speak of a *selection* or a *decision.*

1 A Preliminary Definition

What is the difference between a mere decision or selection and a choice i.e. decision freely made? Here is a common idea: a free choice is a decision such that, up to the moment that it was made, another decision could have been made. The idea behind this suggestion is that the difference between the decisions of yours that are choices, i.e., freely made, and the ones that are not is that how you make the free ones is *up to you.* The only thing that caused you to make the decision was you; nothing forced you to make it one way or another. Let us combine these two ideas:

(1) *A Choice* (i.e., a free choice) is a decision such that up to the
      moment that it was made, another decision could have been made
      and which decision is made is up to the person making it.

This definition is fine as far as it goes. It does not go very far, however. The main problem with it is that the term 'free choice' and the term 'another decision could have been made' are equally puzzling. That is to say, if we are puzzled about what a free choice is, we will also be puzzled about what is meant by the idea that another decision could have been made. The two terms are not exactly SYNONYMS (terms with the same meaning), but they are too close to one another for either to shed light on the other. (Most definitions in a dictionary are like this.)

The unhelpfulness of (1) notwithstanding, it does indicate in a general sort of way what the term 'free choice' means. Free choice seems to be about having alternatives such that, up to the moment of decision, one is not limited to just one of those alternatives. So let's accept (1) for now, general and unhelpful though it is, and ask, Why does free choice matter?

2 Why Freedom of Choice Matters

With some philosophical issues, it can take some effort to see any practical significance in them. Some people react this way to the mind-body problem. They in effect ask, "Who *cares* whether the mind is or is not the brain?" Well, we think that this attitude is wrong even about the mind-body problem. If materialism is right, for example, then there is probably more hope for treatments of mental illness that use medications to change the chemistry of the brain than if dualism is right. But nobody feels indifferent about the problem of freedom of choice.

The issue of freedom of choice has been around in one form or another since at least the time of Aristotle, one of the last and greatest of the classical Greek philosophers. It is at the very heart of many of the most important parts of our personal and social life. If we have no freedom of choice, then it is hard to see how we could possibly be *responsible* for what we do: what justification could there be for blaming us when things go badly, praising and rewarding us when we try hard and/or things go well? The following principle of alternative possibilities seems to lie behind our notion of responsibility:

(2) *Principle of alternative possibilities* If a person couldn't have decided otherwise, then that person isn't responsible for what he or she goes on to do.

If we have no freedom of choice, then almost by definition we could not have decided otherwise. And by (2), if we could not have decided otherwise, then we are not responsible for the decisions we make or what we go on to do.[1]

To see how the issue of freedom of choice can arise, imagine this dialogue:

Student to professor "You have no justification for deducting marks just because my paper was a month late. The power to make choices, genuinely free decisions, does not exist, and writing this paper when I did was the only thing that I could have done."

Professor "Nonsense! I saw you in the student pub at least ten times in the month before the paper was due."

We could ask, of course, how the *professor* happened to be in a position to see that. But the point is this: If the student really had no choice, then it would seem that his protest is entirely justified, and the professor's response is entirely irrelevant. So what if the student wasted a lot of time? If he had no choice in the matter, it would seem very unfair to hold him responsible for doing so. If there is no freedom of choice, it would seem that the most that the professor could justifiably say as she hands out the penalty is, "I know you had no choice, but this penalty will help to make your future behavior more acceptable," or something like that. Of course, the student would have no alternative but to behave as he behaves at that later time too, but his behavior might conform better to some social or ethical norm.

Do we have a choice about the decisions we make, at least some of the time? Are we responsible for at least some of our decisions? And are these questions as closely linked as the common view maintains? Before we try to answer these questions, let us look briefly at two more places where the issue of whether we can ever have a choice in the decisions we make has real practical importance.

One place is the law. To be liable before the courts for punishment for breaking the law, you must not only break the law, you have to be *responsible* for the decision and action that led to it being broken. The way that legal writers express this point is to say that you must have *mens rea* (a guilty mind).[2]

Now, the law does not concern itself with the great issue of whether our decisions are ever free (though arguably it should). The law simply *assumes* that we make free choices most of the time and concentrates on the exceptions. But its treatment of the exceptions is very interesting. The important exceptions to the general assumption that our decisions are freely made are severe mental illness, certain unconscious states such as sleepwalking and automatism (automatic actions that the person is not aware of doing or has no control over), and in some jurisdictions, extreme intoxication.

What is common to all these cases is that the person is held to have had no control over what he or she did. The lack of control can stem from the person's actions being in the control of another or it can stem from the "controller," the mind, not operating properly, as in insanity or maybe intoxication. We do not need to go into the details.[3] The important point is that the principle that an action was the result of free choice unless proven otherwise is one of the fundamental principles of the law.

Another place where we all assume that power of choice exists is a bit more surprising: personal relationships. When someone does us a favor, we feel gratitude. But to feel grateful to someone, we have to assume that they chose to do what they did. Otherwise, saying "Thank you so much for doing that; what a nice thing to do!" would amount to saying "My, you've been well programmed," which does not quite have the same ring to it. Likewise, when someone does something that hurts or injures or offends us, we feel angry, hostile, etc. But this is to hold them responsible for what they have done. You don't blame clouds for raining on you— not if you are rational.

In short, the assumption that we have the power of choice, that we are free to decide as we do, at least a lot of the time, is one of the basic assumptions of our whole way of life. All moral and most legal judgments depend on this assumption's being true, as do personal relationships as we know them. This raises the first big question of this chapter.

Question 1 Do we have the power of choice?

Before we can answer question 1, however, we need to address a second question:

Question 2 What *is* the power of choice?

That is to say, when someone does or does not have the power to make decisions freely, what *is* it that the person does or does not have? What would be required for someone to have the power of choice? Under what conditions would someone lose it?

We have to answer question 2 before we can answer question 1: we have to know what would make a decision free or unfree, what the power of choice is, before we can know whether or not such a power exists. Interestingly, the second question is much harder than the first. Indeed, if we could ever get a clear picture of what would be *required* to have the power of choice, it would probably be relatively easy to determine whether or not we *have* such a power. All we would have to do is to determine whether the required features are there or not. Strangely enough, most of the vast literature on free will, free choice, etc., focuses on whether such a power exists. Relatively little attention has been paid to the prior issue of what kind of power it is.

3   Freedom of Decision and Freedom of Action

When you go for a job interview, I think a good thing to ask is if they ever press charges.

Jack Handey

To approach question 2, the first thing we need to do is to distinguish between FREEDOM OF DECISION and FREEDOM OF ACTION or what is also called LIBERTY. This distinction has got thoroughly muddled in recent times, and it is fundamentally important that we keep it straight. We have already defined freedom of decision in (1) above; it is simply having a choice. We might define freedom of action as follows:

(3) *Freedom of action* Being able to do what one chooses to do.

Usually this definition comes with riders such as, 'without being prevented by the state or other people from doing so or being harmed or penalized for doing so' and 'so long as the action does not harm others'. Freedom of action is the sort of freedom at work in the idea of liberty just mentioned, and the closely related ideas of freedom of speech, personal freedom, and autonomy.

The fundamental difference between freedom of decision, i.e., choice, and freedom of action is this. Freedom of decision is about decisions, freedom of action is about actions. You could have either without the other. On the one hand, you could have complete liberty, complete power to say and do what you want, and yet have no power to choose what you want or how you will act. This would be liberty, freedom of action, without free choice. On the other hand, if you have the power to make choices, in most respects it would not be taken away by losing your liberty, your freedom of action. Suppose that you were locked up in a jail. This would take away your liberty, your power to do what you want. Would it take away your power to make choices? Well, you would retain at least a large part of that power: you would not lose your ability to choose what you will believe, to decide what you would do if you could, etc. All you would lose in prison is the ability to *do* anything about those decisions, i.e., your freedom of action. (That is a large part of what makes prison so awful: a person in prison retains full freedom to decide what he or she would like to do but loses the power to do anything about it.)

As with some of the other terms that we are discussing, we run into a terminological problem here. We are drawing a sharp distinction between freedom of decision and freedom of action. As we are using the terms, freedom of decision concerns selection processes in the mind, and freedom of action concerns external actions. As these terms are used in ordinary discourse, however, the distinction gets blurred. To be "pro-choice" on the abortion issue, for example, is not only to favor letting pregnant women make up their own mind about whether to end their pregnancies or carry to term; it is also to favor giving pregnant women the liberty to *act* on that decision. Thus it involves both elements: freedom to decide and freedom to act on the decision. In our approach, we do make a clear distinction between the process of deciding and the process of acting on a decision. *As we are using it*, the term 'choice' applies only to the process of decision.

The conditions of having liberty, freedom of speech, and personal autonomy; the justifiable extent and limits of liberty; the relation of liberty for each to equality for all; and many related questions about freedom of action are intensively studied and deserve the attention. However, we are going to focus on the other side of the coin: free choice, what it is and whether we have it.

4 Positions and Distinctions

There are three major positions on the nature and existence of the power of choice. They are usually called HARD DETERMINISM, COMPATIBILISM (also soft determinism), and, believe it or not, LIBERTARIANISM. We say 'believe it or not' because this word lands us in one more terminology mess. Above we *distinguished* power of choice from liberty. Now we find that many philosophers *call* one position on the power of choice 'libertarianism'. This terminological confusion is very unfortunate. From now on, when we use the word 'libertarianism', keep in mind that we mean a position on the free-will issue, not the very different issue of liberty or freedom of action.

To introduce these positions, we need to sketch some background. Broadly speaking, we have two very different conceptions of ourselves as persons. One conception is the manifest image of everyday interpersonal and social life. We introduced it in chapter 5. In this image, we think of persons as unified agents of choice and action, agents able to take account of important alternatives, to focus their attention on the important considerations, to identify the important alternatives, and to make a choice. Thinking of people in this way, it is natural to hold them responsible for the actions that ensue.

The other conception is the scientific image also introduced in chapter 5. This image arises out of the work of the sciences on human beings, including biology, cognitive science, and neuroscience. On this conception, we think of persons as a vast system of very tiny units (neurons and other cells), a system that is completely determined to be as it is by its genes and environment and perhaps other prior causes. For the question of free choice, the important part of this conception is that we are completely determined by prior causes to decide as we do. By 'completely determined', we mean that from the same prior causes the same decisions would always follow. Thinking of people as we do in the scientific image, it is natural to worry that they may have *no* power of choice and thus may *never* be responsible for their decisions and actions.

As originally conceived by the philosopher Wilfrid Sellars, the two images of the person were meant to be completely compatible, simply two different ways of picturing or describing the same thing. We discussed this issue in chapter 5. When we explore the conceptions of choice built into the two images, however, they suddenly start to seem less than obviously compatible. The manifest image contains a picture of persons as free choosers. The scientific image contains a picture of persons as causally determined. The three great positions on freedom of decision consist of three positions on these implications of the two images.

Let us start with libertarianism. Libertarians accept the view of the manifest image that we are agents with the power to make free decisions. They also hold that having this power rules out the complete causal determinism of the scientific image. They argue as follows:

Premise 1 Free choice exists.
Premise 2 If free choice exists, then complete causal determinism is not true.
Conclusion Therefore, complete causal determinism is not true.

Thus libertarians reject a crucial element of the scientific conception of the person, an element assumed by virtually everyone who accepts the scientific image of persons, namely determinism.

By contrast, hard determinists accept the causal determinism of the scientific image. They agree on one thing with libertarians, namely that complete causal determinism rules out freedom of decision, but they argue in exactly the opposite way. They argue thus:

Premise 1 Complete causal determinism is true.
Premise 2 If complete causal determinism is true, free choice does not exist.
Conclusion Therefore, free choice does not exist.

Thus *hard determinists* reject a crucial element of the *manifest* image of ordinary social life.

The result? We are at a nasty impasse. It seems that we must give up either a crucial part of our ordinary conception of the person or we must reject a crucial element of what science tells us about persons. Neither alternative is desirable. If at all possible, we would like to keep both. This is where the third position comes in. The third alternative is what we above called *compatibilism*. Compatibilists think that the views on choice and causal determinism of the two images are entirely *compatible* with one another (hence their name).

To see how compatibilists view the problem, notice first that hard determinists and libertarians *agree* on one central point. They agree that free choice and complete causal determinism rule each other out, i.e., are *incompatible* with one another. This is what P2 in both their arguments asserts. The compatibilist rejects P2. For the compatibilist, free choice *would not* be ruled out merely by a decision's being causally determined. How so? Well, for the compatibilist, choosing freely is merely *a way* of being causally determined. If your selection was causally determined in the right way, then it was a free choice: the decision was both entirely causally determined and entirely free. Free choice is *not* ruled out by the mere fact that a decision was causally determined.

How does the compatibilist try to pull this neat trick off? Different compatibilists use different moves, but the general strategy is to define a concept that we might call SELF-DETERMINISM:

(4) *Self-determinism* A selection or decision is causally determined by oneself.

A decision is self-determined when the factors that caused it were aspects of the person who made it, such as her wishes and her values. The compatibilist then distinguishes situations in which a decision is *self*-determined from situations in which factors *outside* the person determined what decision was made. Here is an example of self-determinism:

(5) I engage in a careful process of identifying alternative courses of action, relevant values I hold, my objectives, the interests and situations of others, my beliefs about how various alternatives will play out, and so on. These deliberations cause me to arrive at a certain decision.

For the compatibilist, the situation in (5) is entirely different from such situations as those in (6):

(6) I am caused to make a certain decision by the influence of posthypnotic suggestion or by extreme intoxication or while I am asleep, etc.

What's the difference? Simply this. Even though the decision in both cases is completely causally determined, in the first case it is caused by my conscious deliberation about what to do, in the second case by factors outside my thinking and deliberating, factors over which I have no control. For the compatibilist, this is enough for the situation in (5) to at least open the way to free choice (whether, for a compatibilist, it gets us all the way there is a matter of controversy, as we will see), whereas in a situation such as (6) there is no free choice.[4]

Figure 6.1
Disagreements among the three positions

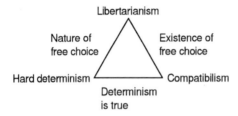

Figure 6.2
Agreements among the three positions

There has been a lot of debate in philosophy over exactly what causality and causal determinism are like. Notice that the compatibilist does not have to concern herself with this question. For the compatibilist, it does not matter what causal determinism is like, so long as it does not rule out self-determinism as defined in (4). Free choice is otherwise compatible with all forms of determinism. The libertarian and the hard determinist need to worry about what causal determinism is like and what its implications are for the possibility of free choice, but the compatibilist does not.

The three "grand positions" can be arranged in two triangles, a triangle of disagreements and a triangle of agreements. In the first (figure 6.1), each of the positions disagrees with the other about something. Each of the three positions also *agrees* with each of the others about something (see figure 6.2). (It is a bit peculiar, however, to say that libertarians and compatibilists agree about the *existence* of free choice (figure 6.2). What are they agreeing on when they disagree so totally about its *nature* (figure 6.1)? When they say that "it" exists, they seem to be talking about two different things.) We now turn to question 2: which of these three positions has the best theory of what a free choice would consist in?

5   The Compatibilist Challenge

To launch into this big question, notice first that we do not really have three positions on the nature of free choice here; we have only two. The reason for saying this is that, much though they disagree about other things, the libertarian and the hard determinist *agree* on the crucial part of the *nature* of free choice. They both hold it to be something that being causally determined would take away. They just disagree on whether causal determinism is true. And that sets our agenda for the rest of this chapter. First we will look at the compatibilist challenge to this traditional view of free choice that the libertarian and the hard determinism both take for granted. This will occupy most of the rest of the chapter. Then toward the end of the chapter we will briefly examine some possible weaknesses in the compatibilist's alternative picture of what free choice is like.

Some people find compatibilism a complete cop-out, nothing more than a way of evading the issue. As we said earlier, one name for compatibilism is 'soft determinism'; some people think that 'soft-headed determinism' would be more appropriate. Since some people do react this way, we will start by showing just how radical the compatibilist challenge to the libertarian's and hard determinist's idea of free choice really is.

Libertarians and hard determinists both maintain that if complete causal determinism is true, there can be no such thing as a free choice. That is to say, if a decision is causally determined to be as it is, something profoundly important to free choice, has to be missing. The compatibilist challenge can be summed up in three words: what is missing? What exactly would being determined in any way whatsoever rule out? Here is their strategy.

First they lay out their best causal-determinism-friendly account of what they take a free choice to consist in. Then they say, in effect, "If you don't like this account, show us what is missing." And their claim, or certainly their dark suspicion, is that *nothing* is missing, that there is no such thing as a kind of decision-making power that simply being causally determined as such would take away. (Recall the similar question that we addressed to the skeptic in chapter 2: if what normal perception gives us does not amount to knowledge of the external world, what exactly is missing?) Being determined *in certain ways* is another matter, of course; for compatibilists, *some* ways of being determined do ensure that a decision could not be free. Their point is that others *do not* and that there is nothing more to free choice than being determined in these ways, for example, by carefully deliberating about what do.

To give some substance to this position, consider the following. Being able to make choices is a power or ability. Now, we have a huge repertoire of powers and abilities: the ability to use language, to jump over barriers, to stand erect without falling, to ride a bicycle, and so on. They number in the many thousands. How many of these abilities would we lose if we were causally determined? The answer: none. Not a single one. Whether we are causally determined to be standing up or causally determined to be lying down, we do not lose our *ability* to stand up. Now, says the soft determinist, how is the ability to make free choices any different? What could possibly make *it* the one ability that being causally determined *would* take away? What a strange idea! This is one way of understanding the compatibilist's challenge.[5]

Earlier we said that philosophers should pay more attention to what free choice consists in. We can now see why. If compatibilism is right, the notion of free choice that has come down to us through the ages, the notion according to which free choice would be taken away if our decisions are causally determined, is totally wrong. In fact, the notion may have no content at all. If there just isn't *anything* relevant to free choice that would be taken away merely by a decision being causally determined, the traditional notion of free choice would be nothing more than a vague image of something-we-know-not-what that is threatened if our decisions are caused. At their most radical, compatibilists harbor just this suspicion. They suspect that the libertarians and hard determinists cannot even *define* anything that would be taken away simply by a decision's being determined, no matter how. If so, libertarians and hard determinists are talking about nothing.

Of course, a bunch of rhetorical questions is not an argument. We will get to the question of whether there are any *arguments* to back the compatibilist's challenge later. For now, we can use their challenge to delineate our task more precisely. First we have to find out what the best available compatibilist picture of free choice looks like. Then we have to examine whether we can define something that would be left out of their picture if complete causal determinism were true.

6 Compatibilists on Free Choice

Early forms of compatibilism simply ran free choice together with freedom of action: if you can do what you want and do not feel forced or compelled to do what you do, they urged, then you have free choice. This account is vulnerable to some powerful counterexamples. Consider the case of the happy junkie.

The happy junkie is heavily addicted to heroin. Because of the power of his addiction, it is absolutely clear that he would not give up heroin even if he tried. However, unlike many addicts, the happy junkie is perfectly happy with his condition. He *likes* being addicted, *enjoys* his life as a junkie, *wants* to continue taking heroin. In short, he is a thoroughly *happy* junkie, just as we said.

Does the happy junkie have free choice? Not a chance. The problem is, at the moment when he is ready to decide to take another hit of heroin, should he try to make a *different* decision, he would not form such a decision, not one that would have any effect on his reaching for the needle, i.e. anything more than a wish or vague intention. Thus, the happy junkie does not satisfy even such a general definition of free choice as (1).[6] But the compatibilist theory just sketched holds that he *does* have free choice. So much the worse for that form of compatibilism. Compatibilism has to be able to do better than that, or it is in trouble.

Compatibilism can do better than that. There are a number of different compatibilist accounts of free choice in the literature, but one of the very best is Frankfurt's (1971) second-order-desire model. On Frankfurt's model, a choice must not only be self-determined (determined by your own desires, beliefs, preferences, etc.), it must be in accord with, if not actually caused by, your second-order desires. To explain this model, consider another addiction: smoking.

When someone addicted to nicotine reaches for the next cigarette, they are, in a certain sense, doing what they want to do. That is to say, they want a cigarette, and they are about to get one. But for most smokers, they are also doing what they do not want to do at a different level. Call the desire for a cigarette a first-order desire—first-order because its object is not another desire. We can now distinguish a second-order kind of desire, where what makes it second-order is that it is aimed at first-order desires. Now see what desires the smoker does and does not satisfy.

The desire that the smoker satisfies is the desire for a cigarette. The desires that the smoker does not satisfy are such desires as the desire *not to desire* cigarettes, the desire *not to give in to the desire* for cigarettes, etc. Second-order desires, says Frankfurt, are the realm of values, life-projects, etc.—in short, almost everything distinctively human. (Indeed, in Frankfurt's view, a being without second-order desires or a being totally incapable of acting in accord with second-order desires would be what he calls a *wanton*, a being totally uncontrolled by higher principles.) Now, says Frankfurt, when the desires "effective in producing [your] behavior" are not in accord with your second-order desires, you are not free. Specifically, you are not free to satisfy your second-order desires. (What if you are not happy with some second-order desire? That is to say, *it* is a desire that you desire not to have. Well, then you'd have a third-order desire about your second-order desire. There is no magic in *second*-order desires. Third- or fourth- or fifth-order desires would do just as well in Frankfurt's model.)

Frankfurt's model is a great improvement on early compatibilist models, but it still needs an additional element: DELIBERATION. Both first- and second-order desires exist in great profusion. They often conflict with one another. (In the case of smokers, for example, most have conflicting desires even at the first level: as well as a desire for a cigarette, they usually have a desire to stop smoking. Both are perfectly good first-order desires.) To sort out the conflicts and discover the optimal decision, we have to engage in a complicated assessment of our desires, our beliefs, our values, our environment, what can be predicted for the future, etc.[7]

Someone who just acted on any old first-order desire in any old way could hardly be said to be making free *choices*. Even if the choice happened to coincide with his or her second-order desires at the moment, there is no reason to think that it would necessarily continue to do so a minute later. For a decision to be free, it must be at minimum the result of assessing relevant first-order desires against other first-order desires in the light of one's best beliefs, all firmly under the guidance of one's second-order desires (one's values, projects, long-term interests, etc.). In short, for free choice, in addition to decisions according with second-order desires, we also need deliberation.

Moreover, the deliberation must be effective. One way to capture this requirement is to say that the deliberation must be connected to the decision in such a way that, were the deliberation to be different, the decision would be different.

Now let us combine these observations about deliberation with Frankfurt's model and call the result the SOPHISTICATED COMPATIBILIST MODEL (SCM). On SCM, a choice would be free if it satisfied the following conditions:

(7) *Free choice$_{SCM}$* A decision is free if the resulting action is in accord with the decider's second-order desires and the decision was caused by the decider's own deliberations in such a way that, were the deliberations different, the decision would be different.[8]

Even if the resulting decision were entirely causally determined by, for example, the decider's desires and deliberations so that from the same deliberations she would always reach the same decision, her decision would be a free choice, according to (7), if it satisfied these conditions.

Let us now test SCM against some possible counterexamples. First, the case of the happy junkie. Even though the happy junkie was a problem for more simplistic compatibilism, he is no problem for SCM. First, the junkie's decisions to reach for another hit are not under the control of his deliberations, they are controlled by the overwhelming desires resulting from his addiction. His craving would cut straight through any countervailing process of deliberation that might happen along. The proof of this is that, should the happy junkie change his mind and deliberate differently (become an *un*happy junkie), it would make no difference to his actions: he would still reach for the needle. Second, it does not matter whether the desires that are effective in the decisions that control his behavior are in line with his second-order desires or not. Even if they were not (even if he had become an unhappy junkie), again he would still reach for the needle.

So let's look at a harder case. We might call this the case of the wired mind.[9] Here is how the wired mind works. An evil genius has control of my mind. However, the control is not exerted in such ham-handed ways as coercion or some form of manipulation that I know about. The evil genius controls me by controlling my *desires* and my *beliefs*. Thus, if he wants me to do something, he makes *me* want to do it, rather than forcing me to do so by some obvious coercive technique, such as holding a knife to my throat. And here's the problem. If the evil genius does his work carefully, the wired mind would appear to satisfy SCM completely. If so, too bad for compatibilism; the wired mind quite clearly does not make its decisions freely. Moreover (and this makes the problem more intense), if complete causal determinism is true, it seems that *we are all wired minds.* Why? Because ultimately we are all in the control of something outside us. Every desire, every belief that I have was caused by factors that ultimately lead either to my genes or to my upbringing and the various environments I have lived in. Is the wired mind fatal for compatibilism?

Well, there are causes and then there are causes. Contrary to appearances, it is far from clear that the wired mind satisfies SCM. The second clause of (7) reads: "the decision was caused by the decider's own deliberations, *in such a way that, were the deliberations different, the decision would be different.*" Now, suppose that somehow or other the wired mind developed some capacity to deliberate independently of the evil genius. To satisfy (7) and therefore to count as an example of SCM, these new deliberations would have to cause new decisions. As the case is set up, however, there is no guarantee of that. If the evil genius wants, he could just crank up the strength of the desires he favors and still get the decision he wants. But if this is possible, then the wired mind's decisions are not under the control of his or her own deliberations. What are they under the control of? It is obvious: the evil genius.

All this just presses another question on us, however: didn't we just say that if we are causally determined, we are all wired minds? If so and if the wired mind is unfree by SCM, doesn't it follow that we are all unfree by SCM? The answer to the first question: no, we said that if we are causally determined, it would *appear* that we are all wired minds. But appearances might be deceiving here. If we are all causally determined, we *get* our desires, beliefs, etc. (and also our ability to deliberate) from our genes and our environments. (From where else could we get them?) But notice: where we get them is one thing, how we use them is another. Even if we *get* our abilities from outside us, it does not follow that something outside us controls how we *use* them. And this is where normal human beings like us differ from the wired mind. When *we* deliberate, the deliberations *are* (or at least *can be*) the entire cause of our decisions, in the sense that, had we deliberated differently, a different decision would have ensued. Of course, ultimately something else still controls our deliberations, something often buried deep in our genes and upbringing, but it is our deliberations that control our decisions, not anything else. So we satisfy (7), but the wired mind does not. And this answers the second question: according to SCM, even though the wired mind does not have the power of free choice, we do—or certainly can. The wired mind is not a counter-example to SCM.

This is not the end of the matter, of course. Things are never that simple in philosophy. There remain at least two powerful objections to SCM, one very abstract and "formal," the other extremely concrete (though a bit hard to state clearly). Before we examine them, we want to say a few more words about compatibilism in general.

7   Implications of Compatibilism

In the same way that some people see compatibilism as providing only a compromise, wishy-washy concept of freedom, they also see it as supporting only a compromise, wishy-washy notion of responsibility. We have already argued that the first suspicion is not justified. Compatibilists mean to give us a full-blown concept of free choice, a concept as rich as the traditional libertarian and hard-determinist concept that they seek to replace. All they want to do is to combat the mythology, as they see it, that we cannot have this full-blown freedom if our decisions are causally determined.

If this is so, if, that is to say, compatibilists mean to give us a concept of free choice as rich as the traditional one, then they may face a problem. The traditional concept of free choice has always been thought to support the traditional concept of moral responsibility. The traditional concept of moral responsibility is the concept that you can justifiably be held responsible—in the sense of being justly praised and rewarded or blamed and punished—for what you have done. One common way of putting this point is to say that the standard concept of responsibility supports the ideas of JUST DESERTS: if you do something as a result of your own free choice, you *deserve* to be rewarded or punished for it.

Now, just deserts is a "backwards-looking" concept. That is to say, it asserts that our moral assessments should make reference to what people have done. The alternative is a "forward-looking" assessment, in which our moral assessments make reference to the *consequences* that our assessment will have. (The difference comes out clearly in the dialogue between the professor and the student at the beginning of the chapter. First the student denies that any backward-looking punishment based on what he has, or in this case has not, done would be justified. The professor then offers a forward-looking justification in terms of modifying the student's future behavior for the better.) There is a problem here for many compatibilists. Or so some philosophers claim.

Many compatibilists, like many other people who believe that all or virtually all behavior is causally determined, hold that there is something irrational, even barbaric, about punishing people on the basis of what they have done. If they were caused to do what they did, what's the point? Punishing people on the basis of what they have done is *retribution*, a concept that stands right beside vengeance in the list of vicious and irrational acts for many of these people. (So the next time you are docked points for a late paper, you can tell the instructor that he or she is merely wreaking vengeance on you, merely inflicting retribution on you. Good luck.) The only justifiable basis for "punishment," these people argue, is some forward-looking basis, some justification in terms of the *consequences* of the punishment. Important consequences include changing the behavior of the person (rehabilitation), changing the behavior of others (deterrence), and the protection of society (public safety).

These questions about the philosophy of responsibility and punishment have been a topic of hot debate in the context of prison reform and elsewhere. We cannot go into them any further here. All we want to point out is that they contain a potential problem for compatibilism. If the compatibilist really believes that she is producing a concept of free choice adequate to capture our *full-blown* traditional concept, then she has to believe that she is producing a concept adequate to support our traditional concept of responsibility. But our traditional concept of responsibility is not forward-looking, it is backward-looking. It holds people responsible for what they *have* done, not to change what they *will* do. On the traditional view, the question of what people *will* do if we do this or that to them is irrelevant to guilt, innocence, and responsibility. We have a strong intuition, however, voiced in the previous paragraph, that if we were caused to decide as we decided, to do as we did, there would be no backward-looking justification for holding us responsible for what we decided and did.

To sum up, the compatibilist has to support the traditional idea that people can *deserve* to be treated one way or another. Otherwise, they will have produced merely a compromise, wishy-washy concept of freedom, not the real thing, just as their opponents suggest. But it is hard to see how the traditional idea of just deserts can survive a conviction that every decision and action is causally determined. Even when the relevant causes are our own desires, beliefs, and deliberations, as in SCM, it would seem that if these factors are sufficient causes of our decisions, then our decisions still could not have been other than what they were, and any backward-looking reward or punishment based on what we deserve as a result of our decisions and actions would be completely unjustified. The only kind of reward or punishment that could be justified would be a forward-looking one. In short, even SCM cannot support our full, desert-based notion of responsibility and provides only a compromise, wishy-washy concept of free choice.

To see if this worry has any merit, we need to turn to the two objections to compatibilism mentioned at the end of the previous section.

8   First Objection: The Joys of Modality

The skeptics who think that the best even SCM can give us is a compromise concept of freedom raise two main objections to the model. In the first of them, which we will examine in this section, the problem is said to lie in the basic idea that free decisions are fully compatible with causal determinism.

This objection is based on a very simple idea: If you were caused to decide as you did, it would seem that *you could not have decided otherwise.* If so, since by (1) we have already seen that the ability to decide otherwise up to the moment of choice seems crucial to our notions of free choice, it seems to follow that there is something amiss at the very heart of compatibilism.

Compatibilists are bound to have an answer to an objection this basic, of course, and they do. Indeed, their answer goes to the heart of their challenge to the traditional view. Unfortunately, both the objection and their answer require us to examine some heady abstractions, so we will start with some preliminaries.

Concepts like 'could have', 'ability to', 'power to', etc., are called MODAL CONCEPTS in the jargon of philosophy. They get this name because they are not about states of affairs directly but about the *modes* in which states of affairs can be thought. Consider the statement 'Apples grow on trees'. Sentences describing *modes* in which we can think about apples growing on trees include, '*It is possible* for apples to grow on trees' (alternatively, 'Apples *could* grow on trees'), '*It is necessary* that apples grow on trees' (alternatively, 'Apples *must* grow on trees'), and, '*It is the case* that apples grow on trees' (alternatively, 'Apples *do* grow on trees').

Modal concepts are notoriously difficult to understand clearly, for reasons that we will not go into. Unfortunately, one of the most difficult modal concepts is found right at the heart of the problem of free choice. It is the concept of possibility, the concept that something *could be.* In the case of free choice, the concept takes the specific form that a choice *could have been* (other than it was), but the specific form inherits all the problems of the general concept. If we want to understand compatibilism and the first objection to it, we have to get clearer about this crucial concept of 'could have chosen otherwise'.

If compatibilists hold that 'could have chosen otherwise' does not require anything incompatible with causal determinism, what could they have in mind? Let's start with one of the simplest "could" concepts. Think of any recent car. This car *could* be going 100 kph (roughly, 60 mph for those still using Imperial measure). Why do we say that? Because it has the *power* to go that speed. How do we know that? Well, if it were started, on level pavement, pointed straight ahead, in gear, with the gas pedal depressed, etc., it *would be* going 100 kph. Yet suppose that the car is parked in a parking garage, going nowhere. Does it still have the power to go 100 kph? Yes, indeed it does: it could have been going down the road at 100 kph, not sitting in the garage. The moral of the story: even something as simple as a car could have been doing, hence right now has the *power* to do, something other than it is doing (see Ayers 1968). Yet cars are completely causally determined. Cars, of course, don't have free choice, but that is not because they cannot do anything other than what they are doing. They can. What denies them freedom of choice is that they do not have the power to *deliberate* about what they will do.

What 'could do' or 'could have been doing' means here is something like 'if so and so were the case, it would do, or would have been doing'. This is sometimes called the HYPOTHETICAL ANALYSIS OF 'COULD'. In the context of free choice, the parallel analysis would run, 'I could have chosen otherwise' means 'If I had deliberated differently, I *would* have chosen otherwise'. Now notice the crucial point: this analysis of 'could have chosen otherwise' is entirely compatible with the choice being caused, so on this concept of 'could', I could have chosen otherwise even if the choice was causally determined.

Put another way, on this analysis, the power of free choice is just like all our other powers. We don't lose our power to get up, open the door, and leave because we are causally determined to sit at the keyboard and finish a paper. Why should we lose our power of making free decisions just because our decisions are causally determined? What could possibly make the power of choice so different from our other powers? On the analysis we are exploring, the power of choice is *not* different from our other powers, and we *do not* lose it if our decisions are causally determined.

This analysis turns the tables on the libertarians. (And on hard determinists, but we will stick to libertarians.) If being able to choose otherwise is compatible with determinism, then there is no such thing as even the *concept* of a kind of power that would be removed by determinism. Now this would be great for the existence of freedom—there would no longer be *any* form of free choice that determinism could rule out, even in principle—but it would be a little tough for the traditional *concept* of freedom. In fact, it would be worse than a little tough. If we could have chosen otherwise *even though our decision was causally determined,* then *we cannot even say what determinism as such is supposed to take away.* If so, the traditional concept of free choice is *completely* vacuous. What Gertrude Stein said about Oakland, California, would be true of the traditional concept of free choice: there is no there there.

Thus, if libertarians even want to stay in the game, let alone win, they have to come up with something better than this hypothetical analysis of ability concepts. What might they offer? We explicated the hypothetical sense of 'could' using the notion of having a power. However, there are two senses of 'could', one favorable to the compatibilist, the other favorable to the liberatarian. Here is the NATURAL POWER sense of 'could':

(8) *Could$_{np}$* A decision taken or an action done by *A could$_{np}$* have been otherwise if *A* has the *power* to decide or act otherwise.

As we said earlier, we have a great many powers, and so a great many ways in which we could have done otherwise than we did, that are not removed in the slightest by our being caused to use some other power at the moment. If all there is to 'could have decided otherwise' is the natural-power sense, i.e., merely having the *power* to have decided otherwise, then libertarianism is vacuous, and compatibilism not only wins but is the only game in town. One promising avenue to get the traditional view at least back in the game is to distinguish another concept 'could' from the natural-power notion. Let us call this new concept the CAUSAL POSSIBILITY sense of 'could':

(9) *Could$_{cp}$* A decision taken or an action done by *A could$_{cp}$* have been otherwise if, even with exactly the same causes as the causes that produced the decision or action, *A* would sometimes decide or act differently.

That is to say, the same causes would not always produce the same effects.

What can we say about this new notion of causal possibility? Well, it does seem to get the libertarian back in the game. The libertarian can now give some *content,* at least, to her idea that if a decision is causally determined, it could not have been otherwise. What she would mean is something like this: Contrary to what the definition of 'could$_{cp}$' demands, if a decision were causally determined and if exactly the same causes were operating, then *exactly the same decision* would always result. If so, then even though the decision could$_{np}$ have been otherwise, it is *not* the case that it could$_{cp}$ have been otherwise. And if this is true, then the idea that if a decision is causally determined, it would not be a free choice again has content. Having content is not the same as being true, of course, but at least we have given the traditionalists something to say.

9 Second Objection: Doesn't Compatibilism Leave Something Important Out?

The compatibilist, though foiled in her more radical challenge, is entitled to ask, "*Why* would a decision's being caused entail that it isn't a free choice? What does my conception of free choice leave out?" This brings us to the second line of objection to SCM. Here the objection is that SCM and all other forms of compatibilism developed so far leave out important aspects of free choices.

The first line of objection, the one considered in the previous section, was an objection to any form of compatibilism, an objection in principle. This second line of objection is an objection merely to the forms of compatibilism that have been developed so far. A better version of compatibilism might be able to get around it, the objector is saying, but no existing one does. The objector then goes on to suggest candidates for what is left out.

This missing element is supposedly removed merely by a decision's being causally determined. The libertarian has to be careful here. If a decision is to be more than a merely random occurrence, it has to be connected to *me,* the person making the decision, in some way. Decisions don't just randomly happen; people *make* decisions. Even if the connection between me and my decisions is not a causally determined one, there still has to be some effective connection between me and my decisions.

So the libertarian does not want to insist upon too much lack of determinism. A world of complete indeterminism would be a world of chaos. And in a world of chaos, we would have no way of knowing whether any given choice would bring about a result of any use to us whatsoever. Even if we had freedom of *choice* in such of world, it would be of no value to us, because there would be no stable way of connecting choices to actions and results. Free choice would have value to us only if the world is stable enough for us to know what will happen (most of the time) if we act on our choices. A few decisions popping up in our heads like "partridges out of the grass" (as Jean-Paul Sartre described one view of free choices), with no settled causal connections to anything else, would, at best, be completely useless to us. In short, from the standpoint of an effective power of choice, large amounts of randomness would be at least as bad as the libertarian's worst nightmare about complete determinism.

This point about randomness can be put in the form of a dilemma for libertarianism:

Premise 1 Every action is either causally determined or not causally determined.

Premise 2 An action that is not causally determined would be random, without antecedents. It would "just happen." So it would not be a free choice in any way that mattered to us.

Premise 3 An action that is causally determined could not have been other than it was, and so could not be the product of any free choice.
Conclusion 1 Actions not causally determined could not be the result of a free choice of any kind that mattered to us. [By P2]
Conclusion 2 Causally determined actions could not be the result of free choices. [By P3]
Conclusion 3 No action could be the result of a free choice of any kind that mattered to us. [By P1, C1, and C2]

Since a libertarian would accept P3, the only plausible way out for her would be to deny P2. This is where she has to be careful. To get around P2, she needs a *touch* of indeterminism but not so much as to run the risk of generating randomness. What she needs is a touch of indeterminism in *just* the right place. A nice trick! The right place is the point at which background conditions like desires and beliefs get transformed into choices. This is where we have to look if we are to have any hope of finding something crucial to free choice that determinism would rule out.

Moreover, not just any old connection will do. The missing element has to do what a causal connection would do, namely to connect desires and beliefs to actions so as to achieve the kind of stability and predictability just discussed. Sartre's decisions popping up in our heads *would not* get around P2 and therefore *would* be caught in the dilemma. Historically, there has been a long list of candidates for the "crucial missing element." Here are three, all of them related to the others.

Agent of Choice
One candidate is the *agent* of choice. An agent of choice is me, the thing that does the choosing. Choices are not made *in* me, choices are made *by* me—and any theory of free choice that hopes to be taken seriously has to account for this fact. In all known compatibilist theories, runs the objection, choices merely happen in me, according to which of the various contending factors turns out to be the strongest causally. Even if there is a "me" watching the process, it would play no role in determining the outcome. Compatibilism gives us no account of what it would be for an *agent* to *make* choices. Making choices requires focused attention. It often requires exertion of effort. Where are elements like these in existing compatibilist theories? So runs the objection.

So far so good; any adequate theory of free choice indeed better have a theory of the agent of choice in it. Everything depends, however, on how this idea of an agent of choice is developed. Compatibilism may be simplistic in its reduction of free choice to causally determined decision making, but we don't want the alternative to turn free choice into an unapproachable *mystery*. So when we fill out the notion of the agent of choice, will it fit with compatibilism, or will it show that compatibilism leaves something out? Interestingly, to date nobody has been able to fill out the notion of the agent of choice sufficiently for us to know what the answer is.

Reasons versus Other Kinds of Causes

When the notion of the agent of choice is filled out, there are a couple of elements that it will have to contain. One is this. Most of the factors that enter into our decision making are *reasons* for us to make or not make a given decision (recall psychological explanation, discussed in chapter 4). But reasons seem to operate in us differently from how causes operate (or how other kinds of causes operate, if reasons are themselves a kind of cause). Reasons operate on us by what they *imply* that we should or should not do, whereas normal causes have their effects by the energy they carry, the force they exert, etc. Put slightly differently, reasons have their "effects" by what they mean to the person who has them.

Here's an example. Suppose that I believe that cheating on exams is wrong. Just sitting in my head, this belief does not by itself affect my decisions or do very much of anything else. So when it does affect my decisions, it is by doing something more than a normal cause would do. A normal cause does have its effects, as we might say, "simply by being there" (in the right circumstances, of course). This point is clearer when we see the alternative: my belief affects me not just by being in my head but by what it *implies* for me. It implies that I should not cheat on an exam. When we introduced the concept of intentionality in chapter 4, we said that it has been put to many uses by philosophers: to mark off the mental, to argue for dualism, and to argue for free choice. The argument we have just given—that reasons, i.e., states with intentionality, influence us by what they imply, not simply by existing—is how intentionality enters into the discussion of free choice. (Recall that this feature of how reasons operate in us was one of things that traditional dualists used to distinguish the mind from anything mechanical, including the brain.)

A further feature of reasons for choice reinforces this distinction between affecting other events by what something *implies* for someone and affecting them by energy or force. Causes that operate by energy or force are (at least in part) *events*. That is to say, something happens, some change takes place that brings about another change. By contrast, a reason need not be an event to have an affect on a decision. Suppose that you believe that cheating is wrong. This belief need not be, and probably is not, an event, some change in you. It may have existed unchanged in you for years. Yet it can still influence your decisions, for example, your decision not to cheat on an exam today even though you have an opportunity to do so.

To sum up, how reasons influence decisions is very different from how normal nonmental causes bring about effects. The former influence by what they imply, not by how much force or energy they contain. This in turn allows reasons to influence decisions even when the reason is not an event.

Now we need to ask, How do implications operate? Crucially, reasons imply something only if they imply it *to someone.* Consider the belief that it is wrong to cheat on exams. For this belief to affect your decisions, it must hold its implications *for you.* There can be all kinds of reasons why you should choose this or that. None of them will have the slightest influence on what you decide unless *you recognize* those implications, unless they mean something *to you.* Even this is not enough. You must also *decide* to be guided by what these reasons imply, and nothing seems to force you to decide to be thus guided. If this is so, there appears on the face of it to be a gap in causal determinism at just the right place.

At the very least, these points together suggest that existing compatibilist accounts leave some aspects of free decision making unexplained. We will close this section with one final suggestion of what compatibilism leaves out. It is a little vaguer than the two we have just explored.

Making an Effort
One important aspect of human decision making that is overlooked not just by compatibilists but by almost everyone working within the scientific image of the person is the element of *trying* or *making an effort* to decide. According to compatibilists, runs this objection, when a choice is made, everything happens mechanically. The factors get identified, they get weighed up, the weights assigned to them cause a decision to be reached, life goes on. Even on sophisticated compatibilist accounts like SCM, deliberation seems to be something that could happen without anyone making any effort: the various first-order desires, etc., compete with one another and with the relevant second-order desires, etc., and whichever has the greatest causal force wins. We could easily imagine all this going on in a computer. But, goes the objection, this is not remotely similar to what real decision making is like. In real decision making, a person often

struggles to spot the relevant elements, *tries hard* to think through the situation carefully, *makes an effort* to reach the best decision, *makes a further effort* to carry it through in the face of conflicting desires and obstacles presented by the world, and so on. Real deliberation and decision making takes effort. It can even be exhausting. It is not easy to see how the compatibilist model can account for any of this.

Nor is it easy to see how these elements could be added to it. Indeed, all the objections we have been considering go together. To give an account of *either* what it is to make a choice on the basis of reasons *or* what it is to try, to make an effort, we require an account of what an *agent* is. No existing compatibilist model offers much of an account of any of these elements.

10   Final Remarks

These objections that compatibilism leaves something out are not necessarily fatal. On the other hand, we have no precise idea how a compatibilist could answer them. We are inclined to think that the best hope for either libertarianism or compatibilism lies in a deep, detailed understanding of human decision making, of the process of an agent recognizing reasons for doing something and acting on those reasons. Which view will such an account favor? We aren't sure. Indeed, there are two ideas that we have not even mentioned. Is responsibility for one's decisions and actions tied as closely to free choice as our discussion has tended to assume? Starting from examples in which we fully assent to some decision we have made even when, unbeknownst to us, we could not have reached any other decision, some philosophers (Frankfurt [1969], for example) urge that what matters for responsibility is that we are happy with our decision, not whether it was free in the sense that we could have decided otherwise. Other philosophers (Strawson [1962], for example) argue that the idea that people are responsible for decisions with which they are happy is so embedded in our everyday practices and so well justified there that no philosophical theory of free choice could affect its justification. We cannot discuss these ideas here, but notice that if either of them were sound, whether we have the power to make "free choices" (again, in the sense that we could have chosen otherwise) would immediately become less important. We could still be responsible for our choices, responsible in the full-blown sense of section 7, even if we don't have the power of free choice.

In general, free choice seems to be one of those topics in philosophy that is still wide open. No one has come up with a convincing account of it yet. We certainly don't think that we have done so in this chapter. Our aims have been much more modest: to shake up people's complacency on the issue and to identify some of the reasons why it is such a hard issue. And that's where we'll leave it.

"Hold on," we can hear you say, "you can't leave free choice like this. You haven't said anything about the most important question, Do we have free choice?" This protest is justified. We haven't answered this question. The reason is simple: until we know what free choice is, what would make a decision a free one, we cannot settle—no, we cannot even *investigate*—whether free choice exists or not. We will close with one glimmer of hope: if philosophers ever figure out what free choice is, it will probably be relatively simple to determine whether it exists. We *suspect* that it does exist. Indeed, it is hard to seriously entertain the idea that it does not exist. We just cannot prove that it does.

Study Questions

1. Recall the student who handed in his essay late because he spent too much time in the pub. Was his argument for why he should not be penalized a good one? Justify your answer.

2. What is the practical importance of the issue of free choice? Is free choice an important condition of the operation of major social institutions and interpersonal relations? If so, how? If not, why not?

3. What is the problem about the *nature* of free choice, what is the problem of the *existence* of free choice, and why do we need to settle the first problem before we can settle the second one?

4. What is the difference between freedom of choice and freedom of action? Could one have either without the other (free choice without freedom of action or freedom of action without free choice)?

5. Hard determinists, libertarians, and compatibilists each agree with one of the other two positions on one thing and disagree with the other position on one thing. Lay out this pattern of agreements and disagreements. Why is the agreement between libertarians and compatibilists a bit peculiar? (Hint: Do they mean the same thing by the words they both employ?)

6. What is the compatibilist challenge, and why is it equally a challenge to the conception of free choice held by both libertarians and hard determinists?

7. Describe Frankfurt's first- and second-order model of human motivations and draw out its implications for the issue of free choice.

8. What is the sophisticated compatibilist model of free choice (SCM), and how does it deal with the objections to earlier, simpler compatibilist models?

9. What is the problem of the wired mind, and why does it seem to raise difficulties even for SCM? Can SCM successfully meet these difficulties? If so, how? If not, why not?

10. Can compatibilism provide a conception of free choice rich enough to ground a meaningful concept of just deserts? (What is the issue of just deserts, anyway?)

11. Lay out the objection to compatibilism that makes use of the modal concept 'could$_{cp}$'. How could a sophisticated form of compatibilism try to meet it? In your view, would it succeed? Justify your view.

12. What is the apparent dilemma that starts from the premise that every event is either causally determined or it is not? How does randomness enter into this dilemma? Can you see any way out of the dilemma that would preserve libertarianism? Can you see any way out of the dilemma at all?

13. Does even a sophisticated compatibilist picture leave out important elements of what is going on when we make free choices? If so, what? Do you see any hope that compatibilism can include these elements in its account? If not, how would you respond to the claims made in this chapter that it does?

Suggested Further Readings

One of the best introductions to the issues surrounding free choice is still Taylor 1963. An excellent older collection of papers covering many points of view is Watson 1982, and an excellent recent one is Pereboom 1997; the latter contains important historical discussions as well as classic and very recent work in the analytic tradition. Two compatibilist models have become contemporary classics, Strawson's (1962) account and Frankfurt's (1971) model, for which Frankfurt 1969 was an important precursor. Dennett 1984 presents a readable but eccentric defense of compatibilism.

Very few philosophers espouse hard determinism or any view that we have no free choice of any significant sort. An interesting and fairly accessible argument for libertarianism, i.e., the view both that free choice exists and that it is incompatible with choices being causally determined, is van Inwagen 1993, chapter 11. (For a fuller presentation of his argument, see van Inwagen 1983.) For the existentialist picture of freedom as a kind of radical indeterminancy and ability to determine oneself, there is no better source than Sartre 1943.

One of the best studies of the complicated modal concepts at the heart of the issue of free choice is still Ayers 1968.

PART III
Relating Knowledge to Mind

Chapter 7

Knowledge of Minds

If trees could scream, would we be so cavalier about cutting them down? We might, if they screamed all the time, for no good reason.

Jack Handey

1 Introduction

In chapter 2, we considered the worry that we cannot know anything beyond our own minds. We were unable to address this worry completely and so put it aside as a puzzling paradox, refusing to concede that we really *don't* know anything about the physical world around us, yet not able to completely justify our belief that we *do* know about the world around us. Even if we grant that we know about some things in the world around us, other important kinds of skeptical problems about our knowledge of things still remain. We will address two of them in this chapter:

• Do we know that anything other than ourselves has a mind?

• Granting that each of us knows of oneself that one *has* a mind, how much does one know *about* one's own self?

The first is the PROBLEM OF OTHER MINDS. We will call the second the PROBLEM OF KNOWLEDGE OF SELF.

Like knowledge of language (chapter 3), knowledge of minds combines the topics of knowledge and of minds. We have left it till now because different theories of the *nature* of mind have different implications for our *knowledge* of minds, so we could not deal with knowledge of minds till we had laid out the various theories of what minds are like.

2 The Problem of Other Minds

The problem of other minds generates a paradox of the strongest kind. On the one hand, nothing seems more obvious than that we know what is going on in the minds of others, most of the time at any rate. Suppose that Ying says to me, "Let's go to a movie!" It would seem obvious that I know a whole bunch of things about her: that she wants to go to a movie, that she wants to go with me, that she has decided to act on this want rather than any other want she may have, that by the signs 'Let's', 'go', 'to', 'a', and 'movie', she intends to say what would normally be expressed in English by the sentence, 'Let's go to a movie', and so on. In short, it seems obvious that we have knowledge of other minds.

On the other hand, it is hard to see how we can know *anything* about the minds and mental states of other. Go back to our friend Ying. What do we actually *know* about her? Even on the assumption that we have knowledge of the world around us in general, all we directly *know* of her is that a string of noises has poured forth from her mouth. As to the rest, the beliefs we form about what she wants, what she means by these noises, etc.—all this seems to be inference: we *infer* that these things are going on in her head, but we do not know about any of them directly. More-over, and this is what gets the problem of other minds really going, it would seem that we have no way whatsoever of confirming these infer-ences. It is not as though we can open up her head and see her wishes and intended meanings directly. But for a belief to amount to knowl-edge, we recall from chapter 2, it must be justified. This leads to the following argument:

Premise 1 We cannot justify our beliefs about other minds, i.e., what is going on in other people "behind their behavior."
Premise 2 A belief must be justified to be knowledge.
Conclusion We do not have knowledge of other minds.

The argument for P1 was just given: we form many beliefs about what others are thinking, feeling, meaning, etc., but we cannot justify these beliefs because we have no direct knowledge of other people's mental states. P2 was explained in chapter 2. We saw there that if we cannot justify a belief, we do not know whether it is true or false.

In summary, here is the paradox:

Statement 1 It seems obvious that we have knowledge of other minds.
Statement 2 It seems impossible to have knowledge of other minds.

Note that the skeptical problem here runs very deep. If the argument just given is sound, we do not even know that other beings *have* minds. For all we know, even the old caricature of behaviorism could be right; perhaps others really are nothing more than complex organisms with rich, highly structured patterns of behavior. To paraphrase what the philosopher Descartes once thought when looking out his window, "Perhaps all these beings walking around on the street below are just robots, just complicated machines with nothing mental going on inside at all."[1]

To make the problem more concrete, let's look at some examples.[2]

Example 1 Think of a time when you and a friend shared ice cream. Focus your imagination on the taste and texture of that delicious, chilly substance. Now ask yourself: how do you know whether your friend experienced the same taste, the same texture, the same sensation of cold, as you did? Couldn't the taste your friend experiences while eating the ice cream be the taste that you get from pancakes and syrup? Indeed, isn't it possible that your friend gets no sensation at all from the ice cream but is merely acting as though she did? How could you know?

Example 2 Find a red pen. Show it to someone else. Now, concentrate on the color sensation you get from the pen and ask, How do you know that your friend has the same color sensation as you have when he looks at the pen? How do you even know that he has any color *sensation* at all? Surely here too you can imagine that the sensation he gets as he looks at the pen is more like the sensation that you get when you look at bananas, or that he acts as though he has the sensation that you get when you look at a red pen but in fact has no sensation at all.

To help us keep them separate, let's give the two problems here names. It is common in philosophy to say that the way something feels or seems to someone is its QUALIA. Now, the problem where the sensations that your friend is experiencing might be totally different from yours let us call the INVERTED QUALIA problem. And the problem where your friend might not have any sensations at all (even though she is behaving as though she does)—let us call this problem the ABSENT QUALIA problem. In the inverted-qualia problem, the risk is that your friend's mind operates very differently from yours, for example, that she has a sensation of green where you have a sensation of red, and you cannot tell. In the absent-qualia problem, the risk is that things do not feel or seem to your friend at all, that your friend does not *have* qualia. That is, the risk is that your friend is a ZOMBIE, a being that behaves like us but has no inner mental life.[3]

So far we have merely asked rhetorical questions about the possibility of inverted and absent qualia and made appeals to intuition: "How do you know ____?" "Surely you can imagine ____." But it's fairly straightforward to construct an argument for the conclusion that we *don't* know how the ice cream tastes to others, or even that it has a taste for others, and that we *don't* know what color sensations other people experience as they look at (what we all call) red pens, or even that they have any sensations. The argument, applied to the ice cream case, runs as follows:

Premise 1 You can imagine that ice cream tastes different to your friend (inverted qualia) or has no taste at all (absent qualia).

Premise 2 You can't show that ice cream doesn't taste different to your friend or even that it has a taste for him.

Conclusion 1 It's imaginable that ice cream tastes difference to your friend or has no taste at all, and you can't show that either is not actually the case. [By P1 and P2]

Premise 3 If something is imaginable and you can't show that it's not actual, then you don't know that it's not actually the case.

Conclusion 2 You don't know that ice cream doesn't taste different to your friend or that it has any taste at all for him. [By P3 and C1]

Conclusion 2 is the one that contains *the problem of other minds.*

3 The Problem of Knowledge of Self

The problem of knowledge of self is a bit different from the problem of other minds. On the question of the minds of other people, it is difficult to show that we really know even something as basic as that others *have* minds. Recall Descartes's worry about whether others might be robots. It is much harder (indeed, probably impossible) to doubt whether you yourself have a mind, for the following reason:

Premise 1 To doubt that you have a mind, you have to engage in the activity of *doubting*.

Premise 2 But doubting is a mental activity, in other words, an activity of a mind.

Conclusion To doubt that you have mind, you must have a mind.

This is a very old argument; indeed, Saint Augustine used something like it in the fourth century, and it underlies Descartes's "Cogito ergo sum" (I think therefore I am) of 1645. But, old or not, it is still a perfectly sound argument. So what is the problem about knowledge of self?

The problem, in a nutshell, is over *how much* you know about your own mind. Let us grant that you know that you *have* a mind (perhaps better, *are* a mind). Well, that puts you in a better position about yourself than Descartes was in about other people when he wondered if he knew even that they have minds. But how much better? How much do you know— *know*, not just believe—about your own mind. How much do you know about yourself?

Again, there is an apparent paradox. On the one hand, it seems obvious that each of us knows a lot about him- or herself. Our friend Ying, for instance, *knows* what she wants her string of words to say, *knows* that she wants to go to a movie (rather than, say, to go fishing), *knows* that she wants to go with you (rather than the person down the hall), and so forth. So it would seem.

On the other hand, have you never been in a position where you *thought* you wanted something and then, when you got it, discovered that you didn't want it very much after all? Have you never been in a position where you thought that you knew how you felt about something but discovered that you really felt something else? (For example, you thought that you were free of racial prejudice but found yourself looking at a mixed-race couple disapprovingly, or you thought that you were angry with a person but were really just jealous of her, and so on.) Anybody who pays attention to what is going on in themselves and is reasonably honest could think of dozens of similar examples.

Here's the problem. If you can sometimes believe perfectly confidently that you want or feel something and turn out to be wrong, how do you know when you are right and when you are wrong? More succinctly, how do you know when your beliefs about yourself are right and when they are wrong? Let's convert these questions into the form of an argument:

Premise 1 Sometimes confident beliefs about yourself turn out wrong.

Premise 2 You have no tools for finding out which beliefs about yourself are correct and which are wrong.

Premise 3 If confident beliefs about yourself sometimes turn out wrong and you have no tools for finding out which beliefs about yourself are correct and which are wrong, then you do not know which are correct and which are wrong.

Conclusion 1 You do not know which beliefs about yourself are correct and which are wrong.

Premise 4 If you do not know which beliefs about yourself are correct and which are wrong, you do not know yourself.

Conclusion 2 You do not know yourself.

Conclusion 2 is *the problem of knowledge of self.* One reaction to conclusion 2 is, "Come on, you can't be serious! I know a lot about myself and so do you." To this our response is, "Certainly you think you do. And so do we all. Now, show that you do." Again we have a paradox: it seems obvious that we have at least some knowledge of ourselves, but we also have a powerful argument that we do not.

In summary form, here's the paradox:

Statement 1 It seems obvious that we have at least some knowledge of our own minds.
Statement 2 It seems impossible that we know anything about our own minds beyond the fact that we have one.

This chapter is all about such paradoxes. We will start with the problem of other minds.

4   Weak, Stronger, and Strongest Skepticism about Other Minds

The central fact that gives rise to the problem of other minds is that we do not seem to have direct access to the contents of other people's minds. All we have direct access to is our own mind, plus others' behavior. As we have seen, there are stronger and weaker versions of the resulting concern. The weakest version is that *sometimes* we cannot know (i.e., justify whatever beliefs we may have about) what the mental states of another person are like. This is clearly true and, unless the problem can be generalized to all cases, is not a source of concern.

A stronger version of the concern is the inverted qualia problem: you can't be sure that your experiences in a certain situation are *ever* similar to the experiences of others in the same situation. So, for example, in the case of the ice cream and the pen, there is uncertainty about what the experience of them feels like to others. If the problem here is general, then that will be true of everything in others' experience.

The strongest version is the absent qualia problem: by generalizing from the ice cream and red pen cases even further, one can argue that you cannot even know that another person is having experiences at all.

Let's start with the argument for the middle concern—you can never know what another person's mental states are like:

Premise 1 You can imagine that ice cream tastes different to your friend (inverted qualia).
Premise 2 You can't show that ice cream doesn't taste different to your friend.

Conclusion 1 It's imaginable that ice cream tastes different to your friend, and you can't show that it's not actually the case. [By P1 and P2]
Premise 3 If something is imaginable and you can't show that it's not the case, then you don't know that it's not the case.
Conclusion 2 You don't know that ice cream doesn't taste different to your friend.

We can immediately see that the argument is valid. Its form is this:

p
q
Therefore, *p* and *q*
If both *p* and *q*, then *r*
Therefore, *r*

Since the argument is clearly valid, what we really need to know is what supports the three premises.

The examples establish P1. P3 seems to be a valid application of a flatly obvious EPISTEMOLOGICAL PRINCIPLE: if something is possible and you can't show that it is not the case, then you don't know that it's not the case. In short, two of the three premises look quite solid. P2, that you can't show that ice cream doesn't taste different to your friend, is more controversial. So it's the crucial claim.

We can defend P2 by noting that we observe only the bodies of other people. When we believe things about their mental states, we do so on the basis of observing their bodies. Put otherwise: what we know *directly* about other people is facts about their bodies and their behavior; we then *infer* their mental states from this evidence. But, it turns out, you cannot give independent justification for this inference.

In effect, the argument for P2 is just like an argument we saw in chapter 2:

The argument for external world skepticism
Premise 1 All you know directly is how things seem to you.
Premise 2 If all you know directly is how things seem to you, then you can't know how things really are outside of you.
Conclusion You can't know how things really are outside you.

This time we alter the argument slightly, and get the following:

The nondirectness argument for other-minds skepticism
Premise 1 All you know directly about others are facts about their bodies and their behavior.

Premise 2 If all you know directly about others are facts about their bodies and their behavior, then you can't know what others' experiences are like.

Conclusion You can't know what others' experiences are like.

The conclusion, that you can't know what others' experiences are like, then provides direct support for P2 of the ice-cream argument: that you can't show that ice cream doesn't, in fact, taste different to your friend. The reason that you can't show this is that you don't have *direct* knowledge of how the ice cream tastes to her; you only have direct knowledge of her body and behavior. But such facts don't rule out the possibility that ice cream tastes to her as pancakes and syrup taste to you.

If the nondirectness argument establishes P2 of the ice-cream argument, what supports the argument nondirectness? Recall the inference rule in (1).

(1) The way things seem → the way things are

It turned out that (1) itself could not be justified in terms of how things seem. To defeat skepticism about other minds, we need to go roughly the other way:

(2) Something outside an agent, namely, behavior → the way things seem to the agent

But how someone is behaving does not justify an inference to how things seem to him or her, not without an additional argument that we have not seen yet. If not, (2) is not a justified inference.

Having argued for the middle conclusion, that you can't be sure that you know how others experience something, we can progress to a stronger conclusion: you can't be sure that there is *any* similarity between your experiences and those of your fellow humans. This is just a slightly more general form of the absent-qualia problem. It is also just a generalization of the ice-cream case. After all, there is nothing especially mysterious about the taste of ice cream. The very same argument could be made for pickles, ginger ale, or oatmeal. In fact, for each correlation between external stimuli and experiences in you, you can wonder whether that correlation obtains for other people, and you can imagine in each case that it doesn't obtain. Likewise for each correlation between external stimuli and experiences in you, you can wonder whether a particular external stimulus is correlated with *any* experience in other people, and you can imagine, in each case, that there is nothing beyond the other person's behavior, that the other is a zombie. All this seems to show that you have no *knowledge* whatsoever of what the mental life of your peers is like. All you have are unjustified beliefs.

5 Responses to the Problem

If the problem of the external world seemed to be an outrageous, purely "academic" problem, one not to be taken seriously by any sensible person, the problem of other minds is apt to seem even more so, especially in the form of the absent-qualia problem. However, being convinced that a problem is silly and impractical is one thing; showing that there is nothing to it is another. So you are convinced that you have knowledge of other minds? Can you *show* that you do? Can you show that your myriad beliefs about other people's thoughts, feelings, meanings, etc., are *justified?* That is our challenge.

Historically, there have probably been five main attempts to refute skepticism about other minds: the argument from analogy, the argument from underlying neurological similarity, behaviorism, an approach related to behaviorism that we will call Wittgensteinianism, and the inference to the best explanation. This is not a very informative array. Happily, there is a better way to summarize approaches to the problem. These approaches divide into two: on the one hand, there are people who, because of their views on the nature of mind, deny that there *is* any problem; on the other hand, there are philosophers who, equally because of their views of the nature of mind, believe that there is a problem of other minds and try to solve it.

The importance, even the existence, of the problem of other minds is directly related to the question of the *nature* of the mind. To take an obvious example, if RADICAL BEHAVIORISM is true and the mind is just the body's behavior and its dispositions to behave, then there is no "problem of our knowledge of other minds." If we know human behavior, we know human minds. The same is true of what is called the IDENTITY THEORY, the theory that the mind is just the human brain: once we gain the right kind of knowledge of the brain, we will have knowledge of the mind. At the opposite extreme, there is DUALISM, the view that the mind and the brain are two radically different things. If dualism is true, then the problem of knowledge of other minds will in all likelihood be real—and very nasty. And in the middle are FUNCTIONALISM, the view that the mind is certain activities of the brain, and NEUROPHILOSOPHY, the view that mind talk has little value and we should focus on the brain and its environment. Functionalists tend to think that there is not much of a problem of other minds, often because they adopt the INFERENCE TO THE BEST EXPLANATION approach to solve it. For neurophilosophers, there is no problem.

For the sake of argument, let's start by assuming that there is a problem, as dualists and others believe, and examine the argument from analogy as a possible solution to it. The argument from analogy is the oldest approach to a solution and one that occurs to most people as soon as they encounter the problem.

6   There Is a Problem: The Argument from Analogy Is the Solution

The argument from analogy runs as follows:

Premise 1 I observe a close correlation between my behavior and what I am thinking and feeling.
Premise 2 I observe others' behavior.
Premise 3 From others' behavior I can infer how they think and feel. [Generalization from P1]
Conclusion I can infer how they think and feel.

The argument from analogy is not only an obvious response to the problem of other minds. It also has merit. Indeed, we use it all the time in everyday life. I observe someone behaving in a puzzling way and ask myself, "What could be motivating this behavior?" To find out, I "put myself in her shoes," that is to say, I imagine what I would be thinking and wishing and feeling if I were behaving that way. I then conclude that she is probably thinking and wishing and feeling something like the same things. This technique for figuring out what is going on in the mind of another person is called EMPATHY, and it is nothing more than an application of the argument from analogy.[4]

Here is why the argument from analogy works when it does. The skeptic supposes that there could be radical differences between the sensations in *you* that accompany external stimuli and the sensations in others that accompany the same external stimuli. But most of the time we do not seem to find any such differences. Most of the time it seems that if the accompanying sensations were radically different, there would be differences in behavior. For example, if ice cream tasted to Mary as pickles taste to you, then Mary's mouth would pucker when she eats ice cream. Or again, if ice cream tasted really spicy to Mary, her eyes would water, and she would perspire when she ate it. But Mary, we may suppose, reacts just as we do when she eats ice cream: her mouth doesn't pucker, and her eyes don't water, etc. So, we conclude, ice cream does not taste drastically different to Mary.

But now ask, when exactly *do* arguments from analogy work? They work when we already have a firm conviction that others have minds and that most of the time what is going on in their mind when they behave in a certain way is similar to what is going on in our mind when we behave in a certain way. When we encounter the occasional knowledge gap, we can then use an argument from analogy to fill it. But how can we *justify* this conviction? Could arguments from analogy be the mechanism for *forming and justifying* our beliefs that the relationship between minds and behavior in others is similar to the relationship between them in us?

Since arguments from analogies are so useful once the system of ascribing minds and particular mental states to others is up and running, it is not easy to see why they couldn't be the tool that we use to set up our beliefs about the relationship in the first place. But they could not be. One problem is this. If the argument from analogy is all that we relied on from the beginning, then we would be generalizing from one case, namely the case of oneself, to the whole rest of humankind. And as Wittgenstein (1953, §293) put it, "How can I generalize the *one* case so irresponsibly?" Here is a comparison. Suppose that you saw a stream in the mountains and discovered that there is a correlation between this stream and carrying gold-laden silt (you cannot see the gold but have discovered that it is there). You then reason as follows: "Every time water takes the form of a stream, there will be gold in it." This reasoning would be so ridiculous that no one would take you seriously for a second. Yet this is exactly the form that the argument from analogy takes: you are reasoning from one case of a correlation between behavior and something inner to all such other cases. Go back to the case of Mary and the ice cream. The objection advanced by this example—that if things tasted different to Mary from how they taste to us, she would react differently from us—assumes a *correlation* between inner experience and outer reactions. But you've observed this correlation only in your own case.

So how *do* we reach our robust, almost unshakeable conviction that others have minds? There is a lot of controversy about this question, but here is one possible answer. This answer also raises a second problem with the idea that the argument from analogy could be our basic strategy for linking behavior and the mind. Babies are able to recognize others as having minds (as caring about them, being angry, watching them, etc.) very early, certainly within the first six months. According to the argument from analogy, they would have to have first observed a correlation between their own behavior and what they feel and then to have transferred this correlation to other people in their environment. But that cannot be right, for at least three reasons:

• Young babies often cannot do the things that they can interpret as backed by feelings, etc., in others.
• Young babies have little ability to observe correlations of any kind.
• Young babies are able to recognize feelings of care, anger, etc., in others *before* they can recognize such feelings—or indeed anything very much—in themselves.

From all this, it would seem to follow that arguments from analogy *cannot* be the mechanism we use to set up our basic conviction that others have minds, though of course we have not said anything about what mechanism we *do* use (some theorists think that this conviction is innate [compare the discussion of innate knowledge of language in chapter 3]).

At this point the argument-from-analogy theorist can try one last move: "OK, so we don't use arguments from analogy to *get* our conviction that others have minds, but we can still use them to *justify* this conviction." Well, it is not clear that the conviction *needs* any further justification. What could justify it better than our everyday encounters with other people (this is a version of Moore's principle, which we introduced as (8) in chapter 2)? Even if justification is needed, however, the argument from analogy could never provide it. As we said above, it generalizes from a single instance, and such reasoning is worthless as a justification of anything.

The argument from analogy faces other problems too. Here's a third. It simply *assumes* that there is no problem about knowledge of one's own self, and it needs this assumption. However, if we do not have knowledge of what we ourselves are perceiving, thinking, feeling, etc., then we would not have knowledge of what is correlated in *us* with *our* behavior, and the argument from analogy would collapse.

A fourth problem. On the argument from analogy, it ought to be impossible for color-blind people to know when others are perceiving colors, for there is nothing in themselves to correlate color-experience behavior with. But that is not the case. Color-blind people are in fact about as good at knowing when others are experiencing color as anybody else.

Indeed, the argument from analogy may BEG THE QUESTION. For me to reason from others' behavior to their mental life on the basis of my behavior and mental life, I must *already have reason to believe that behavior and mental life are linked in the same way in others* (for example, that puckering up behavior is apt to go with acidic tastes in others as it does in me). But, it would seem, that is just what the argument from analogy is meant to allow us to infer.

To sum up, the most that arguments from analogy can do for us is to help us figure out what someone might be feeling in specific instances, when we already have a robust conviction that the person in question feels basically as we do. That's not much. Let's see if there aren't better approaches.

7   There Is a Problem: Underlying Neurological Similarity Is the Solution

This argument is based on the fact that all humans are physically similar; in particular, we have the same kind of brain, the same sorts of nerves, etc. The argument is simple: others who share your physical makeup will feel the same things that you do. But notice, this is just a particular form of the argument from analogy. It runs afoul of all the same problems. As the other-minds skeptic would be quick to ask, "How do you know that other people's neuronal firings produce the same sensations as your neuronal firings?" From your own case? Then you *don't* know that other people's neuronal firings produce the same sensations as your neuronal firings. How could you safely generalize from one case in this way? And so on.

The skeptic's points so far could be summarized as follows: At most, the only correlation between behavioral and/or neural states and mental states that you've observed is in yourself, and you cannot generalize from that one instance to everyone else. Besides which, she may add, it is not so clear that you do know your own mental life so well, especially when you are young, or that you based your ability to ascribe mental states to others when you were young on any such knowledge. What we need is some way to make inference (2):

(2) Something outside an agent, namely, behavior → the way things
    seem to the agent

And arguing by analogy with our own case is not it. Without (2), the fact that you are behaviorally or physically like other humans lends no support to the conclusion that what goes on inside their minds is at all like what goes on inside yours.

8   There Is No Problem: Identity Theory, Behaviorism, and Wittgensteinianism

To satisfy his skeptical doubt, it seems that the skeptic demands nothing less than that we be able to look directly into another's mind. And that, everyone agrees, you cannot do. But perhaps the demand itself is the problem. Perhaps minds are not as the skeptic conceives them, something so separate and cut off from bodies that the mind could go one way, the body another. Perhaps, in short, there are ways to satisfy (2) that do not require the impossible "looking into another's mind." In particular, if true, the *identity theory* would satisfy (2) without such a look.

Identity Theory

As we saw in chapter 4, the identity theory maintains, in broad outline, that the mind is the brain, in the same way that water is H_2O or lightning is electricity. That is to say, every type of mental state or event is one and the same as some type of brain state or event. If this theory is right, the problem of other minds is potentially solvable. When we know enough of the right kinds of things about a brain, then we will know what mental states those brain states and events are. Unfortunately, the identity theory faces some problems—some general ones that we examined in chapter 4 and others specific to its possibilities as a solution to the problem of other minds, which we will examine now.

The first and most obvious problem is that we already seem to know a great deal about other minds, yet most of us know virtually nothing about the brains of the other people we deal with. If so, we are getting our knowledge of other minds from somewhere other than our knowledge of other brains. This does not close either the possibility that knowledge of other brains might be *another* way of getting knowledge of other minds or the possibility that it might be a way of *justifying* our beliefs about other minds, but it does entail that knowledge of other brains is not our primary means of acquiring these beliefs.

Second, some of the most powerful arguments against the identity theory are also arguments that knowledge of brains could never give us knowledge of minds. There is multiple realizability (discussed in chapter 4): any given bit of the brain could be participating in many different mental functions at different times. Then there is the "brain plus" argument that to know what mental states a brain contains, you must know how that state is hooked up to other states of the brain, to the world, to other people, and so on (for more on this, see chapter 8). In short, the old dream of brain reading, of reading the mind off the brain, is probably just that: a dream.

One response to this critique of the identity theory as a solution to the problem of other minds is to suggest that we focused on the wrong thing. Instead of seeking to read the mind off the brain, this line of thought goes, perhaps we should seek to read the mind off *behavior*.

Behaviorism

Behaviorism, if true, would certainly satisfy (2) without any need to look into something behind behavior. Behaviorism is the view that the mind *just is* behavior: what it is to have a mind is to behave and to have dispositions to behave in certain complex ways.[5] For example, what it *is* to know arithmetic, says the behaviorist, is to say or write the right answer and to have a disposition to say or write the right answer when rows of numbers linked by arithmetic signs are put in front of you. Thus, when you see another's behavior, you are *seeing* their mind. There is nothing mental *behind* the behavior at all. The idea that the mind is something behind behavior is the myth of the ghost in the machine, as the British philosopher Gilbert Ryle put it. The idea is just a massive confusion.

Behaviorism obviously denies that the skeptic's demand needs to be met. To *know* what is going on in the mind of another, or even to know that others have minds, we *do not* need to get behind their behavior and directly observe what is going on in their minds. All we need to do is to observe their behavior and what is stimulating them to behave in this way.

Wittgensteinianism

An approach to the problem of other minds that is either a particular version of behaviorism or closely related to behaviorism derives from the work of Wittgenstein. Since this approach also denies that there is any problem of other minds and the problems with it are much the same as with behaviorism, let us introduce this approach too and assess the two of them together.

Wittgenstein's approach to our knowledge of other minds begins with one of his famous aphorisms: "My attitude towards him is an attitude towards a soul. I am not of the *opinion* that he has a soul" (1953, 178e). Now, exactly what Wittgenstein meant by this is far from obvious, and there is room for lots of disagreement. But the general idea seems to be something like this: We do not arrive at the belief that another has a mind by assembling evidence from how they behave (or the way their brain is)

Figure 7.1
The duck/rabbit

and inferring from this evidence that the body in front of us must have a mind. Rather, that another has feelings, thoughts, hopes, wishes, etc., is something of which we are *directly aware*. Unfortunately, at this point the story becomes short on details. Again one can see the general idea: Wittgenstein thinks that the difference between seeing another as having a mind and seeing another as a zombie (a body without a mind) is something like the difference between seeing figure 7.1 as a duck and seeing it as a rabbit. We can see the figure as one or the other, but in neither case do we *infer* what it is a figure of from other information. We just see it one way or the other. Minds are manifest in behavior. (The duck-rabbit case is different from other people in one respect. It is entirely optional whether we see the figure as a duck or as a rabbit, but it is not optional in the same way that we see others as having minds. Indeed, in practice it is virtually impossible not to see others as having minds.)

Wittgenstein's story is a decided improvement on classical behaviorism in a number of respects. Whereas behaviorists have to reduce all mental life to behavior and dispositions to behave, a very implausible reduction, Wittgenstein leaves it open as to what mental life consists in. Indeed, sometimes he seems to go so far as to suggest that this is something about which nothing much can be said. Likewise, Wittgenstein's account fits certain kinds of experience better than the behaviorist account. For example, when we see a young child as happy, sad, playful, attentive, etc., it is not plausible to say that we are simply observing patterns of stimuli-induced behavior—there seems to be more to their feelings than that—yet it is plausible to say that we see the young child's mood directly; we do not infer it from anything else we observe. (It is not as though we have to reason, "Oh, little Samy has his eyes fixed on the page, so he must be paying attention." We seem to see little Samy's attentiveness more directly than that.)

The problem that both behaviorists and Wittgensteinians face is that when you try to fill in their story, it is very hard to do so. For the behaviorist, the problem, in a nutshell, is that there is just too much going on between stimulus and behavioral response to maintain that the mind is nothing more than the behavioral response. For both behaviorists and Wittgensteinians, there is the problem of INTROSPECTION: one person, namely, the person having a given thought, feeling, etc., can become directly aware of the thought in a way *totally different* from the way in which others become aware of them. How can we account for this difference if mental life is just behavior? (Wittgensteinians try to do so, but it is difficult to follow their reasoning.)

Finally, by the age of seven or eight, human beings become very good at feeling one way while behaving in another (covering up one's feelings, playacting, lying, etc.). In these cases, the mental life of the other is *not* something of which anyone else can be directly aware. Behaviorists and Wittgensteinians try to address this problem. Behaviorists talk of conditioned responses to suppress other responses. Wittgensteinians talk about the general system of language for the mind and behavior, urging that we could not learn specific breeches such as lying and acting unless we already had the general system and it worked, and anyway, source "mindedness" is always manifest in the behavior. To assess either response would take us too far afield, but neither looks very plausible on the face of it.

9   There Is a Problem: Inference to the Best Explanation Is the Solution

I guess of all my uncles, I liked Uncle Cave Man the best. We called him Uncle Cave Man because he lived in a cave and because sometimes he ate one of us. Later on we found out he was a bear.

Is there any way out? There is one last approach, one that accepts that there is a problem (that is to say, that we cannot just "read off" the mental life of others from their bodies and behavior) but thinks that it has a solution. It is called the *inference-to-the-best-explanation approach.* It tends to be favored by FUNCTIONALISM and other theories of mind that take natural science as their model. We introduced inferences to the best explanation in chapter 2 and discussed them at length in chapter 3 in connection with how we acquire linguistic knowledge. The problem of other minds is another place where the notion has been put to work.

The notion goes as follows: Why do scientists believe, for example, that electrons exist? Because postulating that electrons exist allows us to explain a whole bunch of observable phenomena. More strongly, electrons give us the *best explanation available* of these phenomena, so we postulate that electrons exist. Now, has anyone ever seen an electron? No. Is it even possible that anyone could see an electron, even with the strongest microscope? No. (They are too small.) So we will never directly observe that electrons exist. Does this inability to observe them make us skeptical about their nature or existence? Not especially.

Now apply this approach to minds. On this approach, the reasoning that we use to ascribe mental states to others is just like the reasoning that we use to postulate the existence of electrons: postulating mental states gives us the best explanation of observable behavior. Thus, when we see someone walking down the street and going into a store and we ascribe to him a *desire* for some milk and a *belief* that the store is a good place to get it, what we are really saying is that postulating this desire and this belief gives us the *best explanation* of the person's behavior, given the context they are in and what we know of their background. And that's the solution to the problem of other minds.

Notice that this approach avoids some of the more obvious problems facing the argument from analogy. Because it is not based on a single case (namely, oneself) but is developed by applying general standards of explanation to a whole bunch of behavior, we do not feel the same need for an independent justification for the inference, any more than we feel such a need in the case of electrons.

Likewise, it avoids the most obvious problems of the various "no problem" approaches. It does not hold that mental states are really something else, as the identity theory and behaviorism both do in their different ways, but on the other hand it does not cut mentality loose from other factors (whether behavioral or neurological), as dualism and Wittgensteinianism tend to do. Let's explore this last point a little further. Most philosophers feel that mentality has to be linked either to brains or to behavior if it is not to float free of our cognitive grasp altogether. Identity theorists try to link it to brains, behaviorists and functionalists to behavior (behaviorists say that it *simply is* behavior; functionalists think that it can only be understood as what causes behavior). Wittgensteinians, by contrast, seem to think that we can apply mental concepts to other people directly, without any intermediary. This makes their view hard to grasp.

The inference-to-the-best-explanation approach avoids this problem. On this approach, we do not observe others' mental life directly. What we observe directly are behavior, context, and background. We ascribe mental states to others in order to *explain* what we observe in these observations.

Unfortunately, the inference-to-the-best-explanation approach faces some problems of its own. The first is something that we just saw create problems for Wittgensteinianism, namely introspection, the direct awareness that each of us has of his or her own mental states. The analogy to postulating electrons seems to break down over introspection. *Nobody* has direct access to electrons, but *each person* has direct access to some of his or her own mental states. And that poses the following problem: for that person, there *is* something better than inference to the best explanation about those mental states. That person has *direct access* to the mental states in question. And the problem that this poses is just the problem that got the whole business of other minds going in the first place: is there any way to get knowledge as good as this of the minds of anyone else?

The response of those who favor the best-explanation approach has to be to invoke the *problem of knowledge of self*. Perhaps the access that introspection gives us to our own mental states is not so good after all. Perhaps we are *not* in a better position with respect to knowing our own mental states than the physicist is with respect to having direct access to electrons. That's the argument.

Of course, this response will seem completely bizarre to many people. More seriously, maybe we're in doubt about what we are thinking or feeling in a few particularly complicated or emotionally loaded cases, but *most* of the time we have no trouble at all introspecting what we are thinking and feeling and wanting and planning, not in the slightest.

How good our access is to our own mental life is connected to one final concern. The following situation *seems* entirely possible. From your behavior the best explanation of how you are acting would be that you are angry. But you are not angry. That is to say, looking at you "from the outside," the best account of your behavior is that you are angry, but as you "look" at yourself from the first-person point of view, you see that you are not angry. If the inference-to-the-best-explanation approach is right, however, this *isn't* a possible position: whenever the best explanation of your behavior is that you are angry, then you just *are* angry—that is what it is to be angry, your own view of what you are feeling notwithstanding. Some people will find this result absurd: surely no one else's account of how to explain your behavior can determine that you are angry when you don't feel angry. So it appears that the best-explanation approach has a rather unpalatable consequence.[6] Unless we can deal with these objections, the approach is in serious trouble. It is time to turn to introspection and the problem of knowledge of self.

10   The Problem of Knowledge of Self

We just sketched two objections to the inference-to-the-best-explanation
approach to the problem of other minds. Both of them depend on introspection sometimes being more justified than inferences from behavior,
etc., to what best explains the behavior, etc. But is this so? Is our awareness of ourselves always, or even sometimes, more secure than inferences
from our behavior, etc., to what is going on in us? Put otherwise, the
contrast between our awareness of our own mental life and our awareness
of the mental life of others is one of the main sources of the problem of
other minds. From the point of view of justifying beliefs about mental
states or events, how real is this contrast?

From the standpoint of forming justified beliefs about what our own
and others' mental life is like, there are a variety of reasons to suspect that
the contrast is less real than it might appear. The first is this. As Kant
already saw two hundred years ago, we are "conscious even [of] our own
selves only as we appear to ourselves, not as we are" (1927 [1781/1787],
B153). What did he mean? When put in argument form, it looks something like this:

Premise 1 When we are aware of ourselves, what we have is a *representation* of ourselves. (Argument: When we are aware of ourselves, we
merely have an *image* or a *description* or a *perception* of ourselves. We do
not somehow pull our very selves magically into our consciousness.)
Premise 2 Any representation can be wrong.
Conclusion Therefore, our beliefs about what we are feeling, seeing,
thinking, etc., can be wrong.

So much seems obvious. Interestingly, for a very long time, most philosophers in the European tradition flatly rejected this apparently obvious
point. They maintained that we cannot be wrong about our own mental
states, not the fairly simple ones at any rate. Some called this INCORRIGI-
BILITY. Thus, they urged, you cannot believe that you are in pain and yet
not be in pain. You cannot seem to yourself to want something and yet
not want it. And so on. What made them think this, among other things,
is that representations of one's own mental states are special in one
important way. Very often the representation and what it represents can
be one and the same. Thus, for example, if I am aware of imagining what
I will have for dinner, it is probably that act of imagining, not any other
representation, that makes me aware that I am imagining.

This difference is not enough to support the idea of incorrigibility, however. To be aware of our mental states, we need the mental state of which we are aware, but we also need to recognize it as something, characterize it in one way or another. As Kant also saw, to be aware of something, we need not just input from what we are aware of but also concepts to describe it (1927 [1781/1787], A51). And when we apply concepts, i.e., when we describe something, we can make mistakes and apply the wrong concepts, change our mind about what concepts to apply, etc., even when we are dealing with our own mental states. In sum, we are aware of ourselves as we appear to ourselves, not as we are.

That there is room for error even about our own mental states is confirmed by a great deal of evidence from cognitive psychology and elsewhere. Indeed, we sometimes even make things up in introspection (CONFABULATION). Here is an interesting example. A subject is hypnotized and told to do something silly in five minutes such as patting his head and burping. He is told that he will obey this command but have no memory of being given it. He is then brought out of the trance. Invariably, five minutes later the subject pats his head and burps. What is interesting is that when asked why he did these strange acts, he *makes up a reason*. ("I did it because I suddenly had an itch on my scalp and felt gas in my stomach." Right.) In short, we can be wrong about what we are introspecting in ourselves in all sorts of ways.[7]

If introspection is prone to all these ills, then though we have *special* access to our own mental states, a kind of access that no one else has, we do not have *specially secure* access from the point of view of justifying our subsequent beliefs about what we are thinking, feeling, etc. And from this it follows that the objections to the inference-to-the-best-explanation approach do not work. Here's why.

The first objection was that, for one person, there is something better for knowledge of mind than inference to the best explanation. The person in question is the person who has the mental state. That person has *direct access* to the mental state in question. True, but as we have just seen, *direct* access is not necessarily *secure* access. We can be wrong about our own mental states too, and when we are, we need to examine our behavior, etc., to see what is really going on in us as much as anyone else does. Normally, we do not do so, of course, but then normally we do not check our judgments about the *external* world either. Normally, we trust both our introspective and our perceptual abilities. It does not follow that either is fully reliable.[8] The other objection was that it was absurd to suppose that the best explanation of our behavior, from a third-person point of view, could trump what we are feeling. But, once we realize that introspection can get what we are feeling wrong, this is no longer absurd —unlikely, perhaps, but not absurd.

Unfortunately, these responses, powerful though they are, do not *entirely* resolve the problem of other minds. There are some mental states where something like incorrigibility does seem to be the case. Think of feeling a short, sharp pain. How could I think I was feeling a pain like that and be wrong? Or think of how something *seems* to me. I can be wrong about how it is, but can I be wrong about how it seems to me? Dennett (1991, chap. 3) stresses this point. If so, it would follow *for these mental states* that I *do* have more secure access to my own mental states than I do to anyone else's. For these mental states, then, we have not resolved the problem of other minds.

11   Conclusion

For most mental states, introspection and the grasp we have of our own mental states do not pose a problem for the inference-to-the-best-explanation approach to the problem of other minds. If so, for these mental states, we have a solution to the problem. It is not a solution that everyone will like, because of its implication that often we do not have direct, guaranteed access to what is going on in ourselves mentally, but it is an solution. Interestingly, it is precisely the approach taken by contemporary cognitive science to the problem. Unfortunately, it does not work for the relatively small group of mental states where we do seem to have specially secure access to our own states.

We will conclude with one last remark. It would be a very good thing to be able to resolve the problem of other minds. We spent chapters 4, 5, and 6 examining what the mind is like. It would be strange to have to turn around and admit that we don't have any knowledge of it. As we have seen, we are not entirely out of the woods on this issue. And more troubles are ahead. We will meet them in the infamous Chinese room in the next chapter.

Study Questions

1. What is the difference between direct knowledge and knowledge by inference? Give examples of each. Do we know other people's mental states directly or via inference?

2. Explain the difference between inverted qualia and absent qualia. Is either one really a concern?

3. Is it possible to know that nonhuman animals have thoughts, feelings, etc.? Is it possible to know that their experiences are like ours? How?

4. What is a zombie? What do zombies have to do with skepticism about other minds?

5. Why might doubting something require having a mind? If doubting does require that one have a mind, is it possible to doubt that one has a mind? What does this suggest about self-knowledge?

6. How does the ice-cream thought experiment raise concerns about inverted qualia?

7. Explain how one's views on mind-body relations intersect with one's approach to skepticism about other minds. In particular, why do radical behaviorists not worry about skepticism of this sort?

8. What is the argument from analogy? What is its relationship to the argument from neurological similarity?

9. Describe the various "no problem" approaches. Do any of them work? Justify your answer.

10. If there is a problem of other minds, is inference to the best explanation the solution? Justify your answer.

11. Is there a reason to suppose that every representation, no matter what its nature, can be mistaken? How does this supposition lead to worries about self-knowledge?

Suggested Further Readings

An accessible treatment of general issues surrounding skepticism about other minds may be found in T. Nagel 1987. In addition, see the Suggested Further Readings in chapters 1 and 2.

On absent qualia and inverted qualia in the philosophy of mind, see Shoemaker 1975 and Block 1978. On direct knowledge versus inference, see Ayer 1956, Austin 1962, Ryle 1949, Sellars 1997 [1956], and Wittgenstein 1953. An introductory explanation of Wittgenstein's views may be found in Kenny 1973. The argument from analogy is explored in detail in Russell 1948. The relevant parts are reprinted in Nagel and Brandt 1965, along with related selections by Norman Malcolm (a follower of Wittgenstein) and A. J. Ayer (an important opponent).

The use of inference to the best explanation to understand the minds of others is explored in many of Dennett's writings. He argues that, appearances notwithstanding, the third-person approach cannot be trumped in general by first-person authority. See especially Dennett 1991.

For Kantian reflections on the limits of self-knowledge, see Brook 1994 and Kant 1927 [1781/1787]. For another point of view, see Descartes 1931 [1637], 1931 [1641]. Descartes suggests, in effect, that it is impossible to doubt that one has a mind, because doubting is a mental state.

Chapter 8

A New Approach to Knowledge and Mind

To me, boxing is like a ballet, except there's no music, no choreography, and the dancers hit each other.

Jack Handey

We began this book with six questions. They introduced theory of knowledge (epistemology) and philosophy of mind by highlighting some of the central issues. The questions were these:

1. What is knowledge?
2. What can we know?
3. How is knowledge acquired?
4. What is a mind?
5. How are minds related to bodies?
6. Can a person ever really know the mind of another?

The first three questions are central to epistemology, while the next two are central to philosophy of mind. The last belongs equally in theory of knowledge and philosophy of mind. These aren't the only questions that we addressed. We also discussed free will and knowledge of language. But, as we said, the above six questions are central to epistemology and philosophy of mind.

In this final chapter we will return to these six questions but in a somewhat different way. Up to now we have addressed them as philosophers have traditionally done. In this final chapter we want to introduce a new, recently developed approach to them, an approach that brings philosophical and scientific thinking on these issues much closer to one another. Let us begin by setting the stage.

For most of human history, researchers did not draw a sharp distinction between philosophy and science. Indeed, until this century, many sciences were thought of as simply branches of philosophy. (To this day, a senior professorship in physics at the University of Cambridge is called the Chair of Natural *Philosophy*). Then about one hundred years ago philosophers started to think that what they did was very different from any science.

Once this split settled in, philosophers started to talk about seeking a kind of knowledge quite different from what scientists seek and using very different methods and kinds of analysis to do so. (Recall the discussion of these themes at the end of part I). As has often been noted, philosophers do not need laboratories to carry out their investigations. This by itself seemed enough to make philosophy quite different from most, if not all, sciences. (Partitioning philosophy off from the natural sciences in this way conveniently overlooks the fact that mathematics, linguistics, theoretical physics, archeology, evolutionary theory, and parts of other disciplines such as economics do not use laboratories for their research, either.)

In addition, many philosophers believed that science, whatever its power elsewhere, offered little to their enterprise. Philosophy might have something to offer the sciences, ran this line of thinking; in particular, philosophy can help science to get its concepts and the general nature of the scientific enterprise clearer. But the sciences have little to offer philosophy. From the other side and contrary to what the philosophers may have thought, many scientists doubted that philosophy had much to offer science. (This was true in particular of experimental psychology. Philosophical analysis of issues about mind and knowledge, such as those we've examined in this book, played little role in their thinking.)

These two notions—that sciences such as psychology have little to contribute to our understanding of traditional philosophical issues such as knowledge and mind and that philosophy of knowledge and mind has little to contribute to the science of these topics—are really bizarre when you think about them for a minute. Philosophy of mind and psychology are both concerned with perception, belief, memory, reasoning, representation, the relation of cognition to the brain, and so on. Philosophy of language and linguistics are both concerned with knowledge of language and the nature of meaning. How could such central parts of our intellectual tradition as psychology and linguistics have little or nothing to contribute to a philosophical understanding of knowledge and mind? And how could philosophy of knowledge and mind, with its 2,500-year heritage of study of these topics, have little or nothing to contribute to psychology and linguistics?

Well, these carefully constructed walls of mutual indifference were bound to collapse, and, we are happy to report, they have. A sense that most of the wide variety of approaches to cognition should work together to enrich one another began to grow about forty years ago. It came together in a very concrete way in the 1970s in the form of a new field of study, COGNITIVE SCIENCE. (For further information about cognitive science, see Thagard 1996 or, for a somewhat more detailed treatment, Stillings 1995). Cognitive science is based on the idea that individual approaches to cognition have to influence and be influenced by the widest variety of other approaches if we are ever to develop a deep, comprehensive understanding of human cognition.

Just to fill this exciting new idea of combining all the approaches to cognition into a single, unified research program out a little, notice how diverse the initiating influences were. One major force behind the creation of cognitive science was the development of the computer. The first programmable computers were built in England during World War II to assist in breaking German military codes. For hundreds of years, philosophers and mathematicians have speculated that the mind might be something like a vast adding machine, a vast computer, but the invention of the computer gave this speculation some substance for the first time. In the early 1970s computers first became fast, powerful, and convenient enough to offer hope of actually seeing these speculations come true. The second major influence could not have been more different. It was Noam Chomsky's discoveries about the deep, complex structures that underlay language. Nowadays, cognitive science combines artificial intelligence, psychology, linguistics, philosophy, neuroscience and other disciplines and is beginning to unite these diverse activities into a single, comprehensive understanding of knowledge and mind.[1]

With this sketch of the context within which philosophy of knowledge and philosophy of mind now find themselves, let's turn to the new approach we mentioned. (A warning: some parts of this chapter are a bit complicated.)

1   Naturalizing Philosophy: How Philosophy Relates to Science

If philosophy of knowledge (epistemology) and philosophy of mind are joining forces with various empirical sciences of cognition in a unified approach to cognition, we need to understand better how philosophical approaches to cognition relate to the approaches found in empirical science. One way to connect epistemology and philosophy of mind to scientific approaches to cognition is to argue that, contrary to the dominant ideas about philosophy of the twentieth century until recently, philosophical approaches to knowledge and mind are, or should be, themselves scientific. The answers that philosophers give to, for example, the six questions at the beginning of this chapter are or should be scientific answers, in one way or another. Perhaps philosophers' answers are a bit more general than the usual scientific ones, but they are scientific all the same.

This approach to epistemology and philosophy of mind is called NATURALISM because it treats them either as, or at least as closely related to, natural science. (The NATURAL SCIENCES include physics, chemistry, and biology, and they study matter in interaction. They are contrasted with the SOCIAL SCIENCES, which study the nature and interactions of human beings. The difference between them is related to the difference between the scientific and manifest image that we examined in chapter 5.) There are at least four ways in which epistemology and philosophy of mind can be related to natural science. They amount to four different kinds of naturalizing. Let us call them WEAK NATURALISM, MODERATE NATURALISM, STRONGER NATURALISM, and STRONGEST NATURALISM.

Weak naturalism The idea that philosophical theories should be *consistent* with what science tells us about the world.

This form of naturalism says nothing about the methods of epistemology or philosophy of mind or even that philosophical theories in these areas are themselves scientific theories. It merely says that, because of the immense success of science over the past centuries, we had better make sure that our philosophical theories are at least consistent with what science has discovered about knowledge and mind. As should be clear, this book is clearly in sympathy with this kind of naturalizing, and we will not say anything more about it.

Moderate naturalism The idea that philosophy of knowledge and language should be *informed about* what empirical scientists have discovered about knowledge and mind.

This form of naturalism urges that what scientists have found out about how knowledge and mind actually work can help philosophers come to better philosophical theories about knowledge and mind, so philosophers had better make sure that they know what the scientists are doing. Again, we agree with this suggestion, as our frequent use of findings and examples from linguistics and psychology throughout the book makes clear. For instance, in chapter 3 we drew on results from theoretical linguistics and from the biological notion of innate capacities to help us understand certain philosophical issues about a priori knowledge of language. In chapter 5 when discussing the old dualist argument that minds cannot be divided but brains can be, we used the results of brain-bisection operations to help us understand how minds can and cannot be divided. Also in chapter 5, we used the example of connectionist computer systems to shed light on the relationship between language and thought. And in chapters 3 and 7, at a more general level, we drew on one of the standard modes of reasoning in science, namely inference to the best explanation, as a promising approach to the problem of other minds. These are all attempts to apply the results of scientific research to a philosophical issue.

We will discuss moderate naturalizing further, mainly to contrast it with stronger and strongest naturalism.

Stronger naturalism The idea that philosophical problems about knowledge and mind (and most everything else) are really scientific ones and can be adequately answered by using only the methods of science, natural science in particular.

This is the view that philosophy has no distinctive methods of its own, none that works anyway. The questions it has beat its head over for 2,500 years are scientific questions and need science to answer them. If we can show that something traditionally studied by philosophers, e.g., perception, can be treated entirely scientifically (for example, as information processing by the vision system or as electrochemical processes of neurons), that would be one way of naturalizing it in this stronger sense.

Strongest naturalism This view accepts stronger naturalizing but goes one step further. It holds that *neuroscience* is the basic science of knowledge and mind and that no theory of either that cannot ultimately be REDUCED to neuroscience is adequate.

Of the positions on the mind-body problem examined in chapters 4 and 5, behaviorists, neurophilosophers and many identity theorists accept that the mind can be naturalized in the strongest way. The difference between stronger and strongest naturalizing can be illustrated using the functionalist theory of mind. On this theory, as we saw, mental descriptions and explanations cannot be reduced to descriptions and explanations in neuroscience. Now, say that a functionalist theory can be developed using nothing but scientific methods. Such a theory would be a naturalist theory of the stronger kind, but because it is antireductionistic, it would not be a naturalist theory of the strongest kind.

In addition to the need to fit epistemology and philosophy of mind into the integrated project of cognitive science, another reason often given for naturalizing epistemology and philosophy of mind in one way or another is that science has made tremendous progress on every front and philosophy has made little progress on most fronts. If so, it makes sense to make sure that epistemology and philosophy of mind fit well with what science has discovered about knowledge and mind.

We have said that there seems to be little to object to in weak and moderate naturalism. What about the stronger and strongest varieties? These are the two views that urge that traditional philosophical questions about knowledge and mind are *nothing but* scientific questions, so using scientific methods is the only way answer to them. Let us group them together and call them s-NATURALISM (for 'strong naturalism').

S-naturalism The combination of stronger and strongest naturalism.

As we will see, even if one accepts weak and even moderate naturalism, there is reason to be a bit skeptical about s-naturalism.

One of the issues over which s-naturalism runs into trouble is VALUES. Natural sciences, almost by definition, are supposed to stick to the facts and avoid making judgments of value. Yet values are at the heart of what philosophers study. It is obvious that values are the main subject matter of ethics, political philosophy, and aesthetics, but they are also central to philosophy of knowledge and of mind. As well as being interested in how people do think, philosophers are interested in how they *should* think, in what *good* thinking is. As well as being interested in how people do form beliefs, philosophers are interested in how people *should* form their beliefs. And, to move up a level, as well as being interested in how we do study knowledge and mind, philosophers are interested in how we *should* study knowledge and mind. Philosophers are also interested in facts about how things *do* work, of course, but they are just as interested in *values*, i.e., issues about how things *should* work. This poses a problem for s-naturalism.

Science is generally concerned with facts. Psychology is the science of most direct interest here. It is concerned with how we do in fact acquire knowledge, how we do in fact know language, how the mind does in fact work. It is generally accepted, however, that studying only how things *do* work is seldom if ever enough by itself to give us a rational basis for deciding how they *should* work. If so, there are sharp limits on how much science can help us with questions of value. (As Hume put it over two hundred years ago, you can never derive an 'ought' from an 'is': you can never settle how people *ought to treat other people,* for example, by studying how people *do treat other people.*)

This limitation creates a serious problem when you try to treat philosophical questions as *purely* scientific. When a topic has a value dimension, it is hard to see how a purely scientific approach is going to give us what we need. Yet, as we just saw, values are a central part of philosophy of knowledge and of mind: philosophers of knowledge and of mind are interested not only in how things do work but also in how they should work.[2]

There are, it should be noted, two distinct ways of being interested in values. On the one hand, someone can be interested in what values a person (or a society) actually operates under. Thus an anthropologist might ask, "What are the core values of the Hopi?" Or a psychologist might inquire about a patient, "What are the norms she is in fact using to guide her decisions?" This is a purely descriptive enterprise. It is not concerned with what values we *should* have, how we *should* form our beliefs, etc. It is only when theorists ask these 'should' questions that they are studying values in a way that is distinctively philosophical. In summary, sociologists, anthropologists, and the like wish to describe value systems as they exist; philosophers are more interested in what values we should have. (We will return to this distinction and make it a bit more precise in the next section.)

With this by way of introduction to the drive to naturalize philosophy and the problems that philosophy's interest in values poses for this effort, let us now turn to some specific issues. Since weak and moderate naturalism are not very problematic, we will focus on s-naturalism. First we will look at knowledge. The drive to s-naturalize knowledge runs up against the problem of values in a very serious way. Then we will look at s-naturalizing our understanding of the mind/body and our knowledge of other minds.

2   Naturalizing Epistemology

Recall the three questions about knowledge with which we began this chapter:

1. What is knowledge?
2. What can we know?
3. How is knowledge acquired?

If we want to s-naturalize these questions, i.e., answer them using nothing but the resources of science, the first obstacle is that knowledge is value-laden. Indeed, values are at the very heart of the philosophical interest in knowledge (epistemology). Suppose that in answer to question 1 we say that knowledge is justified true belief. (This is one of the simplest and most plausible ways to think of knowledge, though, as we saw in chapter 2, the definition needs some further specification.) Now, justification and truth are both matters of value: justified beliefs are *good* beliefs, certainly better than unjustified ones, and similarly with true beliefs. We can debate what the goodness consists in, but terms like 'justification', 'truth', and even 'knowledge' itself are terms of approval, terms that rank things on a scale of better to worse.

Similarly in connection with question 2, when we ask "What can we know?" we are asking, "What can we come to have *justified* beliefs about?"—again, a value question. One common way to express this idea is to say that knowledge has a NORMATIVE DIMENSION; it involves not just factual information but also norms, i.e., standards for judging which beliefs about the facts are justified (i.e., are good) and which are not justified (i.e., are bad, or at best neutral). When we say that a belief is justified or true, we are not only making some factual claim about it, i.e., that it has such-and-such characteristics; we are also praising it because it meets a certain norm of goodness and thereby has a certain value. Thus, if epistemology is in part the study of matters of fact, such as what mechanisms and procedures yield justified true beliefs, it is also and crucially a study of values, of the norms by which we can reach good judgments about when a belief is justified and/or true.

This feature of epistemology has important implications for the issue of s-naturalizing epistemology, indeed for the relationship of epistemology to science in general. The scientific work in question is, principally, the psychology and neuroscience of perception and memory, of reasoning from perception and memory, of the general features of perceptions and memories, and so on—in short, the psychology and neuroscience of how we come to have the beliefs we have. Can such research answer the value questions about knowledge, i.e., can it tell us how to decide what beliefs we *should* accept, etc.?

Attempts to s-naturalize epistemology, i.e., to argue that most or all of the important questions about epistemology can be answered by science, tend to answer our three questions in something like the following way:

1. What is knowledge? Knowledge is whatever comes up to the standards for justified true belief that we as a society have in fact accepted as serving our needs. (And where do our standards for justifying our beliefs come from? How are they justified? As we will see in a moment, there is a big disagreement within naturalism about these questions.)

2. What can we know? To have knowledge is to have justified true beliefs, and science tells us what we can have justified true beliefs about.

3. How is knowledge acquired? Knowledge is acquired by the various information-gathering and belief-forming abilities that we have acquired as earlier species evolved into the species *Homo sapiens* and as those abilities have been refined by our best scientific practice over the centuries.[3]

Now, what about the value dimension in epistemology that we identified above? Question 3 needs a purely descriptive answer. That is to say, it is straightforwardly a scientific question. We will not say anything more about it. Questions 1 and 2 do raise value issues, as we saw. So we will focus on them. Can we answer the questions of value that arise in questions 1 and 2 purely s-naturalistically? To put the question a bit more concretely, could research in psychology and neuroscience into belief fixation, for example, answer the value questions about knowledge that arise in questions 1 and 2? Could such purely scientific research tell us how we *should* decide what beliefs are true, what beliefs are justified?

At this point, the difference between moderate naturalism and s-naturalism (also called RADICAL NATURALISM) becomes important. Moderate naturalizers answer this question with a 'no', s-naturalizers with a 'yes'. Moderate naturalists about epistemology accept that questions about the norms and values for knowledge cannot be either reduced to or answered by scientific investigations alone. Settling questions about norms and values also requires a special kind of philosophical thinking about the good and bad in beliefs, what we ought and ought not to believe. The naturalism of moderate naturalism comes in when we ask such questions as these: 'What procedures will yield beliefs that satisfy these norms of truth and justification?' 'How good are these mechanisms at yielding justified true beliefs?' 'Under what circumstances do these mechanisms work better or worse?' 'When can an agent be held responsible for accepting unjustified beliefs, and when will limitations in the mechanisms result in such shortcomings no matter what we do?' The important point is this. Moderates about naturalizing epistemology, e.g., Goldman (1992), urge that work in the natural sciences, psychology in particular, can teach us a great deal about the *procedures* of belief fixation but also hold that the *norms* cannot be naturalized. Put more succinctly, they hold that scientific work is highly relevant, even necessary, to understanding norms, but it is not sufficient.

By contrast, radical or s-naturalism about epistemology attempts to naturalize the norms too. That is to say, it argues that not only the procedures of belief fixation but also the norms by which we decide which beliefs are good (i.e., justified) and which ones are not *are themselves merely the result of natural processes.* Evolution is the most important such process. Moreover, there is no way to justify them beyond pointing out where they have come from and that they are the practices that we have in fact ended up with (Quine 1969 is often read this way).

Where did our standards for settling the truth or falsity of a belief come from? As we suggested, the most common answer among s-naturalizers is that they came from our evolutionary history. Here is how the story goes. Over the course of evolution, certain beliefs turned out to enhance survival and/or reproduction, others not to do so. We "naturally" value the beliefs that enhance survival or reproduction or both. Moreover, over time certain organisms turned out to be better at arriving at beliefs that enhanced survival and/or reproduction. The procedures by which these organisms selected their beliefs led them to live long enough to reproduce more often than organisms without these procedures, so we gave the beliefs of these more successful organisms a term of high praise: 'knowledge'—i.e., they were deemed good beliefs. We are the most successful example of such organisms ever created. This evolutionary story, says the radical naturalizer, is the only story about the origin of our epistemic norms that it is possible to give.

But what about the *justification* of our epistemic norms? How can we *justify* the standards that we have acquired from evolution, i.e., the standards for deciding when a belief is true or when someone is justified in accepting a belief? Here s-naturalizers continue to offer the same story, but with a twist. The story, again, is this: We accept as justified and/or true those beliefs that enhance survival and/or reproduction. All other beliefs count as unjustified or untrue. The twist is this. Science has spent the last 400 years refining the core values given to us by our evolutionary history to the point where each science now has its own precise methods and standards for deciding what is justified and true in that science. But science has been successful, indeed *incredibly* successful, at enhancing the capacity of much of the human race to survive and reproduce, and has been equally successful at helping us to protect ourselves from other things we don't like, such as hunger, disability, and pain. Thus, if we want to know what standards of truth and justification to accept, we should look to the ones that have worked in science. Indeed, since there is no place to look for such values except to science and its evolutionary background, science is the *only* place where we can find such values.[4]

To return to the question of values and norms, what the sketch of an s-naturalist epistemology that we have just completed reveals is that such an account has to have two parts. In the first part it shows that the *mechanisms* by which we acquire and relate beliefs are purely natural processes in the brain: perceptual processes in the visual cortex, inferential processes in the cerebral cortex, memory creation and recall processes in the hippocampus, etc. In the second part, it shows that the *norms for justifying* beliefs are also nothing but the result of natural processes. These norms can have no other origin, *and* they can have no other justification.

Moderate naturalizers think that radical or s-naturalizers are wrong about the second part. First, says moderate naturalism, science can tell us only that we have such and such norms, that they in fact play such and such roles in our processes of accepting or rejecting candidate beliefs, etc. It can never tell us which norms we *ought* to accept, which applications of norms *really do* yield true and justified beliefs. In a word, moderate naturalizers agree with Hume's dictum, quoted above: an 'ought' can never be derived from an 'is'. Second, moderate naturalizers urge, some of our norms in science could not have come from purely natural processes. Consider some of the weird and wonderful norms at work in physics. When particles are made to collide at high energy in a particle accelerator, it is sometimes enough to accept that a certain reaction is occurring if it is observed as seldom as once in ten million reactions. A strange norm such as this could never have any application in reasoning processes relevant to survival in nature, and so it could not have been built into us by evolution. It seems obvious that physicists did not get this norm from nature. They got it by thinking hard about the standards by which to settle difficult questions, e.g., questions about the ultimate particles that make up matter.

This brings us to a crucial point: even in pure natural science, questions about norms and their justifications arise. This is demonstrated by the observation we just made about the hard thinking about norms that goes on in science. And from this it would follow that radical or s-naturalism is not true even of natural science. The difference between moderate and s-naturalists is this: For the radicals, evolution and science are the final court of appeal—there is nowhere else to go. For the moderates, the norms that evolution and science have given us can themselves be assessed by reference to our epistemic interests, to our current needs, to what it takes to genuinely understand something, and so on. For the moderates, there is a higher court of appeal than evolution and science. The highest court of appeal is philosophical reflection on what matters to us, in the broadest possible sense of 'what matters to us', and on why it matters. As we just saw, by this analysis, even natural scientists are not radical naturalizers.

It is far too early to say which approach to naturalizing epistemology will win the day—if either. Scientific epistemology of any kind is in its infancy. If the moderate approach is right, there will remain a permanent place for a distinctively philosophical kind of reflection on the norms and values involved in belief fixation. If s-naturalism is right, all epistemology will eventually become a purely scientific study.

3   Naturalizing the Mind

Knowledge is not the only traditional philosophical issue that the s-naturalizers have attempted to reduce to natural science. Far from it. The next issue we will examine is the mind-brain problem familiar from earlier chapters. Recall the questions about the mind with which we began:

4. What is a mind?
5. How are minds related to bodies (and specifically, to brains)?
6. Can a person ever really know the mind of another?

To s-naturalize the mind would be to give complete and satisfactory answers to these questions (and others) entirely from science, specifically, from the sciences of psychology and neuroscience. Here too naturalizers face a serious challenge, though one different from the challenge they faced in connection with naturalizing knowledge. With knowledge, the main challenge was over the value dimension, the 'ought's and the 'ought-not's, the goods and the bads, of justified belief. With mind as well, the main challenge, as we will see, is that there is something that cannot be accounted for naturalistically. But the extra element is not exactly normative.[5]

Much of the work aimed at producing a scientific answer to questions 4 and 5 starts from a new question, one that was never asked in traditional philosophical treatments of the mind.[6] That question is this:

(1) How can minds process meanings?

Traditional philosophical treatments of the mind all left this key issue unexamined. They simply took it for granted that the mind works by "processing meanings" and never investigated how it can do this. It is very strange to simply assume this. Isn't the processing of meaning something that we should be trying to understand? Of course minds *somehow* process meanings, but *how* do they do this? That is the burden of question (1). It was lurking behind the scenes near the end of chapter 5. It is now time to examine it.

Question (1) highlights that extra element we just mentioned: the something about the mind that looks like it cannot be treated scientifically. The something in question is *meaning*, sometimes called 'content'. How, one wants to ask the s-naturalizer, can meaning be studied scientifically? In particular—and here we run directly into the problem posed by (1)—how can one construct a scientific model of the processing of meanings? Let's try to make this question for naturalizers a bit more precise.

First, what is meaning, as talked about here? There is one obvious sense in which our thoughts have meaning: they matter to us; we care about them. Another way to put this is to say that they are significant and important to us. But when philosophers ask (1), they have something more specific in mind. Recall the notion of INTENTIONALITY introduced in chapter 4. As the doctrine of intentionality tells us, thinking a thought has two elements: the act of thinking and what is being thought about. The nature of the second element, the CONTENT of the thought, is what is in question in (1). What are mental contents like? Two things seem clear.

First, mental contents stand for (picture, represent) something else. If I am thinking about what graduate school to attend, then that thought pictures or represents a graduate school to me—a graduate school in general, not any particular graduate school. Since the thought is in my head and graduate schools are outside it, there has to be something in my head that stands for or represents something outside it. This is the first thing that is meant by saying that the mind processes meanings: our mental states are about something; they have INTENTIONALITY.

Second, the contents of mental states are connected to the contents of *other* mental states by what they mean. Someone cannot, for example, consistently believe that everyone dies *and* that Rob will live forever, because what 'Everyone dies' *means* is that no one lives forever, Rob included (too bad for Rob). As was suggested in chapter 4, relationships of meaning (semantic relationships) may be quite different from cause-and-effect relationships. So the second thing that is meant by saying that the mind processes meanings is this: the contents of mental states are connected to the contents of other mental states by what they mean, e.g., by relationships of implication.

To make the objection to s-naturalizing the mind clearer, recall that in much current research the mind is thought of as a computer. One obvious way for a radical naturalizer to show how *minds* process meanings would be to lay out how a *computer* could process meanings. But—and this is a key point—if it turns out that computers cannot process meanings, then for the s-naturalizer there must be something suspect about the idea that minds process meaning (however implausible it is to say this).

Now we ask, Do computers process meanings, in the sense just elaborated? It is, to say the very least, not clear that they do. All they process are streams of electrons that encode strings of 1s and 0s, usually in the form of switches being on or off, logic gates being open or closed. It is very plausible to hold that all the meaning in what they do is provided by us when we interpret the results of their activity.

To see this, think of a small calculator that adds, subtracts, multiplies, and divides. Does it do arithmetic? In one important sense, it does not. It has no notion of numbers, it does not know what '+' means, it can't tell whether what occurs on the one side of an '=' sign is really equal to what occurs on the other side. All it does is shunt streams of electrons, set off when its keys are pushed, through various gates until they get to the end of the process and cause certain tiny lights in the display to go on. It is we who interpret some of the keys as entering numbers, others as giving arithmetic instructions, and it is for us that the patterns of light mean the answer.

Now generalize the question. Can *any* computer do more than this, no matter how big or fast? The answer is, at the very least, quite unclear. (We will say a bit more about this issue in the next section in connection with s-naturalizing our knowledge of other minds.) And now comes the crucial question for the project of s-naturalizing the mind: Can science treat us as anything more than a computer in this respect? If computers just crunch meaningless patterns of electrons and the meaning comes from an outside interpretation, how can science model humans as doing anything more? For notice what scientists say that *we* are: our brain is just a massively complex pattern of neurons; all our "thinking" too is supposedly merely a matter of electrochemical activity in us—in our case, it consists of highly coordinated changes in the rates at which neurons fire and then cause other neurons to fire. If the streams of electrons in computers don't add up to processing meaning, how do the streams of firing frequencies in us add up to processing meanings? In sum, it seems that there cannot be a scientific account of the processing of meaning in computers and that, from a scientific perspective, humans are no more than biological computers. If so, the cost of naturalizing the mind, paradoxically enough, is that we have to locate the meanings that minds process somewhere else.

We may summarize the argument that led us to this surprising implication as follows:

Premise 1 Human minds process meanings.

Premise 2 Computers, no matter how complex, cannot process meanings.

Conclusion 1 Processing meaning as human minds do cannot be done by a computer.

Premise 3 But brains are no more than complex biological computers.

Conclusion 2 Brains cannot process meanings. [By P2 and P3]

Premise 4 If minds process meanings but brains cannot, then meanings must involve more than the brain.

Conclusion 3 Meanings must involve more than the brain.

Motivated by the problem of meanings in computers and this sort of argument, a new approach to (1) has sprung up in the past twenty-five years or so, one totally different from anything in traditional philosophy of mind. The key idea in this approach is the idea that, in Hilary Putnam's memorable phrase, "Meanings just ain't in the head" (1975). Rather, blind computational processes in computers, blind firings of neurons in us, get meaning by being hooked up to the world outside the computer or the brain. The traditional idea that meanings are in the head is called INTERNALISM ABOUT MEANINGS. The new picture of meaning is called EXTERNALISM ABOUT MEANINGS. Recall question 4, What is a mind? On the externalist picture, the answer to question 4 is that the mind is a complex system made up of *both* the brain *and* its relationships to its world. (It was to allow for this possibility that we introduced the notion of 'brain plus' in chapter 4.)

One paradoxical result of the new externalist picture is that, in one clear sense, minds *don't* process meanings. Like computers, the mind also processes merely uninterpreted strings of some sort. Thanks to evolution (or perhaps culture), these strings happen to stand for other things outside us. But the mind is not "processing this relationship"—whatever that would be. It is merely processing the string itself. (See Fodor 1994 for detailed development of this idea.)

Externalism opens the door wide for s-naturalism. Externalism moves one of the most difficult issues about the mind, namely meanings, over to the mind's relationship to its environment. It then argues that these relationships are just perfectly ordinary cause-and-effect relationships, not some special relationship of implication such as we discussed earlier. And so s-naturalism is off and running. If what is inside the mind is nothing but blind, mechanical processes and the mind's relationships to the world are nothing but straightforward cause-and-effect relations, there should be nothing in the way of a purely scientific, completely naturalistic account of the mind. Externalists can be seen as urging that P1 and P2 hinge on the FALLACY OF EQUIVOCATION. In one sense, neither the human mind nor computers process meanings; instead, they process strings that happen to correlate with items of the environment. In another sense, minds do process meanings, precisely by processing strings, but in *this* sense of 'process meanings', computers too can process meanings. So, on one of these two readings of 'process meanings', P2 is true but P1 is false; on the other reading of 'process meanings', P1 is true but P2 is false. Whichever way one reads 'process meanings', there is no problem for s-naturalism.

To be sure, on the externalist picture, a naturalistic or any other adequate account of the mind will be a bit more complicated than we might have expected. To study the mind, for externalists, it is not enough to study just what is inside human beings. We also have to study how they are hooked up to their environment. More specifically, we have to study how what *is* entirely inside them, namely neurons and their activity, is hooked up to the world. If so, to understand the mind, we have to understand it as a complex brain/world system.[7]

This brings us to question 5, How are minds related to bodies? Specifically, how are they related to the brain? Much of what we have said above in connection with meaning and the mind is relevant here because an s-naturalistic theory will also be a completely materialistic theory. So let's focus on the question of how different kinds of materialistic theory sit vis-à-vis s-naturalism about the mind. We now need to bring back the distinction between *stronger naturalism* and *strongest naturalism*. As we said earlier in this chapter, behaviorism, identity theory, and neurophilosophy fall under strongest naturalism with no difficulty. Behaviorism and neurophilosophy both deny that minds exist, so they are trivially strongest naturalism. Identity theory is also a form of strongest naturalism because, on this theory, all mental kinds are identical to, and therefore reducible to, brain kinds.

But what about functionalism? For functionalists, every token of a mental event is identical to some token brain (or brain plus) event, but mental types are not identical to any types described in the language of the brain. If so, we get the following picture. On the one hand, functionalists view the mind as nothing more than the functioning of the brain (or brain plus). Thus they view their account of the mind as science: it is just as scientific as any neuroscience. On the other hand, they deny that the account of the mind they give can be REDUCED to any account in terms of the brain or any other nonmental scientific theory. Is this a naturalizing account or not? Well, it is moderate or stronger naturalism, but it is not strongest naturalism. It is *derived* from science and developed using the *methods* of science, etc. But since it denies that a correct scientific account of the mind can be reduced to neuroscience or any other natural science, it is not strongest naturalism.

Is this a problem? Well, if not being naturalistic in the strongest way is a problem, then lots of other good science has a problem, too. That's because lots of other good sciences—including acoustic phonetics, economics, and archeology among many other disciplines—are not reducible to neuroscience either. Since the requirement that good theories be naturalistic in the strongest way rules out not just functionalism but a lot of other perfectly good sciences, we think that the requirement that theories satisfy strongest naturalism is too strong. (And where questions of value are involved, requiring even stronger naturalism may be to ask too much, as we saw.) So functionalist accounts of the mind may well be adequately naturalistic, even if they are not naturalistic in the strongest way.

Which flavor of naturalism is more likely to be right, the moderate stronger naturalism of functionalism or the strongest naturalism of neuroscience? It is really too early to tell, but two recent developments mildly favor merely moderate or stronger naturalism and functionalism. The first is cognitive science. Functionalism is virtually the official philosophy of cognitive science. If cognitive science really is as promising as it seems to be and if it presupposes functionalism, then its development as a science offers some support to functionalism.

The second recent development involves a fascinating practical turn that functionalism has taken. It has become the heart of a very promising approach to the devastating disorder called AUTISM. Recall the idea of explanatory dualism on which functionalism is built:

Explanatory dualism To understand ourselves, we need two very different kinds of explanation: psychological explanations and mechanistic explanations.

And recall the example we gave of this dualism: our friend Pavritra walking down the hall and pouring herself a cup of coffee. As we saw in chapter 4, what Pavritra does can be explained in two very different ways, one in terms of what moves she makes, the other in terms of what action these movements perform. One explanation would say,

(2) Pavritra walked down the hall because her brain sent certain signals to her leg muscles, her leg muscles contracted and relaxed in a certain highly coordinated way around her knees, ankles, and toes, and so on.

The other explanation would say,

(3) Pavritra walked down the hall because she wanted a cup of coffee and thought that there might still be some coffee left in the pot in the coffee room.

The explanation in (2) is a *mechanistic explanation,* explanation by mechanical causes (here muscle movements, changes in brain chemistry, etc.). In contrast, (3) is a *psychological explanation,* explanation by reference to Pavritra's *reasons* for doing what she did: what she wanted, what she believed about how she could satisfy her desire, etc. Functionalists, as we saw, maintain that to understand ourselves, we need both kinds of explanation, one to make sense of ourselves as cognitive systems, one to make sense of the processes and structures that implement these systems.

Here is how psychologists have applied the notion of psychological explanation to autism. The system of concepts that we use in psychological explanations is what we earlier called *folk psychology,* our ordinary concepts for beliefs, desires, intentions, emotions, and so on. As Simon Baron-Cohen (1995) and others have demonstrated, children acquire these concepts very early. The first signs of them appear well before the first birthday, and children have the full system of concepts by the age of three or four. These theorists explain all this by saying that even very young children have a theory of mind, i.e., a rich, systematically organized system of procedures for figuring out what people are feeling, thinking, etc., from how they are behaving. Now in the case of autism there is a lot of evidence that this system of procedures called folk psychology is damaged or missing, so these people are not able to recognize others as having minds. This is a large part of what makes it so difficult for them to relate to other human beings. People with autism cannot relate to other people as *people.*

This theory of autism is controversial, of course, like everything else in contemporary cognitive science. Whatever its ultimate value, it is an interesting application of the idea of psychological explanation at the heart of functionalism. Is it naturalistic? That depends. On the one hand, it is as scientific as you could wish, so it accords with moderate or stronger naturalism. On the other hand, there is no reason to think that its account of autism in terms of the so-called "THEORY THEORY OF MIND" could ever be reduced to any account given by neuroscience. If so, it is not naturalistic in the strongest sense.[8] Given the power of this theory, if it is not naturalistic in the strongest way, this is some evidence for functionalism.

To sum up, we have been exploring attempts to naturalize the mind, in particular, attempts to answer questions 4 and 5 in purely s-naturalistic terms.

4. What is a mind?
5. How are minds related to bodies?

We noted that both kinds of s-naturalistic answers to these two questions face an obstacle from the fact that minds process meanings. How, we asked, can there be a scientific account of such a phenomenon? One possible answer was externalism, a view according to which meaning derives from a relationship between internal symbols and external things. On this assumption, so-called "meaning processing" would be restricted to operations on the internal symbols, in a manner very reminiscent of a computer. But such operations would be meaningful in some sense, precisely because (unbeknownst to the processor, as it were) the internal symbols do in fact stand for external things. We then turned to question 5 and asked how the various materialist theories of mind-body relations—identity theory, behaviorism, neurophilosophy, and functionalism—fit with the two forms of s-naturalism. We concluded that whereas the first three all accord with strongest naturalism, functionalism satisfies only stronger naturalism at most. We then examined two things that tip the scales mildly in favor of moderate or stronger naturalism.

4   Naturalizing Knowledge of Other Minds: The Problem in Robots

I wish a robot would get elected president. That way, when he came to town, we could all take a shot at him and not feel too bad.
Jack Handey

We turn now to question 6:

6. Can a person ever really know the mind of another?

Indeed, can anyone know that another person even *has* a mind? What's happened to the problem of our knowledge of other minds in recent research is very interesting. Theorists have certainly made an attempt to give a naturalistic account of how we know other minds, but this is not the most interesting recent development. The most interesting recent development is that the problem of knowledge of other minds has suddenly popped up in an entirely new place! And it is just as troublesome here as it was before.

The usual approach to naturalizing our knowledge of other minds is, as we saw in chapter 7, to argue that our knowledge of other minds is just another example of *inference to the best explanation*. Other people's mental states are just another instance of something in nature that we cannot observe but that we can infer from something else we can observe, in this case, behavior. This is our general method for gaining knowledge about hidden processes, and it should be good enough here. We observe others' behavior and infer what mental states and processes would best explain the behavior. End of story.

This approach certainly s-naturalizes knowledge of other minds, but like all radical s-naturalizing approaches, it has its limitations. The analogy is supposed to be to things like electrons. No one has ever seen an electron and no one ever will, not even under the most powerful microscope. We *postulate* that they exist, however, because doing so gives us very powerful explanations and very accurate predictions about things that we can see. As we suggested in chapter 7, one dissimilarity in the analogy is introspection: unlike other hidden processes, in the case of minds *one* observer, namely the person who has the mental states, appears to have direct, noninferential access to the process, access that no one else has. But we will not pursue this dissimilarity here.

Instead, we want to look at something more interesting. The old problem of other minds has recently appeared in an entirely new place. This new context will throw up a new and striking limitation of the naturalizing approach, but let us first examine the new context in its own right. It is quite interesting. The new context is ARTIFICIAL INTELLIGENCE (AI). Just as its name would suggest, AI is about producing intelligence by artificial means, producing artificially constructed machines that behave in ways that would require intelligence in us. Let us look at two examples of how the problem of other minds arises in AI.

About 1950 the British mathematician Alan Turing described a test for determining whether an artificial system has intelligence. A contemporary variation on his test has come to be called the TURING TEST. The Turing test is very simple: put a subject in front of two input and two output devices—typically two keyboards and two monitors. Have each monitor get its input from an agent. And have each keyboard send its output to one of the agents. In this setup the subject can type questions and receive answers, composed by the agents, on a monitor before her. (For instance, she might type on keyboard 1, "Where do you live?" And agent 1, the agent who gets the output of keyboard 1, might reply on monitor 1, "I live in Montevideo." Or she might type, "Do you like hockey?" on keyboard 2. And the agent might post the following to monitor 2: "Are you kidding? I love hockey! I grew up in Montreal.") Next step: make one of the agents a human being, and make the other a computer. The goal of the subject is to figure out which one is which. Now, according to the Turing test, a computer is intelligent if, from its role as one of the agents in this game, its performance cannot be distinguished from the performance of a human being. (What that means is that the computer is as likely to be labeled the human by the subject as the real human is.) In essence, if the subject cannot tell which agent is the computer and which is the human being, then the computer passes the test. (This test has become part of the lore of the AI community. There is even a Turing-test contest held every year in the United States.)

The Turing test, obviously, is purely behavioral. (It was first proposed in the heyday of behaviorism.) All we are testing is whether the system can *behave* intelligently. Even more narrowly, it is restricted to purely linguistic behavior. The test tells us nothing about what is going on in the system. Now suppose that we change the test slightly. Instead of determining which system is artificial, we simply tell the subject which system is artificial and ask the subject to answer this question 'When the system is acting enough like you to pass the Turing test, is it like you "on the inside," i.e., is it behaving the way it is because it is thinking thoughts, feeling feelings, having desires?' What is the subject now supposed to do? We are asking her, in effect, to solve the problem of other minds—for a computer!

Suppose that the Turing test has revealed that the artificial system can discriminate and respond to the world closely enough to how we do. We are now asking whether the system is acting as it does because it is processing *meanings,* whether it is *aware* of the world, of what it is doing in the world, of itself, and so on.[9] Notice that the first and biggest issue in this new version of the problem of other minds is exactly the same as the one in the original version: what would we need to know to be able to decide, one way or the other, whether the computer has a mind like us?

Here's another place where the problem of our knowledge of other minds appears in new clothes. John Searle (1980) has mounted a famous thought experiment, called the *Chinese room,* against the very possibility that computers as we know them can think (or be conscious, though the latter may not be the primary issue for him). What Searle denies is that any computer that we know of now could be like us mentally. Here is how the Chinese-room thought experiment goes.

Put someone who knows no Chinese into a room. Suppose it is you. Now we give you a large book of rules (it would have to be *huge*) for transforming Chinese symbols into other Chinese symbols. Crucially, the symbols don't mean anything to you. (As far as you are concerned, the "symbols" are just pretty designs.) We tell you that Chinese symbols will come in through a slot on the left. When they do, you are to match them with the 'if' part of an 'If . . . , then . . .' rule in your book, then pull the symbols in the 'then' part out of a box in front of you, and shove these new symbols out a slot to your right. We then set you to work. Within a few weeks, you get pretty good at the task. Symbols (maybe better, designs) are flying in from the left and flying out to the right. As it happens, the Chinese symbols coming in on the left encode complex intellectual problems, and the Chinese symbols going out on the right encode solutions to them. Of course, you know none of this: all the symbols are, to repeat, completely meaningless to you.

Now, says Searle, the position you are in inside the room is exactly the position any known computer would have to be in. We might turn computers into good symbol crunchers, but mere symbol crunching can never amount to understanding anything. So far we do not have a problem of knowledge of other minds, just an argument against STRONG AI of a certain form. (The argument, recall, is that someone, namely you, can shuffle designs around well enough to pass the Turing test without understanding anything. So design shuffling of the sort characteristic of familiar computers, even if it leads to very sophisticated behavior, is not sufficient for understanding.) But now ask, "What would we need to add to whatever is in the Chinese room to go from blind symbol matching to genuine understanding and consciousness?" More specifically, "How can we tell from *outside* the room that whatever is in the room had gone from blind symbol matching to conscious understanding of the symbols' meanings?" Now we are back to the familiar problem of other minds.

To see that the problem raised by the Chinese room really is just the problem of our knowledge of other minds all over again, notice that you can ask exactly the same question about another person: "How could we tell from the outside that there is a conscious being inside for whom the symbols have meaning, not just a blind, stupid machine mechanically manipulating symbols according to their shape?" In short, the problem of our knowledge of other minds is right at the center of a number of the philosophically most challenging issues arising out of contemporary work on artificial intelligence.

Earlier we said that introspection is one dissimilarity in the attempt to naturalize our knowledge of other minds by treating it as just another case of inference to the best explanation. We also said that the new context in which the problem of knowledge of other minds has arisen would throw up another striking dissimilarity to the inference to best explanation approach. We can now see what it is. The problem is this. Can we solve the problem of whether there is meaning and consciousness inside the Chinese-speaking room by inferring to the best explanation? This move would not seem to help us. Here, we think, is why. The real problem with the Chinese room—and also with other people—is that *we do not know what behavior would be needed* to justify an inference to meaning and consciousness. And this is exactly what makes the problem of other minds in people so hard: we do not know what behavior would justify us in inferring that they are like us on the "inside."

Until we know what would *justify* an inference from some observed behavior to some underlying mental state or event as the best explanation of the behavior, inference to the best explanation is of no use to us. Here are the questions for which we need answers: *What* behavior is entirely compatible with there being nothing inside but a blind, stupid machine mechanically manipulating symbols according to their shape? *What* behavior could best be explained by inferring a conscious intelligence inside? Until we know these general *principles* for *making* the inference, we have no idea when to make the inference and when not—whether with Searle's Chinese Room or with other people. And if we ever find these principles, we can use them to infer the best explanation of behavior we are observing both in machines and in people. Once we find them, the problem of other minds will be solved. So either way, inference to the best explanation cannot play any major role in the problem of other minds.

Here's another way to put the point we've just made about inference to the best explanation. Recall the distinction between mechanical and psychological explanations (chapter 4). When we are faced with complex behavior, whether from the Chinese Room or from other people, it is likely that there will always be a mechanical explanation of this behavior. (It will be extremely complicated in many cases, and often we will not know what it is, but probably there will always be one.) On this explanation, the system mechanically manipulating symbols without any understanding will be enough to explain the behavior. And the question will become, What kind of behavior (and perhaps other factors) would also require a psychological explanation, one in terms of the behaver's reasons, i.e., one that attributes at least some degree of understanding to the behaver? Until we know the answer to this question, we have no idea when to infer understanding, consciousness, etc., and when not.

Indeed, prior to finding what kinds of behavior *require* understanding, etc., to be explained, we cannot even be sure that we ourselves are more than "blind, stupid machines mechanically manipulating symbols according to their shape." Some theorists both inside philosophy and out have urged that we are nothing more (see, e.g., Dennett 1987 and Fodor 1994).

Time now to pull together the implications for s-naturalism. Searle's argument that mere symbol crunching can never be enough for meaning or consciousness is also an argument against one common way of s-naturalizing the mind. One way to s-naturalize the mind, as we saw earlier, is to compare it to a computer, indeed to argue that we don't have anything more by way of "real" or "intrinsic" meanings in us than a computer does. (Recall that in chapter 4 when discussing intentionality as a mark of the mental and in chapter 5 when discussing intentionality as an argument for property dualism, we suggested that the intentionality of pictures may be merely derived from us, whereas our intentionality may be original with us. The approach we are now discussing says that all intentionality is derived, including our own [see Dennett 1987, chap. 8].) If Searle is right in the two things he maintains, i.e., that known computers cannot have meanings and that we do, then this approach has to be radically mistaken. There has to be something more to meaning and consciousness than mechanistic processes in a computer could ever achieve.

There are a variety of approaches to this extra element. Searle's own approach is a version of neurophilosophy—he just adopts a different form of naturalism. He calls it *biological naturalism*. It says, in effect, Turn to the brain. There is something about the brain that gives it the meaning and consciousness that computers cannot have. Unfortunately, Searle has never been able to say very much about what this special substance might be like. (Indeed, it is hard to tell whether he adheres to s-naturalism of some sort or merely moderate naturalism. Certainly his approach is different from *standard* neurophilosophy. Standard neurophilosophers would say that we should give up meaning and consciousness talk altogether.) Another approach to other minds is to look to the system's functions: get the functions rich and complex enough, introduce language use, vision, locomotion, etc., and meaning and consciousness *will* emerge, though not in any way that can be straightforwardly reduced to neuroscience. Finally, any and all of these approaches can be combined with the idea that the "missing element" that distinguishes real thinkers from mere symbol manipulators can be found in the system's hookups to its environment. All these approaches seem likely to fit within some form of s-naturalism without difficulty.

5 Philosophy and Naturalism

A quick review before going on. We began this chapter by considering attempts to s-naturalize epistemology—that is, attempts to answer questions about what knowledge is, how it is obtained, what its limits are—by turning to science. A key obstacle to this project was that philosophical questions about knowledge inevitably raises value issues, and these are precisely *not* the sort of issues that science is designed to answer. We proceeded to describe two ways around this worry. One response, moderate naturalism, was to grant that there would always be a residue of normative issues in epistemology, issues that cannot be addressed scientifically, but to maintain, nonetheless, that work in the natural sciences can teach us a great deal about what knowledge is and about the mechanisms whereby knowledge is obtained. The other response, s-naturalism, was to insist that even values and norms can be treated scientifically, in the sense that they too derive from natural processes like evolution. Having introduced naturalized epistemology, we turned to attempts to s-naturalize the mind. Here again we noted a couple of obstacles facing the naturalizer. One was, can there be a scientific theory of meaning and processing of meaning? Another was, Given our special access to our own conscious states and given Searle's Chinese-room thought experiment, are scientific arguments like inference to the best explanation adequate to give us knowledge of other minds, natural or artificial?

We now want to consider a final objection to the whole s-naturalizing strategy of addressing traditional philosophical problems with purely neuroscientific accounts. The objection, simply put, is that philosophy is too different from science and the accounts that it gives are too different from scientific accounts for s-naturalism to work. Indeed, the two kinds of account may not even be in competition. Science and philosophy are simply doing different jobs. Recall that at the end of chapter 3 we considered and for the most part rejected the idea that philosophy has a distinctive subject matter. What is now being suggested is that philosophy has distinctive methods and gives distinctive accounts. For people who think this way, the separation of philosophy from science in this century was exactly the right thing to do.

We think that this objection is sometimes plausible, sometimes not, depending on the topic under consideration. In connection with the study of norms and values, it seems to be right. When we turn from *what is* to *what ought to be*, it does indeed seem that we need a kind of thinking not found in the natural sciences. Psychology, for example, can tell us how we do think but has little to say about how we should think. What *good* reasoning is like is a job for logic and philosophy of science and other philosophical thinking about values and norms, not for psychology, as the founder of modern logic, Gottlob Frege, already knew.

On the other hand, when the issue is something like the mind-body problem, a problem where the issues are largely about facts, things are less clear. Here it seems that philosophical analysis of the kind we examined in chapters 4 and 5 and scientific investigations of cognition and the brain of the kind we've sketched a few times in this chapter are discussing the same issue and are using at least complementary methods to do so. If so, at least in this area of inquiry, science and philosophy may be aspects of a single enterprise. Indeed, cognitive science has contributed a lot to our understanding of mind and brain. Both the main current views, functionalism and neurophilosophy, owe a great deal to scientific work on cognition and the brain. Equally, such clarity as philosophy has been able to achieve about the problem of meaning in connection with the mind owes a lot to reflection on AI systems.

In short, once we get beyond thinking about value issues, it is harder to pin down major differences between philosophy and science than many philosophers have thought. (Most scientists think that they see big differences, however.) Until this century, philosophy and science were thought to be on a single continuum. In the first half of the twentieth century, as we discussed at the beginning of this chapter, philosophers worked hard to show that philosophy is very different from science. Now the pendulum is swinging back. Except for issues about values, many philosophers again think that philosophy is not so different from science after all. We will close this chapter with a brief look at one part of this debate.

Here is a way that has been used to try to pin down the supposed difference between science and philosophy: Scientists study facts; philosophers study concepts. Scientists find patterns in the world and invent theories to account for them; philosophers study meanings, i.e., the relationships between concepts. The idea was this. Scientists study things like the relationship between force and acceleration or heating and boiling and other things that can be expressed in straightforward propositions about matters of fact, propositions such as these:

(4) Water boils at 100 °C at sea level.

(5) Sugar dissolves more rapidly in hot water than in cold.

Philosophers, by contrast, study the way concepts and propositions relate to one another. Here are some simple examples of the relationships:

(6) Bachelors are unmarried men.

(7) Two thousand milliseconds is more than one second.

(8) Red objects are colored.

(9) If Pedro ate a bagel, then Pedro ate (i.e., ate something).

Compare (4) and (6). The difference was supposed to be that (6) is true because 'bachelor' and 'unmarried man' mean the same thing, so that one can know that (6) is true just by knowing the meanings of the words, whereas to know that (4) is true, one needs to know some nonlinguistic facts about the world. Philosophers call truths like (4) SYNTHETIC TRUTHS and truths like (6) ANALYTIC TRUTHS. Philosophers then applied this distinction and the view of concepts that goes with it to much more complicated concepts, asking questions like, What do we mean by 'representation'? What is the meaning of 'meaning'?

Of course, for (4) and (6) to be different in the way just sketched, there must *be* two different kinds of truths, i.e., truths of fact and truths of meaning. Starting from about 1950, some philosophers began to question this. The problem was simple: To analyze concepts in this way, we need a notion that two things, the concept and what we offer as an analysis of it, mean the same. The name for meaning the same thing is SYNONYMITY. It turned out to be very difficult to describe such a notion in any way that did not already presuppose it (see Quine 1953). If we cannot say what having the same meaning consists in, however, then there is no point in building the methods of philosophy on the notion. And if that is so, then the methods that will work in philosophy may very well not be as different from the methods of science as philosophers used to think.

We are skating very rapidly over a very large and controversial topic here, but the short of it is this. Contrary to what many philosophers in this century have believed, philosophical methods may *not* be fundamentally different from the methods of experimental science (except the branches of philosophy concerned with values). Far from being a special domain devoted to the analysis of concepts, philosophy may be just another way of describing and theorizing about the world. And the difference between philosophy and science may be merely a matter of degree, not some matter of fundamental difference in principle. It may merely be that philosophy is concerned with bigger, more abstract questions than most of (experimental) science and that philosophers tend to make more general claims less rooted in immediate empirical evidence than (the rest of) science.

If philosophy does turn out to be merely speculative science (from which it also follows that science is simply a more experimental, detailed kind of philosophy), philosophy could still be centered on concepts. Concepts are the tools with which we study the world, so we have to be interested in concepts. Our study of the world will only be as good as our tools (and how well we use them). However, interest in concepts is by no means exclusive to philosophers. To the contrary, if philosophy is just the most abstract kind of science and science is just a more experimental, detailed kind of philosophy, one would expect working scientists to be as interested in concepts, some of the time at least, as philosophers. And that is just what we find: when scientists get bogged down because the concepts they are using are not working right, they leave their lab bench and talk about conceptual issues as much as any philosopher would. (For more on the methods of philosophy, see Brook 1999.)

Certainly philosophers *focus* on conceptual issues and are *more* sensitive to issues of conceptual structure, etc., than (other) scientists. And certainly experimental scientists *focus* on experimentation and observation of the facts and are *more* sensitive to issues having to do with the facts than philosophers. But that might be all there is to the difference. If so, except for value issues, the argument against s-naturalism from the supposed differences between philosophy and science would not be very strong.[10]

6   Conclusion

The aim of this book has been to introduce a number of the most important issues having to do with knowledge and mind. Here are the main topics that we have considered:

• Contemporary views of the nature of knowledge and problems with those views
• Traditional skeptical challenges to the claim that we know what we think we know
• Special problems of knowledge and mind that arise in connection with our knowledge of language

• The traditional mind-body problem and traditional and contemporary responses to it
• The question of how to settle what we should think about the mind-body problem
• The problem of freedom of choice
• The problem of our knowledge of other minds
• The recent naturalistic move of attempting to give a purely scientific solution to traditional philosophical problems and the connected topic of contemporary cognitive science

Along the way we have tried, a couple of times, to say a bit about what philosophy is and how to do it. We hope that you have enjoyed the ride.

Study Questions

1. How is the development of cognitive science related to the emergence of the computer? What is the relationship between cognitive science, computers, and functionalism?

2. What is it to take a naturalizing approach to a philosophical question? Are there any areas in which is it an *unpromising* approach? Why?

3. With respect to naturalizing epistemology, where do moderate and s- or radical naturalizers disagree over questions of value? How does the argument go? Can you see any reason to favor one side over the other?

4. What is the problem of meaning or mental content in the mind? How did it arise with the development of computers? What are the two main approaches to solving it?

5. Is functionalism a naturalistic theory of mind? Identify the ways of naturalizing according to which it is and the ways of naturalizing according to which it is not. Could it nevertheless be a scientifically adequate theory?

6. How is functionalism supported by recent findings on autism?

7. Describe the Turing test and Searle's Chinese room, then show how they raise the old problem of other minds in a new context.

8. What are some of the alternatives for addressing Searle's skepticism about symbol crunching ever adding up to processing of genuine meaning or mental content?

9. How did philosophers attempt to justify their feeling that philosophy is very different from any experimental science? What was the problem with this approach?

10. Discuss the following: The naturalizing road runs in both directions. For example, what's going on in AI, when the problem of other minds pops up, shows that an inevitable result of assimilating philosophy to science is that scientists find themselves facing variations on good old philosophy problems.

Suggested Further Readings

On cognitive science and how it works, see Thagard 1996. For treatments that go into more detail, see Stillings et al. 1995 and Dawson 1998. Baron-Cohen 1995 is the definitive summary of the "theory theory" of mind. As for evolutionary psychology, Pinker 1997 is an excellent introduction.

On moderate versus radical naturalism, see Quine 1969 and Goldman 1979, 1992. Kornblith 1985 gathers these and other papers in an excellent collection. It contains an extensive bibliography by topic.

The literature on externalism has become highly technical. One of the works that started it all is Putnam 1975. An important though difficult book that develops a fully naturalistic theory of the mind from an externalist perspective is Dretske 1995. See also Fodor 1994.

On psychological explanation, folk psychology, and the "theory theory" of mind, see the Suggested Further Readings for chapter 4.

On the Turing test and the Chinese room, the seminal works are Turing 1950 and Searle 1980. There is an excellent play about Alan Turing called *Breaking the Code* by Hugh Whitemore (1987).

On all the topics of this chapter, see Dennett 1987 and Fodor 1994. One of the best reference works on everything to do with cognitive science is *The MIT Encyclopedia of the Cognitive Sciences* (1999). It is available on paper or on CD and on the Internet with some restrictions at http://mitpress.mit.edu/mitecs/.

On the methods of philosophy, see Brook 1999 and references given there.

The Internet now contains thousands of interesting and highly relevant sites dealing with philosophy and cognitive science. Links to some good sites, sites that will lead you to most everything else on the Internet, can be found at http://www.carleton.ca./~abrook. Click the heading 'Philosophy and Cognitive Science'.

Notes

Chapter 1

1. If a word is in SMALL CAPITAL LETTERS, it is defined in the Glossary at the end of the book. For the sake of readability, we only small-cap the first occurrence of a term (with some rare exceptions where a term comes back in after a long absence). So if you are not sure of the meaning of a term, check for it in the Glossary even if it is not in small capitals. Often you will find it defined there.

2. The first time we refer to someone, we will give birth dates for thinkers who are dead. We will not give dates for living thinkers.

3. It's also worth noting that philosophers don't spend all their time *criticizing* other people's arguments. Especially in history of philosophy, the job is often to sort out exactly what the argument is. This requires a charitable attitude rather than a critical attitude, divining what the argument might reasonably be saying. You might well ask why philosophers don't just state their arguments clearly, so that no filling-in is required. (Then they could spend *all* their time criticizing!) The reason is that any complex argument is bound to be an ENTHYMEME, that is, an argument with some implicit premises. It's usually not possible to state everything that one is taking for granted in a dispute. And yet sometimes background assumptions really are required for the argument to succeed. Hence the reader's job is often to hypothesize what the writer might reasonably be taking as implicit premises.

Chapter 2

1. More exactly, *one* way to support P1 is to suppose that there's nothing in the mind at birth. Another way would be to allow that, though there are innate mental contents, none of them is a source of knowledge, because, e.g., none is justified. By the way, as we noted above, there are many variations on the empiricist theme. In what follows we are essentially discussing a simplified classical form of empiricism, of the sort one might find in John Locke. Other forms of empiricism would not support P1. For instance, some present-day empiricists say that all knowledge comes from experience but simultaneously insist that what we experience with the senses are not "seemings" but ordinary objects—like tables, chickens, etc. This view, called direct perceptual realism, will be discussed below. (Thanks to Tim Kenyon and Dave Matheson for pushing us on these points.)

2. *Can't* one learn about cows by examining skateboards? For instance, can't one learn, by careful study of skateboards, that they aren't cows? Not without *some* knowledge of what cows are. And that cannot be had just by contemplating skateboards.

3. This line of argument, and several cogent critiques of it, may be found in Audi 1998, chap. 1.

4. What's intended here is 'verifiable in principle'. Thus sentences that have not yet been verified, or that cannot be verified for practical reasons, are still taken to be meaningful. (Examples of sentences that are not verifiable in practice but are nevertheless verifiable in principle include sentences about distant planets or about the bottom of the Atlantic, etc.)

Chapter 3

1. The clearest example is the problem of knowledge of other minds; it is equally a problem about knowledge and a problem flowing from the nature of the mind. We discuss it in part III.

2. The difference has to do with whether the 'who' being asked about is the subject or the object of the second verb. Thus the first sentence might be paraphrased as: "You want to meet who?" Here 'who' is the direct object of 'meet'. In contrast, the second would be paraphrased as "You want who to talk?" Here 'who' is the grammatical subject of 'talk'.

3. It is not the case, by the way, that babies' brains are just more flexible or "smarter" than adult brains. In fact, acquiring language doesn't seem to require much general intelligence at all. One of the truly striking discoveries about language acquisition of the last quarter century is that even children whose learning abilities are severely impaired can pick up grammar about as well as normal infants. Even when their general learning abilities are depressingly bad, their ability to acquire grammar can still be excellent. (And vice versa, actually. There appear to be genetically inherited language *deficits* that don't necessarily correlate with general intelligence. See Gopnik 1990 for the original material and Pinker 1994, chap. 10, for an interesting introduction.)

4. There is a nice anecdote, brought to our attention by Ian Slater, that illustrates how observation requires assimilation of what is observed. Sir Karl Popper apparently once asked a room full of people simply to "observe." Of course, they hadn't a clue what they were supposed to do. Popper's point was precisely that you have to observe *with respect to something*. And that requires thinking.

5. Language has practical uses too, of course. And some of them are far from obvious. Take complicated trains of thought and their place in avoiding nasty mistakes: "What if ____? Well then ____. But that would mean ____. So I better not ____." As Dennett (1995, chapter 13) points out, sophisticated planning requires anticipating obstacles way down the road, and that requires trains of complex and detailed imaginings, which in turn seems to require language. Ditto for many kinds of social interaction. Without language, stocks couldn't exist, let alone change hands; marriage (as opposed to mere pairing off) wouldn't be possible; illegality would be unthinkable; and so on.

6. This sort of idea is developed and defended in Davidson 1975. Several of the points in this paragraph and the next are based on that paper. See the Suggested Further Readings for more works on thought and talk.

7. As Maite Ezcurdia has pointed out to us, it is not clear whether Fodor himself would approve of the parallel we draw between binary computer code and the language of thought. It may be that Fodor intends LOT to be a "higher-level language," with the result that, rather than LOT supporting images, both LOT and imagistic representation are supported by something syntactically more fundamental.

Chapter 4

1. We thank Tim Kenyon and Jill McIntosh for impressing on us the importance of introducing this complication from square one. The difference between brain and brain plus does not amount to alternative versions of *materialism* because this dispute is not about alternative ways of conceiving of the relation of mind to matter but about alternative views of what the relevant matter is.

2. We leave out the complication 'brain plus' because few if any identity theorists have ever thought that the mind is, i.e., is identical with, anything more than the brain.

3. At any rate, dualists who believe that the mind and the body *interact* believe that there is a relationship of cause and effect between the mind and the body: desire a drink (mental) and you will head for the fridge (bodily); have light from a sunset hit your retinas (bodily) and you will see a vivid scene (mental). We are stressing this two-way relationship because historically there have been philosophers who have, strangely enough, *denied* that the mind and body are in a relationship. There have been a number of such theories, in fact, running under names such as EPIPHENOMENALISM (the body can affect the mind, but not the other way around) and PREESTABLISHED HARMONY (mind and body never connect, but God created them so that they operate in perfect harmony for the whole of bodily life). We won't go into these views. It is difficult to make good sense of the idea of something not made out of matter, i.e., not occupying space and not having physical energy, interacting with something that occupies space and has energy like the body. The strange views we're just sketched arose as a response to this problem—a fairly desperate response, we'd say.

4. True enough, bodily resurrection is talked about in the Christian Bible, and we find a kindred idea, the idea of bodily reincarnation, in religions such as Buddhism and Hinduism. But to make sense of this, we have to suppose a creature with godlike powers who miraculously recreates the body. How else could the molecules that are scattered over a wide area as the body decays and turns into fertilizer get reunified and reanimated as a living being?

5. The qualification allows for the possibility of a radically changed adult not really "being the same person" over the life of the body. For example, consider a very old person with a severe Alzheimer's-like disease, or a male priest who used to be a female professional assassin. We don't need to take a stand on whether we

have one single person in either or both cases. It is enough for our purposes that there is a single person for at least a long stretch of bodily life.

6. Whether our intentionality is entirely original with us is controversial. Some theorists think that it is not, that we got it from evolution (Dennett 1987, chap. 8; Dretske 1988). (Thanks to Jill McIntosh for impressing the importance of the issue upon us.)

7. Philosophers have known about these two types of explanation for a very long time. The first recorded account of the difference between them goes back to the Greek philosophers 2,500 years ago. Aristotle already knew about the difference; he called it the difference between efficient and final causes. What he called 'efficient causes' are the mechanical processes that bring something about. What he called 'final causes' are the goals, purposes, or reasons for which a thing was done.

8. Pain involves not just C-fibers but also T-fibers and requires sorting the signals in something called the Wall-Melzack gate, processing in the old low-brain and the newer cerebral cortex, and so on. For further reading on this topic, see Melzack 1973 and Dennett 1978a.

9. Not everything the brain does is relevant, of course; the brain processes oxygen and eliminates waste and does all sorts of other things that have nothing to do with the mind.

10. There are many flavors of behaviorism. Some of them make only very modest claims. For instance, some varieties claim only that a good place to start our study of human beings is with their behavior, or that it is important to understand stimulus/behavior correlations. Some behaviorists make the stronger claim that behavioral evidence is the *only* kind that should be used, and that understanding stimulus/behavior correlations is as much as psychology can hope for. (These are forms of METHODOLOGICAL BEHAVIORISM: they make claims about how the empirical study of mind *should* proceed.) A more radical version of behaviorism, which is the form that we have in mind, says not only that psychologists should limit themselves to studying behavior but also that there really is nothing to study beyond behavior and dispositions to behave. This ontological claim can be read in either a "Minds exist" or a "Minds don't exist" way. On the former reading, minds exist because having a mind just is behaving in certain ways, though there is no more to mentality than behavior. On the latter reading, minds don't exist because, it is supposed, if there really were minds, they would have to be "more than behavior" and there is really only behavior. For more on problems with behaviorism, see the Suggested Further Readings.

11. We should note that the theory sketched in the text, according to which minds don't exist because there is only behavior, represents B. F. Skinner at his most radical. Skinner's thinking on the mind in particular and behaviorism in general went through many variations—from the modest to the extreme and back again.

12. Idealists, we expect, would mostly agree with functionalists here: we need dual explanations, but that does not reflect any important metaphysical duality in the things or properties that exist. There aren't too many idealists around to ask, however, so it is hard to be sure.

Chapter 5

1. For Sellars, the philosopher who introduced the idea of these two images, the two, we want to stress, are completely compatible, alternative ways of describing the same reality. We are not arguing with him about this. Our point is that the two images can *lead* theorists in two different directions, depending on which one appears to be more adequate.

2. The nature and importance of this difference in burden of proof was illustrated very clearly by the O. J. Simpson case. In the criminal trial, where the burden of proof was on the prosecution, the jury found that the case against Simpson had not been proved beyond a reasonable doubt, and they acquitted him. In the subsequent civil case (where the charge was not murder but that Simpson had wrongfully caused death), all that was required was that on the balance of probability, it was more likely that Simpson had caused the death of his ex-wife and her friend than not. In the jury's view, the balance of probabilities were that he had caused the death of his ex-wife and her friend, so they found him liable.

3. Of course, one can turn this into a valid argument by changing P2 so that it reads, 'Life ultimately does have meaning'. P1 and the revised P2 now really do entail the conclusion. (The argument form is our old friend *modus tollens*: if p then q; not q; therefore, not p.) But now the worry is, What supports the claim that life does have meaning? What evidence can be brought in favor of this hypothesis, other than the "evidence" of our wishing it so?

4. It's based on some remarks in T. Nagel 1987. He does not endorse the argument.

5. The argument has a fairly common form: if p then q; if r, then q; p or r; therefore, q. The argument is in the form of a DILEMMA: p and r are the only possibilities, and if *either p or r* is true, the consequent of interest, q, follows.

Chapter 6

1. There is an interesting question about what to say if you *think* that you have alternatives, but unbeknownst to you, you really do not: all but one choice has been foreclosed, though you do not know it (see Frankfurt 1969). We will return to this issue briefly of the end.

2. There is one exception to this rule: STRICT-LIABILITY offenses. Strict-liability offenses are offenses where just doing the deed is enough to justify punishment. Whether one intended to do the deed, or even knew that it was being done, is irrelevant. Strict-liability offenses are relatively rare and usually concern fairly trivial things like letting the time on a parking meter run out. For all other offenses, to be responsible for breaking the law, you must both commit the offense and be responsible for your action.

3. The law holds a person not responsible when, due to a "diseased mind," they are incapable of appreciating "the nature and quality" of their action, in particular that it was legally or morally wrong. We cannot go into this extremely interesting issue here.

4. What we have just said here is enough to show that determinism does not necessarily lead to FATALISM. Fatalism is the idea that nothing one thinks, decides,

or favors will make any difference. That is, the causal chains determining how the world works completely bypass one's mental life. About the big events of politics and history, fatalism may have a certain appeal. Here we have in mind claims such as that, given the economics and politics of Europe, World War I was bound to happen. For everyday decisions such as whether to get a cup of coffee or a soft drink, whether to stay home and work on an essay or go to a film, etc., it is hard to see how fatalism could be true. Equally, determinism does not entail EPIPHENOMENALISM, the view that all the causality is from the outside in and the actions of the mind have no effect on anything. This kind of determinism is sometimes associated with the Stoics of Roman times and is closely related to fatalism as just introduced. If it were true, epiphenomenalism might threaten the existence of free choice as defined by compatibilism. However, it would also rule out self-determinism, something that the compatibilist insists upon for decisions to be free, so they do not have to worry about it. In any case, epiphenomenalism is not true. It is false, and obviously so: what I think and feel and desire sometimes does affect the world outside me.

5. The logic of choice, ability, and what are called opportunity concepts is exceedingly complicated. We are only skimming the surface here. For a good account, see Ayers 1968.

6. So long as the happy junkie is still happy, that is to say, still desires to have the craving for heroin, is he responsible for the actions by which he procures it? The answer to this question is not so clear. After all, he is doing what, all things considered, he wants to do, that is, he is doing things to satisfy a desire that he is happy to have. Frankfurt (1969) and some other papers in Pereboom 1997 discuss these interesting in-between cases. We will come back to this issue of the end of the chapter.

7. If not an optimal decision, at least a decision that is good enough. We often seek to make decisions that are good enough, satisfactory—not the best possible decision, the optimal decision. The two strategies involved are called *optimizing* and *satisficing*.

8. As Jill McIntosh has pointed out to us, weakness of will may be a problem for SCM. Weakness of will is (perhaps among other things) acting in ways that fall short of one's second-order beliefs and values. One way around the problem might be to say that when weakness of will is present, free choice is to that extent curtailed.

9. The wired mind is derived from a counterexample laid out by Richard Taylor in his *Metaphysics* (1963). Taylor's seminal work on free will is the foundation of a lot of the thinking on free choice of one of us (Brook), though the views we hold differ from his in some places.

Chapter 7

1. Note that it is much harder (though not impossible, we think) to wonder this about oneself. This is the asymmetry between the problem of knowledge of others and that of knowledge of oneself.

2. It would, of course, be easy to think of other examples.

3. The name 'inverted-qualia problem' is a generalization of the problem that purportedly arises for color sensations, where it is called 'the inverted spectrum problem'. The name 'absent-qualia problem' is used for the problem as it arises for all sensations. As these names indicate, the problem of knowledge of other minds and the problem of knowledge of others' consciousness are closely linked. Of course, there is more to minds than consciousness. A lot of mental life is not conscious. Thus, the problem of knowledge of other minds is broader than the problem of knowledge that others are conscious.

4. The meaning of the term 'empathy' has become blurred recently to include sympathy. Empathy and sympathy are quite different from one another. Sympathy is caring about another, especially feeling sorrow, pity, concern, acceptance, etc., for another when the other person is experiencing difficulties. Empathy is merely figuring out what the other person is feeling, whether or not you sympathize with the person or even care at all.

5. As we said in note 10, chapter 4, there are many flavors of behaviorism. Some of them are no more than suggestions for where to start our study of human beings: with behavior. Some make claims about what is important to understand: stimulus-behavior correlations. Some make claims about what the mind is like: nothing but behavior and dispositions to behave. The latter variety is *radical behaviorism* and is the form of behaviorism that we have in mind.

6. This objection was first formulated by Hilary Putnam (1964) over thirty-five years ago.

7. One of the better discussions of the fallibility of introspection is P. M. Churchland 1984.

8. The theorist who has carried through this approach to knowledge of self most comprehensively is Dennett (1991).

Chapter 8

1. Initially neuroscience played little role in cognitive science, for reasons we examined at the end of chapter 5, but that has changed dramatically in the past decade. Neuroscience now plays a huge role in cognitive science. More recently still, researchers have begun to investigate the historical and social dimensions of the mind, with the result that cognitive anthropology, social psychology, and sociology are playing an ever-growing role in our understanding of the mind (we are using 'the mind' and 'cognition' to mean roughly the same thing).

2. We are over-simplifying a bit here. Some natural scientists take an interest in how scientists *should* arrive at their beliefs, in how a natural system like an organ *should* work, etc. When they do, however, it is not clear that they are using scientific methods. In fact, if we are right, what they are doing seems to be distinctively philosophical.

3. Sometimes naturalizers think that this approach commits them to saying that the only kind of knowledge that individuals have is knowledge from observation and experimentation, since that is the only kind of knowledge that science provides. It would follow that claims for nonempirical knowledge (in, for example,

linguistics) could not be correct. In fact, such a commitment should not be part of naturalism. One could find out, *on scientific grounds*, that there is knowledge which is very unlike scientific knowledge: innate knowledge of language, for example. Since such a discovery would be scientific, it would be consistent with naturalism.

4. An important aside. Notice one of the main arguments used in this kind of radical naturalizing: the argument from what evolution has built into us. This kind of appeal to evolution to explain features of the human mind is called EVO-LUTIONARY PSYCHOLOGY. Evolutionary psychology is the attempt to understand the structures and functions of the human cognitive system, as it is now, by seeing why it evolved to have these structures and functions over a very long period of time, usually from the time when the line of descent of our ancestors diverged from that of the chimpanzees, etc., about six million years ago (Pinker 1997). If philosophy of knowledge and of mind ever get assimilated into the sciences of knowledge and mind, it will be due in no small part to evolutionary psychology.

5. Some theorists have urged that there is a normative problem for naturalizers in connection with the mind too, not just in connection with knowledge. It beyond the scope of what we are trying to do in this book to examine that issue (see Davidson 1980 and Dennett 1987).

6. By 'traditional philosophical treatments' here we mean, roughly, theories that existed prior to the twentieth century, e.g., dualism and idealism.

7. Such inclusive theories are known by names such as SITUATED COGNITION and ECOLOGICAL COGNITION. As we become more sensitive to the role of environment in the mind, recognizing indeed that the environment might even be *part* of the mind, these approaches become ever more attractive.

8. The theory theory of our ability to form a picture of others' minds contrasts with something called the SIMULATION THEORY OF MIND, in which it is alleged that we come to a view about what is going on in another's mind by putting ourselves in their position and simulating what would be going on in us in such a position.

9. Notice that the question about whether the system is processing meanings is quite different from the question of whether it has awareness. The latter is the question, in T. Nagel's (1974) suggestive phrase, of whether there is "something it is like" to be that system and have that system's states. There are almost certainly unconscious states, states that it is not like anything to have, that nevertheless have meaning.

10. An attempt has even been made within cognitive science to naturalize free choice. It has not got far enough yet to merit a section of its own in this book, but we want to say a word about it. Radical naturalizers about free choice urge that when we see the rich, fluid, sophisticated ways in which the best information-processing and decision-making systems can process information to reach decisions about complicated matters, we will see these decisions as free (see, e.g., Goldman 1990). Yet these decision-making systems are completely causally determined, so our fears about causally determined decision making excluding free choice are simply based on too crude a notion of complex decision making.

This naturalizing move seems to face a serious problem. To develop a naturalistic theory of something, you must have some fairly clear initial idea of what that thing is. In connection with free choice, we do not have that initial idea. Put bluntly, there is no initial agreement on *what is needed for a choice to be free.* Till we settle this issue, we don't know what a naturalistic (or any other) theory of free choice is supposed to be a theory *of.* There is good reason to think that this initial understanding is not going to come from a more complete understanding of decision-making systems.

The reason is this. Free choice is not just complex decision making. Free choice opens the way to moral praise or blame and personal responsibility. That is to say, the concept is deeply embedded in our practices and institutions, indeed in our whole way of life. No science of decision making is going to take us very far in our attempt to understand what features of choices are required to justify these practices. As we said at the end of chapter 6, we view the problem of the conditions under which a decision is free as a wide open issue.

There is also a moderate naturalizing approach to free choice that argues merely that knowing more about how we actually make choices and form intentions will *assist us* in understanding what is needed for a choice to be free. This moderate approach is not problematic.

Glossary

Throughout the book we have highlighted terms that may be unfamiliar. Here is a list of those terms in alphabetical order together with short definitions of them. A word in SMALL CAPITAL LETTERS within an entry is defined in another entry. We have entered terms as they occur in the text, not in the more usual 'base term, qualifier' format.

Absent qualia   The idea that there could be creatures that behave just like us but have no QUALIA, i.e., are ZOMBIES.

Absolute idealism   The view that the whole universe, including all "matter," is one vast mind.

Analogy   Reasoning that proceeds by comparing something whose structure is unclear or controversial to a situation having a similar structure that is clear.

Analytic truths   Sentences true in virtue of logic and/or meaning alone.

Anthropomorphizing   Treating something as being human in some respect when it is not.

Argument form   The result when one substitutes variables for specific parts of an argument. Put otherwise, the "shape" of an argument. (For example, 'If p, then (q and r); if q then s; p; therefore, s' is the shape exhibited by 'If Joey smokes, then Joey will get cancer and Joey will spend time in the hospital; if Joey gets cancer, then Joey will die young; Joey smokes; therefore, Joey will die young.')

Artificial intelligence   The attempt to create computers that can perform tasks that would require intelligence in a human.

Autism   A condition usually appearing early in childhood in which, among other things, the child cannot relate to other human beings very well and sometimes cannot relate to other people as people at all.

Begging the question   Assuming as a premise what one seeks to establish as a conclusion.

Behaviorism   In general, the idea that behavior is fundamental to the study of living organisms. (See RADICAL BEHAVIORISM and METHODOLOGICAL BEHAVIORISM.)

Brain plus   The brain plus whatever else is needed for a material system to constitute a mind. Two candidates for the extra element are a stable social setting and a physical world.

Burden of proof   The idea that sometimes there is a stronger evidential requirement on one disputant in a debate than there is on the other. For example, the prosecutor has the burden of proof in a criminal trial: if each side presents an equally good case, the defense wins.

Category mistake   Putting different kinds of concepts together that make no sense together, such as a mathematical concept and a color concept, with results that are neither true nor false (for example, the square root of two is purple).

Causal possibility   A decision taken or an action done by an agent could$_{cp}$ have been otherwise if, even given exactly the same causes as the causes that produced the decision or action, an agent would sometimes decide or do differently. (See NATURAL POWER.)

Circular reasoning   A form of reasoning in which one uses A to support B and then turns around and uses B to support A.

Cognitive science   The program of unifying philosophy, linguistics, psychology, computer science, neuroscience, and other approaches to cognition into a single integrated science.

Cognitive system   A system that processes information about the world, itself, its body, etc.

Compatibilism (also called "soft determinism")   The view that free choice and causal determinism are compatible with one another.

Computer metaphor   The view that the computer is a useful, even accurate, model for how minds function.

Confabulation   The activity of making up explanations when we do not know why we have done something.

Connectionist systems (also known as NEURAL NETWORKS)   Computational systems that do not contain discrete, separate symbols or explicitly represented rules for transforming symbols.

Consciousness (as discussed here)   The same as SPECIAL ACCESS, i.e., introspectibility. (See INTROSPECTION.)

Content   In a mental state, what is being believed, perceived, thought about, etc.—what the mental state is about.

Criterion   A feature or group of features that are central to all and only things of a certain type.

Deductive argument   An argument in which if the premises are true, the conclusion must be true.

Deliberation   Assessment of our desires, beliefs, values, and environment in order to decide what to do.

Descriptive ethics   The study of the values that people in fact hold. (See also NORMATIVE ETHICS.)

Dilemma   A situation in which we are faced with two or more alternatives and we have no satisfactory way to choose between them.

Dispositions Tendencies to react to some situation by virtue of structures or causal connections existing in an object. For example, glass has a disposition to break when hit with a rock. (Behavior resulting from dispositions is contrasted with behavior caused by the application of rules.)

Dualism In general, the idea that there are two radically different kinds of thing/ property/event/etc. (See SUBSTANCE DUALISM, PROPERTY DUALISM, and EXPLANATORY DUALISM.)

Ecological cognition The theory that to understand the mind, we have to understand it as a complex brain-world system.

Eliminative materialism The doctrine that our conviction that people have minds is just a theory like any other and a rather bad theory that deserves to be eliminated in favor of neuroscience.

Empathy Figuring out what is going on in another person by imagining what one would be thinking, wishing, feeling, etc., in that person's situation.

Empirical question A question that requires evidence from observation and experimentation to answer and cannot be answered by argument or reflection alone.

Empiricists Philosophers who maintain that genuine knowledge is derived from sensory experience.

Entailment A relationship between premises and conclusion in which, if the premises are true, the conclusion must be true.

Enthymeme An argument with some implicit premises.

Epiphenomenalism (about the mind) The view that the body can affect the mind but not the other way around.

Epistemological principle A principle that is a reliable guide to good reasoning.

Epistemology The philosophical study of the nature, extent, and origin of human knowledge.

Evidential support The premises of an argument offer *evidence* for the conclusion, i.e., if the premises are true, the conclusion is *more likely* to be true.

Evolutionary psychology The attempt to understand the structures and functions of the human cognitive system by reference to how it evolved.

Existential claim A claim that something of interest exists.

Explanatory dualism To understand ourselves, we need two very different kinds of explanations: PSYCHOLOGICAL EXPLANATIONS and MECHANISTIC EXPLANATIONS.

Externalism about meanings The idea that CONTENT comes from the brain's relationship to the world.

Fallacy of equivocation The meaning of a key term (or terms) changing between two premises in an argument.

Fatalism The idea that nothing one thinks, decides, or favors makes any difference to what will happen.

Folk psychology The view that beliefs, desires, emotions, values, etc., are what explain human behavior.

Free choice   Commonly held to be a decision such that, up to the moment that it was made, another decision could have been made, such that which decision is made is up to the person making it; that is, a decision that embodies FREEDOM OF CHOICE and FREEDOM OF DECISION.

Freedom of action   Being able to do what one chooses to do.

Freedom of choice   The power to make FREE CHOICES.

Freedom of decision   The power to make FREE CHOICES.

Free will   The rather vague idea that something called 'the will' has FREEDOM OF CHOICE.

Functionalism   The mind is certain functions of a complex system, for example, the brain; each and every particular mental state or event is some physical state or event of that system; but states described as mental cannot be reduced to states described any other way, so the mental requires its own proprietary language.

Hard determinism   The doctrine that free choice and causal determinism are incompatible with one another and every event is determined, so there is no free choice.

Hypothetical analysis of 'could'   Interpreting 'I could have chosen otherwise' to mean 'If I had deliberated [or whatever] differently, I would have chosen otherwise.'

Idealism   The view that the basic stuff of the universe is idealike or mindlike. (See ABSOLUTE IDEALISM and SUBJECTIVE IDEALISM.)

Identity theory   The view that every mental state and every mental event of a given *kind* is (is identical to, is one and the same thing as) some brain state or some brain event of a given *kind*.

Incorrigibility   The idea that we cannot be wrong about our own mental states, not the fairly simple ones at any rate.

Induction, inductive argument   Reasoning in which the premises are evidence for the conclusion but not conclusive proof of the conclusion. That is to say, if the premises are true, the conclusion is more likely to be true but is not guaranteed to be true. (See INDUCTIVE MERIT.)

Inductive merit   The property of premises providing significant evidentiary support for a conclusion.

Infer   When we make one proposition the basis for accepting another proposition, we are said to infer the latter from the former.

Inference to the best explanation   Inferring to what best explains something we are observing. For example, inferring that someone is having such-and-such mental states because postulating these mental states best explains the person's observed behavior.

Intentionality   The property of being about something else.

Internalism about meanings   The traditional idea that CONTENT is something "in the head" (or the mind).

Introspection The direct awareness that everyone has of his or her own mental states.

Inverted qualia The idea that the sensations one person is experiencing might be totally different from the sensations another person is experiencing, even though they are seeing the same thing and their sensations result in the same behavior.

Just deserts The idea that one can deserve praise or blame, reward or punishment, because one has done something as a result of a free choice.

Knowing how Having abilities, e.g., knowing how to swim, catch a ball, or ride a bicycle.

Knowing that Propositional knowledge: believing certain truths, possibly on the basis of a cognitive learning process.

Language of thought (LOT) The proposed universal code in which all human beings think.

Libertarianism The doctrine that free choice and causal determinism are incompatible with one another but free choice exists, so not everything is causally determined.

Liberty Another, more common name for FREEDOM OF ACTION.

Linguistic competence A body of linguistic knowledge.

Linguistic performance The actual linguistic behavior arising from the interaction of various bodies of knowledge and other factors. (See LINGUISTIC COMPETENCE.)

Logical positivism A philosophical position of many philosophers in the first half of this century that held that the meaning of a statement is the observations by which the sentence may be verified (see VERIFICATIONISM) and that all knowledge is constructed out of simple constituents, usually sensory ones.

Manifest image The view of a person as a single, unified center of consciousness and decision making. (See SCIENTIFIC IMAGE.)

Materialism (about the mind) The view that mind is the brain or certain aspects of the brain or BRAIN PLUS.

Mechanistic explanation The kind of explanation at work when we explain something by causes such as muscle movements, changes in brain chemistry, etc.

Metaphysics The philosophical study of issues about the nature of things that are so general and basic that the natural sciences cannot investigate them. (See also ONTOLOGY.)

Methodological behaviorism The claim that the empirical study of mind should start from behavior.

Modal concepts Concepts about the "modes" in which states of affairs can obtain: necessary, possible, actual. A state of affairs can be necessary, possible, or actual.

Moderate naturalism The idea that philosophy of knowledge and language should be *informed about* what empirical scientists have discovered about knowledge and mind. (See WEAK NATURALISM, STRONGER NATURALISM, and STRONGEST NATURALISM.)

Modus ponens   An argument of the form 'If p then q; p; therefore, q.'

Monism   The view that everything is, or is made up of, one kind of stuff.

Moore's principle   If you find yourself believing two incompatible things, reject as false the less obvious of the two.

Multiple realizability   The idea that a given function can be performed in otherwise very different systems. For example, the function of keeping time can be realized by very different physical systems: sun dials, egg timers, quartz movements, etc.

Nativist   A theorist who believes in innate knowledge.

Naturalism   Attempting to give answers to philosophical problems using the methods of the NATURE SCIENCES. (See WEAK NATURALISM, MODERATE NATURALISM, STRONGER NATURALISM, and STRONGEST NATURALISM.)

Natural power   A decision taken or an action done by an agent could$_{np}$ have been otherwise if that agent has the power to decide or do otherwise. (See CAUSAL POSSIBILITY.)

Natural sciences   Physics, chemistry, biology. Contrasted with the SOCIAL SCIENCES.

Necessary conditions   Conditions that must be in place for something to exist or take place. For example, having a part useful for sitting on is a necessary condition for something to be a chair.

Neural networks (also known as CONNECTIONIST SYSTEMS)   Computational systems that do not contain discrete, separate symbols or explicitly represented rules for transforming symbols.

Neurophilosophy   A complicated successor view to ELIMINATIVE MATERIALISM that, like its predecessor, privileges neuroscience over other approaches to understanding human beings. Usually argues that the mind does not work by manipulating symbols.

Nonspatiality   The idea that the mind does not have a precise location or any location at all.

Normative dimension   The dimension of an issue or area of study that is about standards—for example, for judging which beliefs, actions, etc., are justified.

Normative ethics   The study of what people ought to do. The contrast is with DESCRIPTIVE ETHICS, the study of the norms and values that people actually have.

Occam's razor   The principle that we should not multiply entities needlessly, that we should not believe that something exists unless we have some reason to do so.

Ontology   The philosophical study of issues about the nature of things so general and basic that the natural sciences cannot investigate them. (See also METAPHYSICS.)

Personal identity   Being one and the same person over a period of time.

Personal immortality   A person's continuing as the person she is now beyond bodily death.

Philosophy of mind   The philosophical approach to general questions about the mind such as the nature of the mind, the relation between mind and body, the nature and existence of free will, and so on.

Phonology   Rules for pronouncing units of language.

Phrase book   A book of sentences and subsentential units such as phrases and clauses.

Pleonasm   A phrase in which one part is redundant.

Pluralism   The view that there are more than two fundamentally different kinds of substances/properties/events/etc.

Poverty-of-stimulus argument   Language users end up with more information about their language than is available to them in their environment; the best available explanation of this fact is that the "missing" information is innate.

Preestablished harmony   Mind and body never causally connect, but God created them so that they operate in perfect harmony.

Problem of knowledge of self   Granted that each of us knows of oneself that one *has* a mind, the question of how much one knows *about* one's self. (See PROBLEM OF OTHER MINDS.)

Problem of other minds   The philosophical issue of whether we can know that others have minds and/or what is going on in their minds. (See PROBLEM OF KNOWLEDGE OF SELF.)

Productivity   The ability to combine words into novel wholes (e.g., phrases, sentences) according to grammatical rules.

Property   In the ONTOLOGY of objects and properties, objects are individual items, properties are the various things true of those items. Thus a chair is an object. Being red, having four legs, being useful to sit on are properties. A given property can be shared by many objects.

Property dualism   The view that the human person is a single, unified object, but that this object has two radically different kinds of properties: mental properties and material properties.

Psychological explanation   Explaining behavior by referring to the agent's reasons.

Qualia   Appearing to one as something; felt qualities. (See ABSENT QUALIA and INVERTED QUALIA.)

Radical behaviorism   The theory that what we call the mind is really only behavior and organisms' DISPOSITIONS to behave.

Radical naturalism   Another name for S-NATURALISM.

Rationalists   Philosophers who hold that genuine knowledge is based not on the senses but on something internal to the mind, e.g., reasoning powers and/or innate ideas.

Reductio ad absurdum   Accepting a hypothesis for the sake of argument and then showing that it has absurd consequences.

Reduction   Showing that a kind of thing described in one way consists in elements described in a deeper and more general way in all or virtually all cases.

Representation   When an object, state, or event is about something else, it is called a representation; examples in the mental realm are thoughts, imaginings, and perceptions.

Scientific image   The view of a person as a vast assemblage of cells tied together in a complex system. (See MANIFEST IMAGE.)

Self-determinism   A selection or decision being causally determined by oneself.

Semantics   What the parts of language (e.g., words) and the wholes constructed out of those parts (e.g., sentences) mean.

Simulation theory of mind   The view that we decide what is going on in another's mind by putting ourselves in their position and simulating what would be going on in us. (See THEORY THEORY OF MIND.)

Situated cognition   The theory that to understand the mind, we have to understand it as a complex brain-world system.

Situation   The ontological unit consisting of an object (or objects) having a property (or properties). Also called a state of affairs. For example, Mary's owning a large chicken is a situation.

Skepticism   The view that human beings cannot know anything, either in general or in certain areas of inquiry.

S-naturalism   The combination of STRONGER NATURALISM and STRONGEST NATURALISM.

Social sciences   The study of the nature and interactions of human beings (see NATURAL SCIENCES). The difference between the social sciences and the natural sciences is related to the distinction between the MANIFEST IMAGE and the SCIENTIFIC IMAGE.

Solipsism   The view that nothing exists except one's mind and its states.

Sophisticated compatibilist model (SCM)   A complex form of compatibilism (the view that free choice is not necessarily ruled out by causal determinism). On SCM, a choice is free if the resulting action is in accord with the decider's second-order desires and the decision was caused by the decider's own deliberations in such a way that, were the deliberations different, the decision would be different.

Sound argument   A VALID ARGUMENT that has true premises.

Special access   The access I have to myself and my states, which is different from the access that I have to you and yours.

State of affairs   See SITUATION.

Strict-liability offenses   Offenses where just doing the prohibited act is enough to justify punishment; whether one intended to do the deed and whether one even knew that it was being done are irrelevant.

Strong AI   Artificially intelligent systems that not only exhibit behavior that would require intelligence in us but that also have understanding, perception, consciousness, etc.

Stronger naturalism   The idea that philosophical problems about knowledge and mind (and most everything else) are really scientific ones and can only be adequately answered by using the methods of science, natural science in particular. (See WEAK NATURALISM, MODERATE NATURALISM, and STRONGEST NATURALISM).

Strongest naturalism   This view accepts stronger naturalism but goes one step further. It holds that neuroscience is the only justifiable approach to cognition. (See also WEAK NATURALISM, MODERATE NATURALISM, and STRONGER NATURALISM).

Subjective idealism   The view that all that exist are myself and my states. (See SOLIPSISM.)

Substance dualism   The view that the human person is made up of two distinct substances: a material body and an immaterial mind.

Sufficient conditions   Conditions that guarantee that something will exist or take place.

Symbolic process   A process that starts with strings of symbols—strings of words structured by the syntax of a language, for example—and transforms these strings of symbols into other strings of symbols according to rules.

Synonyms   Two or more terms having the same meaning.

Syntax   Rules for constructing linguistic wholes (e.g., sentences) out of minimal parts (e.g., words). (See also PRODUCTIVITY and SEMANTICS.)

Synthetic truths   Sentences whose truth is not merely a matter of linguistic meaning.

Theory theory of mind   The theory that as young children we form a theory that others have minds, i.e., beliefs, desires, emotions, etc. (See SIMULATION THEORY OF MIND.)

Thought experiment   The activity of trying to figure out the nature of something by imagining situations concerning it, rather than by doing hands-on experiments on it.

Token   One occurrence of some TYPE of thing.

Token identity   The idea that every token of one type is a token of another type but the types cannot be reduced to (mapped onto) one another (see REDUCTION). (See also TYPE IDENTITY.)

Turing test   A test in which a subject is put in front of two input and two output devices, one pair of which is connected to another person, the other to a computer; the task for the subject is to determine which is which.

Type   Things having properties in common such that we give those things and their having the same properties a name in common (type: dog; TOKEN: this dog in front of me).

Type identity   The view that types of one kind can be reduced to (mapped onto) types of another kind (see REDUCTION). (See also TOKEN IDENTITY).

Valid argument   An argument in which, if the premises are true, the conclusion must be true.

Values   Standards, principles, or norms for determining what we ought to do in some domain.

Verificationism   The philosophical/semantic doctrine according to which the meaning of a sentence is the means by which it may be verified.

Weak naturalism   The idea that philosophical theories should be *consistent* with what science tells us about the world. (See MODERATE NATURALISM, STRONGER NATURALISM, and STRONGEST NATURALISM.)

Weeble   A truly fabulous cat, famous throughout the world [Rob's definition], not known, however, for soaring intelligence [Andy's supplement].

Zombie   A being that behaves like us but has no inner mental life.

References

Alston, William P. 1964. *Philosophy of Language*. Englewood Cliffs, N.J.: Prentice-Hall.

Armstrong, David M. 1963. Is Introspective Knowledge Incorrigible? *Philosophical Review* 72: 417–432. Reprinted in Rosenthal 1991.

Armstrong, David M. 1968. *A Materialist Theory of Mind*. London: Routledge.

Arnauld, Antoine, and Claude Lancelot. 1975 [1660]. *Port-Royal Grammar: General and Rational Grammar*. The Hague: Mouton.

Audi, Robert. 1998. *Epistemology: A Contemporary Introduction to the Theory of Knowledge*. London: Routledge.

Austin, John L. 1962. *Sense and Sensibilia*. Oxford: Clarendon Press.

Ayer, Alfred J. 1946. *Language, Truth, and Logic*. New York: Dover.

Ayer, Alfred J. 1956. *The Problem of Knowledge*. London: Macmillan.

Ayer, Alfred J., ed. 1959. *Logical Positivism*. Glencoe, Ill.: Free Press.

Ayers, Michael R. 1968. *The Refutation of Determinism*. London: Methuen.

Baillie, James. 1997. *Contemporary Analytic Philosophy*. Upper Saddle River, N.J.: Prentice-Hall.

Baron-Cohen, Simon. 1995. *Mindblindness: A Essay on Autism and Theory of Mind*. Cambridge: MIT Press.

Bennett, Jonathan. 1971. *Locke, Berkeley, Hume: Central Themes*. Oxford: Oxford University Press.

Blackburn, Simon. 1984. *Spreading the Word*. Oxford: Oxford University Press.

Block, Ned. 1978. Troubles with Functionalism. In *Perception and Cognition: Issues in the Foundations of Psychology*, edited by C. W. Savage. Minnesota Studies in the Philosophy of Science, no. 9. Minneapolis: University of Minnesota Press. Reprinted in Block 1981.

Block, Ned. 1981. *Readings in Philosophy of Psychology*. Two volumes. Cambridge: Harvard University Press.

Bonjour, Laurence. 1985. *The Structure of Empirical Knowledge*. Cambridge: Harvard University Press.

Brentano, Franz. 1995 [1874]. *Psychology from an Empirical Standpoint*. London: Routledge.

Brook, Andrew. 1994. *Kant and the Mind*. Cambridge: Cambridge University Press.

Brook, Andrew. 1999. Does Philosophy Offer Distinctive Methods to Cognitive Science? *Proceedings of the Twenty-first Conference of the Cognitive Science Society*, pp. 102–108. New York: Lawrence Erlbaum Associates.

Carnap, Rudolf. 1932. The Elimination of Metaphysics through Logical Analysis of Language. Reprinted in English in Ayer 1959.

Chisholm, Roderick M. 1955. Sentences about Believing. *Proceedings of the Aristotelian Society* 56: 125–148.

Chisholm, Roderick M. 1989. *Theory of Knowledge*. Third edition. Englewood Cliffs, N.J.: Prentice-Hall.

Chomsky, Noam. 1959. A Review of B. F. Skinner's *Verbal Behavior*. *Language* 35: 26–77.

Chomsky, Noam. 1965. *Aspects of the Theory of Syntax*. Cambridge: MIT Press.

Chomsky, Noam. 1966. *Cartesian Linguistics*. New York: Harper & Row.

Chomsky, Noam. 1969. Quine's Empirical Assumptions. In *Words and Objections: Essays on the Work of W. V. Quine*, edited by D. Davidson and J. Hintikka. Dordrecht: Reidel.

Chomsky, Noam. 1975. On Cognitive Capacity. In his *Reflections on Language*. New York: Pantheon. Reprinted in Block 1981.

Chomsky, Noam. 1980. *Rules and Representations*. New York: Columbia University Press.

Chomsky, Noam. 1986. *Knowledge of Language*. New York: Praeger.

Chomsky, Noam. 1988. *Language and the Problems of Knowledge: The Managua Lectures*. Cambridge: MIT Press.

Chomsky, Noam. 1990. Language and the Problem of Knowledge. In *The Philosophy of Language*, edited by A. P. Martinich. Oxford: Oxford University Press.

Chomsky, Noam. 1993. *Language and Thought*. Wakefield, R.I.: Moyer Bell.

Churchland, Patricia S. 1986. *Neurophilosophy*. Cambridge: MIT Press.

Churchland, Patricia S., and Paul M. Churchland. 1983. Stalking the Wild Epistemic Engine. *Noûs* 17: 5–18. Reprinted in Lycan 1990.

Churchland, Patricia S., and Terrence J. Sejnowski. 1992. *The Computational Brain*. Cambridge: MIT Press.

Churchland, Paul M. 1984. *Matter and Consciousness*. Cambridge: MIT Press.

Churchland, Paul M. 1995. *The Engine of Reason, the Seat of the Soul: A Philosophical Journey into the Brain*. Cambridge: MIT Press.

Clark, Andy. 1989. *Microcognition*. Cambridge: MIT Press.

Copleston, Frederick. 1946. *A History of Philosophy*. Volume 1: *From the Pre-Socratics to Plotinus*. New York: Doubleday.

Copleston, Frederick. 1960. *A History of Philosophy*. Volume 4: *Modern Philosophy from Descartes to Leibniz*. New York: Doubleday.

Craig, Edward, ed. 1998. *Routledge Encyclopedia of Philosophy*. London: Routledge.

Cummins, Robert. 1989. *Meaning and Mental Representation*. Cambridge: MIT Press.

Dancy, Jonathan. 1985. *An Introduction to Contemporary Epistemology*. Oxford: Basil Blackwell.

Dancy, Jonathan, and Ernest Sosa, eds. 1992. *A Companion to Epistemology*. Oxford: Basil Blackwell.

Davidson, Donald. 1975. Thought and Talk. In *Mind and Language: Wolfson College Lectures, 1974*, edited by S. Guttenplan. Oxford: Oxford University Press.

Davidson, Donald. 1980. *Essays on Action and Events*. Oxford: Oxford University Press.

Davis, Steven. 1976. *Philosophy and Language*. Indianapolis, Ind.: Bobbs-Merrill Co.

Dawson, Michael. 1998. *Understanding Cognitive Science*. Oxford: Blackwell.

Dennett, Daniel C. 1975. Brain Writing and Mind Reading. In *Language, Mind, and Knowledge*, edited by K. Gunderson. Minnesota Studies in the Philosophy of Science, no. 7. Minneapolis: University of Minnesota Press. Reprinted in Dennett 1978c.

Dennett, Daniel C. 1977. Critical Notice: *The Language of Thought*, by Jerry Fodor. *Mind* 86: 265–280. Reprinted as "A Cure for the Common Code?" in Dennett 1978c.

Dennett, Daniel C. 1978a. Why You Can't Make a Computer That Feels Pain. *Synthese* 38: 415–456. Reprinted in Dennett 1978c.

Dennett, Daniel C. 1978b. Skinner Skinned. In Dennett 1978c.

Dennett, Daniel C. 1978c. *Brainstorms*. Cambridge: MIT Press.

Dennett, Daniel C. 1984. *Elbow Room: The Varieties of Free Will Worth Wanting*. Cambridge: MIT Press.

Dennett, Daniel C. 1987. *The Intentional Stance*. Cambridge: MIT Press.

Dennett, Daniel C. 1991. *Consciousness Explained*. New York: Little, Brown.

Dennett, Daniel C. 1995. *Darwin's Dangerous Idea*. New York: Simon & Schuster.

Descartes, René. 1931 [1637]. *Discourse on the Method of Rightly Conducting the Reason*. In Haldane and Ross 1931.

Descartes, René. 1931 [1641]. *Meditations on First Philosophy*. In Haldane and Ross 1931.

Devitt, Michael, and Kim Sterelny. 1987. *Language and Reality: An Introduction to the Philosophy of Language*. Cambridge: MIT Press.

Dretske, Fred I. 1988. *Explaining Behavior*. Cambridge: MIT Press.

Dretske, Fred I. 1995. *Naturalizing the Mind*. Cambridge: MIT Press.

Edwards, Paul, ed. 1967. *Encyclopedia of Philosophy*. New York: Macmillan.

Flanagan, Owen J. 1984. *The Science of the Mind*. Cambridge: MIT Press.

Fodor, Jerry A. 1975. *The Language of Thought*. New York: Crowell.

Fodor, Jerry A. 1978. Propositional Attitudes. *Monist* 61: 501–523. Reprinted in Fodor 1981.

Fodor, Jerry A. 1981. *Representations*. Cambridge: MIT Press.

Fodor, Jerry A. 1983. *The Modularity of Mind*. Cambridge: MIT Press.

Fodor, Jerry A. 1987. *Psychosemantics*. Cambridge: MIT Press.

Fodor, Jerry A. 1994. *The Elm and the Expert*. Cambridge: MIT Press.

Fodor, Jerry A., and Zenon Pylyshyn. 1988. Connectionism and Cognitive Architecture: A Critical Analysis. *Cognition* 28: 3–71. Reprinted in part in Haugeland 1997.

Frankfurt, Henry G. 1969. Alternative Possibilities and Moral Responsibility. *Journal of Philosophy* 66: 829–839. Reprinted in Frankfurt 1988.

Frankfurt, Henry G. 1971. Freedom of the Will and the Concept of a Person. *Journal of Philosophy* 68: 5–20. Reprinted in Frankfurt 1988.

Frankfurt, Henry G. 1988. *The Importance of What We Care About: Philosophical Essays*. Cambridge: Cambridge University Press.

Frege, Gottlob. 1892. On Sense and Reference. In *Translations from the Philosophical Writings of Gottlob Frege*, edited by P. Geach and M. Black. Oxford: Basil Blackwell. Reprinted as "On Sense and Nominatum" in Martinich 1996.

Fromkin, Victoria, and Robert Rodman. 1993. *An Introduction to Language*. Fifth edition. New York: Harcourt, Brace, Jovanovich.

Geirsson, Heimir, and Michael Losonsky. 1996. *Readings in Language and Mind*. Oxford: Blackwell.

Gettier, Edmund L. 1963. Is Justified True Belief Knowledge? *Analysis* 23: 121–123.

Goldman, Alvin I. 1979. What Is Justified Belief? In *Justification and Knowledge*, edited by George Pappas. Dordrecht: Reidel. Reprinted in Kornblith 1985.

Goldman, Alvin I. 1990. Action and Free Will. In *An Invitation to Cognitive Science: Visual Cognition and Action*, edited by Daniel Osherson et al. Cambridge: MIT Press.

Goldman, Alvin I. 1992. Epistemic Folkways Meet Scientific Epistemology. In *Liaisons: Philosophy Meets the Cognitive and Social Sciences*. Cambridge: MIT Press.

Goodman, Michael F., and Robert A. Snyder, eds. 1993. *Contemporary Readings in Epistemology*. Englewood Cliffs, N.J.: Prentice-Hall.

Gopnik, Myrna. 1990. Feature-Blind Grammar and Dysphasia. *Nature* 344: 715.

Graybosch, Anthony J., Gregory M. Scott, and Stephen M. Garrison. 1998. *The Philosophy Student Writer's Manual*. Upper Saddle River, N.J.: Prentice-Hall.

Hacking, Ian. 1995. *Rewriting the Soul*. Princeton: Princeton University Press.

Haldane, Elizabeth S., and George R. T. Ross, eds. and trans. 1931. *The Philosophical Works of Descartes*. Volume 1. Cambridge: Cambridge University Press.

Hamlyn, D. W. 1970. *The Theory of Knowledge*. London: Macmillan.

Handey, Jack. 1992. *Deep Thoughts: Inspiration for the Uninspired*. New York: Berkley Books.

Handey, Jack. 1993. *Deeper Thoughts: All New, All Crispy*. New York: Hyperion.

Handey, Jack. 1994. *Deepest Thoughts: So Deep They Squeak*. New York: Hyperion.

Harris, Roy, and Talbot J. Taylor, eds. 1989. *Landmarks in Linguistic Thought: The Western Tradition from Socrates to Saussure*. London: Routledge.

Haugeland, John, ed. 1997. *Mind Design II: Philosophy, Psychology, Artificial Intelligence*. Revised and enlarged edition. Cambridge: MIT Press.

Hempel, Carl F. 1950. Empiricist Criteria of Cognitive Significance: Problems and Changes. Reprinted in Ayer 1959 and in Martinich 1996.

Hobbes, Thomas. 1996 [1668]. *Leviathan*. Edited by J. C. A. Addison. Oxford: Oxford University Press.

Hook, Sidney, ed. 1968. *Language and Philosophy: A Symposium*. New York: New York University Press.

Horgan, Terence, and John Tienson. 1996. *Connectionism and the Philosophy of Psychology*. Cambridge: MIT Press.

Hume, David. 1978 [1739]. *A Treatise of Human Nature*. Edited by L. A. Selby-Bigge. Second edition edited by P. H. Nidditch. Oxford: Clarendon Press.

Jacquette, Dale. 1994. *The Philosophy of Mind*. Englewood Cliffs, N.J.: Prentice-Hall.

Kant, Immanuel. 1927 [1781/1787]. *Critique of Pure Reason*. Translated by Norman Kemp Smith. London: Macmillan. Page references to the original German pagination.

Kenny, Anthony J. P. 1968. *Descartes*. New York: Random House.

Kenny, Anthony J. P. 1973. *Wittgenstein*. Cambridge: Harvard University Press.

Kim, Jaegwon. 1996. *Philosophy of Mind*. Boulder, Colo.: Westview Press.

Kolak, Daniel, and Raymond Martin. 1991. *Self and Identity: Contemporary Philosophical Issues*. New York: Macmillan.

Kornblith, Hilary. 1985. Naturalizing Epistemology. Cambridge: MIT Press.

La Mettrie, Julien O. 1994 [1748]. *Man a Machine*. Translated by R. A. Watson and M. Rybalka. Indianapolis, Ind.: Hackett.

Lehrer, Keith. 1990. *Theory of Knowledge*. Boulder, Colo.: Westview Press.

Locke, John. 1965 [1685]. *An Essay Concerning Human Understanding*. Abridged and edited by J. W. Yolton. LaSalle, Ill.: Open Court.

Lucey, Kenneth G. 1996. *On Knowing and the Known: Introductory Readings in Epistemology*. Amherst, N.Y.: Prometheus Books.

Lycan, William G., ed. 1990. *Mind and Cognition: A Reader*. Oxford: Blackwell.

Marks, Charles E. 1980. *Commissurotomy, Consciousness, and the Unity of the Mind.* Cambridge: MIT Press

Martin, Robert M. 1987. *The Meaning of Language.* Cambridge: MIT Press.

Martinich, A. P., ed. 1996. *The Philosophy of Language.* Oxford: Oxford University Press.

Melzack, Ronald. 1973. *The Puzzle of Pain.* New York: Basic Books.

Morton, Peter A. 1997. *A Historical Introduction to the Philosophy of Mind.* Peterborough, Ont.: Broadview.

Nagel, Ernest, and Richard B. Brandt, eds. 1965. *Meaning and Knowledge: Systematic Readings in Epistemology.* New York: Harcourt, Brace and World.

Nagel, Thomas. 1971. Brain Bisection and the Unity of Consciousness. *Synthese* 22: 396–413. Reprinted in Rosenthal 1991.

Nagel, Thomas. 1974. What Is It like to Be a Bat? *Philosophical Review* 83: 435–450. Reprinted in Block 1981.

Nagel, Thomas. 1987. *What Does It All Mean?* Oxford: Oxford University Press.

O'Connor, John. 1969. *Modern Materialism: Readings on Mind-Body Identity.* New York: Harcourt, Brace and World.

Parfit, Derek 1984. *Reasons and Persons.* Oxford: Oxford University Press.

Pereboom, D. 1997. *Free Will.* Indianapolis, Ind.: Hackett Publishing Co.

Perry, John. 1978. *Dialogue on Personal Identity and Immortality.* Indianapolis, Ind.: Hackett.

Piatelli-Palmarini, Massimo, ed. 1980. *Language and Learning: The Debate between Jean Piaget and Noam Chomsky.* Cambridge: Cambridge University Press.

Pinker, Steven. 1994. *The Language Instinct.* New York: William Morrow.

Pinker, Steven. 1997. *How the Mind Works.* New York: W. W. Norton.

Place, U. T. 1956. Is Consciousness a Brain Process? *British Journal of Psychology* 47: 44–50. Reprinted in Lycan 1990.

Plato. 1973 [ca. 399 B.C.]. *Theaetetus.* Translated by John McDowell. Oxford: Oxford University Press.

Plato. 1981 [ca. 390 B.C.]. *Phaedo.* Translated by G. M. A. Grube. Indianapolis, Ind.: Hackett.

Popkin, Richard. 1964. *A History of Skepticism: From Erasmus to Descartes.* New York: Harper & Row.

Pullum, Geoffrey K. 1989. The Great Eskimo Vocabulary Hoax. *Natural Language and Linguistic Theory* 2: 275–281.

Putnam, Hilary. 1964. Robots: Machines or Artificially Created Life? *Journal of Philosophy* 61: 668–691. Reprinted in O'Connor 1969.

Putnam, Hilary. 1967. The 'Innateness Hypothesis' and Explanatory Models in Linguistics. *Synthese* 17: 12–22.

Putnam, Hilary. 1975. The Meaning of 'Meaning'. In *Language, Mind, and Knowledge*, edited by K. Gunderson, Minnesota Studies in the Philosophy of Science, no. 7. Minneapolis: University of Minnesota Press. Reprinted in Geirsson and Losonsky 1996.

Quine, W. V. O. 1953. Two Dogmas of Empiricism. In his *From a Logical Point of View*. Cambridge: Harvard University Press. Reprinted in Baillie 1997.

Quine, W. V. O. 1969. Epistemology Naturalized. In his *Ontological Relativity and Other Essays*. New York: Columbia University Press. Reprinted in Kornblith 1985.

Rorty, Richard. 1979. *Philosophy and the Mirror of Nature*. Princeton: Princeton University Press.

Rosenberg, Jay F. 1984. *The Practice of Philosophy*. Second edition. Englewood Cliffs, N.J.: Prentice-Hall.

Rosenberg, Jay F. 1996. *The Practice of Philosophy*. Third edition. Englewood Cliffs, N.J.: Prentice-Hall.

Rosenthal, David M., ed. 1991. *The Nature of Mind*. Oxford: Oxford University Press.

Rumelhart, David E., and J. McClelland, eds. 1986. *Parallel Distributed Processing: Explorations in the Microstructure of Cognition*. Two volumes. Cambridge: MIT Press.

Russell, Bertrand. 1912. *The Problems of Philosophy*. Oxford: Oxford University Press.

Russell, Bertrand. 1948. *Human Knowledge: Its Scope and Limits*. London: Routledge.

Ryle, Gilbert. 1949. *The Concept of Mind*. New York: Harper and Row.

Sartre, Jean-Paul. 1943. *Being and Nothingness*. Translated by Mary Gregor. New York: Philosophical Library.

Schlick, Moritz. 1932. Positivism and Realism. Reprinted in Ayer 1959.

Searle, John R. 1980. Minds, Brains, and Programs. *Behavioral and Brain Sciences* 3: 417–457. Reprinted in Haugeland 1997.

Sellars, Wilfrid. 1997 [1956]. *Empiricism and the Philosophy of Mind*. Cambridge: Harvard University Press.

Shoemaker, Sydney. 1963. *Self-Knowledge and Self-Identity*. Ithaca: Cornell University Press.

Shoemaker, Sydney. 1975. Functionalism and Qualia. *Philosophical Studies* 27: 291–314. Reprinted with revisions in Block 1981.

Smart, J. J. C. 1962. Sensations and Brain Processes. In *The Philosophy of Mind*, edited by V. C. Chappell. Englewood Cliffs, N.J.: Prentice-Hall.

Solomon, Robert C. 1998. *The Big Questions*. Fifth edition. Fort Worth, Tex.: Harcourt Brace.

Stainton, Robert J. 1996. *Philosophical Perspectives on Language*. Peterborough, Ont.: Broadview Press.

Stich, Stephen P. 1975. *Innate Ideas*. Berkeley: University of California Press.

Stich, Stephen P. 1996. *Deconstructing the Mind*. Oxford: Oxford University Press.

Stillings, Neil A., ed. 1995. *Cognitive Science: An Introduction*. Second edition. Cambridge: MIT Press.

Strawson, P. F. 1959. *Individuals*. London: Methuen.

Strawson, P. F. 1962. Freedom and Resentment. *Proceedings of the British Academy* 48. Reprinted in his *Freedom and Resentment and Other Essays*. London: Methuen.

Taylor, Richard. 1963. *Metaphysics*. Englewood Cliffs, N.J.: Prentice-Hall.

Thagard, Paul. 1996. *Mind: An Introduction to Cognitive Science*. Cambridge: MIT Press.

Turing, Alan M. 1950. Computing Machinery and Intelligence. *Mind* 59: 433–460. Reprinted in Haugeland 1997.

Van Inwagen, Peter. 1983. *An Essay on Free Will*. Oxford: Clarendon Press.

Van Inwagen, Peter. 1993. *Metaphysics*. Boulder, Colo.: Westview Press.

Vendler, Zeno. 1972. *Res Cogitans*. Ithaca: Cornell University Press.

Watson, Gary, ed. 1982. *Free Will*. Oxford: Oxford University Press.

Weston, Anthony. 1987. *Rulebook for Arguments*. Indianapolis, Ind.: Hackett.

Whitemore, H. 1987. *Breaking the Code*. Oxford: Amber Lane Press.

Whorf, Benjamin Lee. 1956. *Language, Thought, and Reality*. Edited by J. B. Carroll. Cambridge: MIT Press.

Wilson, R., and F. Keil, eds. 1999. *The MIT Encyclopedia of the Cognitive Sciences* Cambridge: MIT Press.

Wittgenstein, Ludwig. 1953. *Philosophical Investigations*. Translated by G. E. M. Anscombe. Oxford: Basil Blackwell.

Wittgenstein, Ludwig. 1969. *On Certainty*. Edited by G. E. M. Anscombe and G. H. von Wright. Translated by D. Paul and G. E. M. Anscombe. Oxford: Blackwell.

Index

We have entered terms in the usual 'base term, qualifier' format and also, when it seemed useful, as they occur in the text. Where a term is defined in the Glossary, we have included the page number of the definition.